MURIEL'S WAR

Also by Sheila Isenberg

A Hero of Our Own: The Story of Varian Fry (2001)

With William M. Kunstler, *My Life as a Radical Lawyer* (1994)

Women Who Love Men Who Kill (1991)

MURIEL'S WAR

An American Heiress in the Nazi Resistance

Sheila Isenberg

palgrave
macmillan

First published in 2010 by
PALGRAVE MACMILLAN®
in the US—a division of St. Martin's Press LLC,
175 Fifth Avenue, New York, NY 10010.

Where this book is distributed in the UK, Europe and the rest of the world,
this is by Palgrave Macmillan, a division of Macmillan Publishers Limited,
registered in England, company number 785998, of Houndmills,
Basingstoke, Hampshire RG21 6XS.

Palgrave Macmillan is the global academic imprint of the above companies
and has companies and representatives throughout the world.

Palgrave® and Macmillan® are registered trademarks in the United States,
the United Kingdom, Europe and other countries.

ISBN: 978–0–230–61565–6

Unpublished journals by Stephen Spender © 1980, 1986. Reprinted by kind
permission of the Estate of Stephen Spender.

NEW COLLECTED POEMS by Stephen Spender © 2004. Reprinted by kind
permission of the Estate of Stephen Spender.

Josef Breitenbach's portrait of Muriel Gardiner © The Josef and Yaye
Breitenbach Charitable Foundation, New York.

Library of Congress Cataloging-in-Publication Data

Isenberg, Sheila.
   Muriel's war : an American heiress in the Nazi resistance / Sheila Isenberg.
     p. cm.
   Includes index.
   ISBN 978-0-230-61565-6
    1. Gardiner, Muriel, 1901–1985. 2. World War, 1939–1945—Underground
movements—Austria. 3. World War, 1939–1945—Personal narratives,
American. 4. Austria—History—1938–1945. 5. Anti-Nazi movement—
Austria. 6. Americans—Austria—Biography. I. Title.

D802.A9I74 2010
940.53'436092—dc22   2010025050

A catalogue record of the book is available from the British Library.

Design by Newgen Imaging Systems (P) Ltd., Chennai, India.

First edition: December 2010

10 9 8 7 6 5 4 3 2 1

Printed in the United States of America.

For Chris, always

Sound, sound the clarion, fill the fife!
Throughout the sensual world proclaim,
One crowded hour of glorious life
Is worth an age without a name.
—"The Call," Thomas Osbert Mordaunt (1730–1809)

CONTENTS

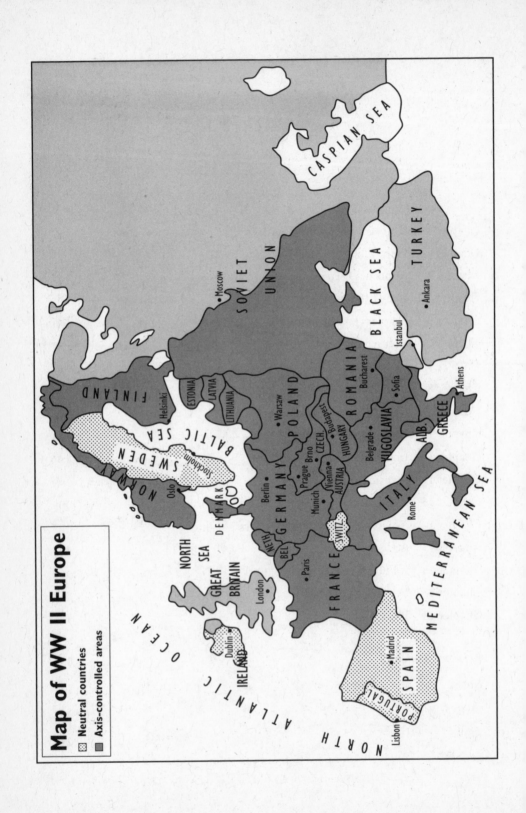

Map of WW II Europe

- ▨ Neutral countries
- ■ Axis-controlled areas

NORTH ATLANTIC OCEAN

IRELAND
Dublin

GREAT BRITAIN
London

NORTH SEA

NETH
BEL
DENMARK

NORWAY
Oslo

SWEDEN
Stockholm

BALTIC SEA

FINLAND
Helsinki

ESTONIA
LATVIA
LITHUANIA

SOVIET UNION
Moscow

CASPIAN SEA

GERMANY
Berlin
Munich

FRANCE
Paris

SWITZ

Prague
Brno
CZECH

Vienna
AUSTRIA

POLAND
Warsaw

Budapest
HUNGARY

ROMANIA
Bucharest

Sofia

Belgrade
YUGOSLAVIA

ALB.

GREECE
Athens

BLACK SEA

Istanbul

TURKEY
Ankara

ITALY
Rome

SPAIN
Madrid

PORTUGAL
Lisbon

MEDITERRANEAN SEA

PROLOGUE

Wednesday, March 9, 1938

It was an unusually warm spring and Viennese waltzes wafted from the open café doorways. A preoccupied American woman, ignoring the day's glories, paced back and forth for an hour, stopping occasionally to glance out the window. But the cobblestoned streets were empty, and Muriel Gardiner saw nothing. All she could do was replay in her head the reports she had heard. The *Wehrmacht* troops were reported to be massing at the Austrian border: the *Anschluss*, Hitler's long-threatened takeover of his native country, was at hand.[1]

At 36, Muriel had assumed that she was inured to this kind of anxiety, born of imminent danger.[2] Four years earlier she had become involved in dangerous anti-Fascist underground work that could easily have led to her arrest and imprisonment, or worse. Since that time, Muriel had functioned both carefully and courageously "in the face of all reason," as her friend Anna Freud would later write.[3] Muriel hid militants, Jews, Socialists, and "undesirables," and she provided them with financial backing and false documents to help them flee to safety. In some cases, she escorted them over the border herself.

But today felt different. Today felt like the end of everything.[4] The Austrian Nazi Party, though illegal under the law, had gained so much power recently that its members moved about the city arrogantly, smug in their certainty of soon uniting with their German counterparts. They had reason to be proud: Hitler's Austrian overseer, Wilhelm Keppler, had reported to the *Führer* that the Austrian Nazis "were in excellent shape."[5] The Brownshirts had suddenly become the most powerful forces in the Austrian government.

Thursday, March 10, 1938

After a night of only two or three hours of restless sleep, Muriel had breakfast with her lover, Joseph Buttinger, head of the Revolutionary Socialists, then bid him farewell. On this particular morning, she didn't know if she would ever see him again, but she pretended as she said goodbye that it was a parting like every other one and hoped that he would not run into the pro-Nazi thugs roaming the streets.[6] She watched out the window as Joe headed toward the Heitzinger Bridge over the river Wien to meet "Little Otto" Bauer.

Little Otto Bauer—his nickname distinguished him from Otto Bauer, the intellectual Marxist head of the Social Democratic Party—was a Social Democratic leader who had written a pamphlet called "The Inevitable Collapse" about the inescapable breakdown of Social Democracy in Austria. He had hoped to circulate the pamphlet among their comrades, but now he realized it was too late because the German invasion was upon them. When they met, Joe and Little Otto employed an old underground trick for communicating without being caught. They stared into the water while they talked, studying their shadows to make sure no one was watching them.

"All packed?" he asked Joe. "Hitler will strike before Sunday."[7] Joe agreed that the future appeared bleak for their country. Little Otto repeated his question, saying, "There's nothing for it now but to pack our bags. Hitler will make mincemeat of everything."[8] In previous days, Joe had made the rounds, talking to Socialists at the Café Meteor, visiting others too afraid to leave their homes. None of these men knew where Joe lived. Many didn't know his real name—to them, he was "Gustav Richter." They had no idea that he had been hidden in Muriel's tiny apartment at No. 8 Lammgasse—and sometimes in a small cottage she owned in the Vienna Woods—for more than three years.[9]

Muriel had her own cover for her anti-Fascist work. She had a second apartment at No. 2 Rummelhardtgasse, near the University of Vienna, which she had expanded by buying the apartment next door and then breaking down its walls. A rich expatriate, she lived there with her young daughter, Connie, now seven, and her daughter's nurse, Fini. Her cover also included her enrollment as a university medical school student. Pretending to be unconcerned with politics, Muriel went to classes, saw an analyst, and cared for her child.

For the rest of that Thursday and into the night, Joe and the other Revolutionary Socialists worked to come up with a plan by which they would maintain the party during the German invasion. If that proved impossible, they also discussed how they would revive it afterward. Muriel planned to rendezvous with Joe later at his hideout in her Lammgasse apartment.

Friday, March 11, 1938

Muriel knew of Austrian Chancellor Kurt von Schuschnigg's referendum, optimistically planned for Sunday, March 13. It was a desperate last stand that the

Austrian government would stage against Hitler, asking citizens to cast their ballots in favor of a free nation, rather than one subsumed by Germany. But as the day went on, based on what she was hearing from comrades around Vienna, Muriel believed that the vote would never take place and that Hitler would prevail.

While waiting for Joe to return home that evening, Muriel destroyed any incriminating papers that Nazi intruders might find in her apartment. Tearing up all documents and leaflets touting Socialism or decrying Fascism, she began flushing the scraps down the toilet. Within minutes, however, the plumbing began to hiss loudly. Fearful that the neighbors might hear, she placed an inverted flowerpot under the lever in the tank to quiet the noise and then continued her task, burning the papers first, then flushing the ashes. The phone rang. It was her friend Berta Bornstein, a psychoanalyst and member of Sigmund Freud's inner circle.[10]

"I hope you are taking Connie away for a change of air," said Bornstein. "I don't think it's that urgent," Muriel responded. "I'm sure it is," replied Bornstein. "I'm so afraid Connie will get pneumonia otherwise." From this purposely ambiguous conversation, Muriel realized the *Anschluss* was actually under- way.[11] The phone rang again and this time it was Joe, asking Muriel in code if it was safe to come home. Five minutes later, just after nine o'clock, he entered the apartment.[12]

"I think you should go. Right now. Take the morning train to Switzerland. And take Connie and Fini with you," Muriel said to him quietly. "Remember, it was agreed between you and the leaders of the party and all the colleagues that you would leave immediately after the Nazis came."[13] She herself had always intended to stay in order to finish medical school and to continue helping com- rades, but remaining in Vienna was simply too dangerous for Joe as a Social Democratic leader.

"I know, but I have some things to do first," Joe responded. "I've got to see everyone I can, and tell them they should contact you, that you will meet them." They argued: he did not want to go nor did he want to leave her behind. She insisted that, as an American medical student who could not easily be linked to the anti-Fascist movement, she was safe. Finally, hours later, Joe agreed to leave the country. Muriel would stay, at least for a few months, to help their comrades to safety.[14]

Saturday, March 12, 1938

Muriel woke Connie at dawn and told the child that she and Fini were going on vacation, skiing in Arosa, Switzerland, and that Joe and their British friend

Tony Hyndman were taking them there; she would see her mother soon, Muriel reassured her. Connie would be safe in Arosa, Muriel knew, but Joe was another story. He was wanted by the Nazis and needed a secure hiding place—Paris seemed to be his best bet. Muriel watched as the group quickly packed, then stood at the window as they left the flat and started walking toward the train station. No one turned to wave to her; it was too dangerous. She dropped the curtain and retreated into the apartment, determined not to cry.[15]

By midmorning that Saturday, Hitler's troops were goose-stepping across the border and, within hours, Austria was taken. Determined not to give in to her feelings of abandonment and fear, Muriel repeated aloud the reasons why she had stayed behind, why she remained in Vienna with Hitler when everyone she loved was getting as far away as they could. "I am not going to leave," she would tell friends. "I am going to stay and see what happens and do what I can…As an American I could do a lot."[16] Along with others of like mind who felt they had a great moral responsibility to resist Nazism and struggle to prevent a world war, Muriel would at least try to make a difference.[17]

Sunday, March 13, 1938

The very next morning, Muriel was at the window again when she saw a frenzy of men and women, some with babies in their arms, singing, laughing, flag waving, and shouting the Nazi cry "Sieg Heil!" The cobblestone streets swarmed with what seemed to be the entire city, ebbing and flowing like a river, their joy unconstrained. In the coffeehouses, German martial music played rather than waltzes. Vienna rejoiced as Austria officially became part of the German empire: one nation led by one Führer, protected by one invincible army.[18]

But who could say how many Viennese remained at home, watching behind drawn curtains, as Muriel did? Those in the streets represented only a segment of the population—though Muriel knew it would be a majority. She knew this from living in her adopted country for the last 12 years. But she also knew that there were many thousands of citizens who did not welcome the arrival of Hitler and his German army, who feared him and were horrified at the death of their nation Österreich—Austria—and its absorption as "Östmark" into Hitler's powerful German state.[19]

Later that day, 150 leading Viennese Jews were arrested by Brownshirts. Nazis would swiftly put anti-Jewish measures in place, and the Austrian-German administrators would launch immediate and absolute restrictions against Jews. Though anti-Semitism had long been part of the Austrian culture, now, for the first time, Germany began the process of Aryanization, the confiscation of Jewish property to benefit the German state.[20]

Muriel had been preparing for this type of challenge all her life. Standing straight and tall, she left the window, all but a wisp of fear dispelled. Now that Joe was gone, Muriel would take his place as the leader, in fact if not in name, of the Revolutionary Socialists. Until now she had worked under her code name, "Mary." Things would be different: Joe had spent his last days before fleeing sharing her real name and address with comrades who remained behind.[21] If, in the past, he had shielded her, protecting her identity and keeping her profile low, now—with her encouragement—he had placed her in grave danger. Soon, frantic Austrians would be at her door, begging for money, for documents, for safe passage out of what would quickly become a hell on Earth.

Thinking of her daughter, and of the children her efforts might save, Muriel began to reflect upon her own sheltered childhood and the family that had raised her. How would her parents and grandparents judge what she had done, what she was about to do? Would they feel she had wasted their legacy, her vast inheritance? Or would they feel that she had brought honor to herself and her family? How to tell? And, at this point, did it matter?[22]

CHAPTER 1

CHICAGO:
SWIFTS AND MORRISES

Separated by an ocean, a religion, and a heritage, Muriel's grandfathers, one a Yankee and the other a boy from a German *shtetl*, were born only months apart. On her mother's side, Gustavus Swift, a canny New Englander, arrived on June 24, 1839, one of a dozen children in the William Swift family of West Sandwich, Massachusetts, on Cape Cod.[1] Earlier that year, across the sea, Muriel's paternal grandfather, Moritz Beisinger, was born to a poor Jewish family in Hechingen, a village in the Black Forest. Though at first glance there were few similarities between them, both boys were shaped by powerful fathers. Determined that his son should take a more lucrative path than he had raising cattle in the Black Forest, Moritz's father sent his 12-year-old child to America to apprentice to an uncle, a peddler living in New England. Immediately changing his nephew's name to Nelson Morris, the well-meaning relative willingly taught him the business. But Nels, as he was now called, did not take to such a demeaning job and disliked this radically different environment, so he ran away.[2] As he worked his way from town to town doing a variety of jobs, his experience echoed the words made famous by newspaperman Horace Greeley, "Go West, young man, go West and grow up with the country."[3] Like others before and after him, with many stops on the way, Nels headed ever westward and, in 1853, after an exhausting sequence of boats and trains, landed in Chicago. He was fifteen.[4]

There, he soon got a job working for John B. Sherman, who would later found the Union Stock Yards. Immediately at home in the familiar environment of livestock and butchering, Nels called on his background and was soon buying and selling, not cattle, but dead hogs and hogs considered unusable. He sold them to renderers, companies that produced by-products from slaughter-ing factories, and thrived as his income increased.[5]

Back on Cape Cod, Gus Swift, too, had his eye on Chicago. As a boy, he had quit school to work for a local butcher in West Sandwich. Realizing there was no future in such a small community—at least not the one the ambitious boy envisioned for himself—Gus told his father he wanted to move to Boston. In an effort to get him to stay at the family's farm, Gus's father gave him $25 to remain on the Cape. But, clever and even a bit disingenuous, Gus instead used the money to purchase a cow from a nearby farmer and quickly relocated, tak-ing his livestock with him.[6]

He slaughtered the cow and sold cuts of beef door to door. With the profits, he soon had enough cash to open his own butcher shop in Brighton, outside Boston city proper. Within a short time, he had opened a chain of butcher shops on the Cape, having learned early that if you sold people what they needed rather than what they wanted, presented it attractively, and priced it low, you could earn more than a living wage. At this point, though, New England was not lucrative enough, and the recently married young man expanded his business to other cities, all the while fixed on Chicago, the nation's leading meatpacking hub. Meatpacking, a powerful economic force in Chicago since the days of fur traders and trappers, cowboys and ranchers, was now totally centered in that northwestern hub.[7]

Because of its central location Chicago became the focal point of the nation's trains by the late 1860s; the great storied railroads of American history roared through the city, belching black smoke and cinders with a reverberat-ing thunder. The stockyards flourished. Success came with a price, however, and the egregious overflow of wastes from the yards into the Chicago River polluted the drinking water and caused Chicago to ban slaughterhouses in the city. Officials allocated what would eventually be a tract of 475 acres south of the city for the construction of a huge new stockyard. Realizing that it would benefit their bottom line, the railroads absorbed the cost of creating the Union Stock Yards in December 1865, thus ensuring their own and the meatpacking industry's financial success.[8]

Meanwhile, Nels Morris had already helped supply meat to the hungry Union Army during the Civil War, an enterprise leading to such financial gain that he had been able to found his own business, Morris and Company.[9] With innate shrewdness and an obsessive drive for wealth, Nels had quickly become a success, with a vast business and personal fortune.

A decade later, in 1875, Gus Swift finally arrived in the windy city. Lured by the Union Stock Yards, Gus knew well Chicago's reputation as a gritty town where a man could make his fortune with sweat and hard work. With the money he had saved from his businesses on the East Coast, the 36-year-old founded Swift and Company,[10] an enterprise that would become an American institution, built on the blood and muscle of slaughtered livestock and an underpaid immigrant labor force.

By the year of Gus's arrival, telegraph lines, telephone lines, and transatlantic cable, which had been laid in 1860, had enabled meatpacking to become the world's first global business.[11] Even so, the city seemed to be waiting for Gus: only six years after he set foot in the stockyards, he altered the meatpacking industry forever by overseeing the creation of the first long-distance refrigerated railroad car.

A man who didn't like being controlled by anything, including Mother Nature, Gus balked at seasonal limitations on fresh meat shipments. He hired an engineer to develop a refrigerated car, thus enabling him to ship his meat in all weather and make a fortune. Gus's other methods were also innovative, so much so that Henry Ford copied the leading meatpackers' efficient disassembly lines for his own assembly lines.[12] Gus changed the way pigs were slaughtered by perfecting a more efficient killing machine, the Hereford Wheel. As Rudyard Kipling would write after seeing it in action, "They were so excessively alive, these pigs. And then they were so excessively dead."[13] In 1885, Gus incorporated Swift and Company with capital of $300,000. A year later, his company was valued at $3 million.[14] It kept growing, until, by 1902, it was worth more than $25 million.[15]

Outside of business, where they were ruthless capitalists, both of Muriel's grandfathers were devoted family men, inspiring most of their offspring to enter the family business. Nels, a non-observant Jew, nevertheless married within his faith, in 1863 taking Sarah, "one of the five beautiful Vogel sisters,"[16] as his bride. They had three sons, including Muriel's father, Edward, and two daughters, both of whom would marry well: Augusta became Mrs. M. L. Rothschild, and Maude, Mrs. M. C. Schwab.

"My dear beloved wife and children have been my all," Nels wrote to his son Ira. "You know my views of organized religion. I have no use for darkness, no fears of the hereafter."[17] It would be two generations before a bravely defiant Muriel would provocatively and briefly adopt the religion of her Jewish forbears.

Gus Swift, too, had a large family, with ten children, including Muriel's mother, Helen. Helen had been born to Gus and his wife, Annie Mae Higgins, in 1869. After a sister died of tuberculosis, Helen remained one of two girls among seven brothers, most of whom would join their father's business. Like Nels, Gus considered family to be the center of his life, along with his business: by 1892, the Swift patriarch employed thousands to slaughter and ship more than half a million cattle a year. Both Nels Morris and Gus Swift had similar business methods. Gus, known as the Yankee of the yards,[18] was a meticulous, perfectionist empire builder. Yet, as his personal wealth increased, he continued living simply, never moving from his original home at 4548 Ellis Avenue. In true Yankee fashion, Gus made many charitable contributions, but always privately. His family, especially his granddaughter Muriel, would follow this example of giving generously without asking for recognition.

Like his fellow meatpacker Gus Swift, Nels Morris, rumored to be illiterate all his life, also remained an uncomplicated cattle broker whose routine included riding horseback into his stockyards daily to inspect the slaughtering.[19] And also like Swift, despite his focus on the dollar, Nels saw himself as a visionary: "I have opened the wild western prairies and made them useful..."[20]

Dubbed "Foxy Grandpa" by his grandsons after a character in the Sunday comics, Nels was indeed clever.[21] By 1880, he, along with his equally avaricious long-term rivals, Gus Swift and Philip Armour, formed a beef monopoly called the "greatest trust in the world." These "overlords of beef" controlled the economics of all businesses they dealt with, from railroads to farms, holding prices down on goods and services received, and raising prices on items sold.[22]

By the first year of the twentieth century, both of Muriel's grandfathers' personal wealth had increased vastly, their multimillion-dollar Chicago meatpacking empires yielding enormous returns. As was common in this era, these tycoons identified money with positive qualities and good character. But because they focused only on acquiring riches, they appeared to lack and had little time for intellectual pursuits and showed little contemplation of life. Gus Swift and Nels Morris reflected an unbridled American aptitude for capitalism and urban values such as hard work, creative business methods, and resourcefulness.[23]

But even meatpacking wasn't enough for these men. In an eerily farsighted move, the beef barons created a futures market in hogs that would lead to today's jumbled web of commodity markets. One could buy or sell, gamble and speculate, on the future price of hogs—a market for "men who don't own something, selling that something to men who don't really want it."[24] In the waning years of the nineteenth century, the beef barons also helped make Chicago a major financial center as they became major stockholders and owners of important Chicago banks.[25]

Because of their wealth and the enormity of their businesses, Gus and Nels had admirers, but it often seemed as if their detractors outnumbered their fans. Investigated and eventually charged by the government for their monopoly of the meatpacking industry, the men were also despised for their heartless business methods and single-minded pursuit of wealth at the cost of human lives. Yet they somehow managed to continue their activities and avoid prosecution, raking in more money than ever. As Upton Sinclair wrote in *The Jungle*, a book partly about Muriel's family, "One could not stand and watch very long without becoming philosophical, without beginning... to hear the hog-squeal of the universe."[26] Because of their concrete belief in capitalism, neither Nels nor Gus were moved by the radical movements of the late 1800s and early 1900s, the rise of labor unions, the struggles of workers. Nels wrote, late in life, that "it was the duty of capitalists to keep labor employed." He believed that capital would "win every conflict," but his son Ira would not be so certain.[27]

In 1890 it might have appeared to the outside world that two of the three leading Chicago meat barons had forced a marriage upon their children in order to ensure the continuing existence of their empire. Instead, and however unlikely, this was a real romance. Gus Swift's daughter Helen, a tall, proud beauty with black hair, blue eyes, and fair skin, and Edward, Nels Morris's oldest son and second-in-command, had fallen deeply in love. The union between Helen and Edward had nothing to do with dynasty building: the two patriarchs remained so competitive that soon after the marriage, Gus Swift set up a trust fund for his daughter because "he was planning to put his son-in-law out of business," as a relative would recall.[28]

Muriel would always be impressed with her parents' loving relationship. "From everything I observed in my childhood, as well as what my mother later told me," Muriel wrote in notes for a memoir, "I believe this was a love match on both sides." Having heard the still-bandied-about speculation that the marriage had been a mere business arrangement, she once asked her mother, "Did you think you loved him?" Helen was completely taken aback. "I did love him," she replied. "We were both very much in love. I always loved him."[29]

From childhood, Muriel's father was passionate about the stockyards and the meatpacking business. Like his own father, Edward was "devoted to the task of making... [and] conserving" money,[30] as his brother Ira would write, and was destined to inherit the family empire. Muriel's mother, Helen, was a millionaire in her own right. Helen and Edward's wedding ceremony, on October 2, 1890, was simple but unusual; the couple had no attendants but arranged for dual clergymen, a rabbi and a Unitarian minister. Neither family objected to the marriage on religious grounds because the Morrises were non-observant Jews, the Swifts non-observant Protestants, and Edward himself had become a Freethinker, defined as one who rejects authority in religious belief.

At her parents' home, within a few blocks of the stockyards, Helen wore a white silk gown adorned with feathers and lace, and was joined in marriage by rabbi and minister to Edward, her father's competitor. After this rather forward-thinking ceremony, guests ate supper in a large tent and danced to a mandolin orchestra. Valuable gifts were displayed in three rooms of the Swift house, none more impressive than a $5,000 check (about $122,000 today) from Gus Swift, along with a hefty pile of "gold coin to act as a weight for the paper," according to newspaper coverage of the society nuptials.[31]

Helen and Edward left immediately for a European tour that would last several months. Upon their return, they lived with Helen's parents while their own house was being built. Soon, settled in their new home on South Michigan Avenue, Edward once again took up the reins of Morris and Company where he would work six and a half days a week for the rest of his life. The couple would move twice more, but they always remained on the South Side of Chicago. Edward chose to live on the South Side, as had his father and father-in-law before him, because of its proximity to the stockyards. Helen did not necessarily agree with this decision. With its vast yards, factories, and other industries, the South Side also had a few stately and elegant areas with enormous homes as befitted such wealthy business owners as the Morrises and Swifts, but it was also the site of the unfortunate slum known as "Back of the Yards."

Helen's role as a society matron was to tend home, "a small castle," as Muriel described it, and a growing family, consisting of two boys, Nelson and Edward Jr., and two girls, Ruth and Muriel.[32] Nelson, the oldest, was born in 1891, and a decade later, on November 23, 1901, Muriel arrived.

Edward Sr. gradually took over more and more responsibility in Nels's business, increasing the family fortune enormously. "I like to turn bristles, blood, and the inside and outside of pigs and bullocks into revenue,"[33] Philip D. Armour once remarked, likely speaking for his friendly rivals Gus Swift and Nels Morris. Now the second generation—Muriel's father, Edward Morris Sr., and her uncle, Louis F. Swift, maintained the successful monopoly by working closely with the Armour family in an intricate web of secret deals and negotiations. Their death grip on American meat prices resulted from blacklisting that was carried out without waver or ambivalence. "This aroused the admiration of captains of industry in all other fields and gave Chicago long ago its atmosphere of violence," as one author would write.[34] If Muriel as a young child did not know the ugly side of her father's trade, she surely would come to understand it as she grew up and heard the stories.

Despite Edward Sr.'s hard work and dedication, his generation could never live up to the energy and innovation of his father's contemporaries: there was "a great difference between the types of men required to build a great business and to carry it on," according to Louis Swift.[35] Helen Swift Morris pointed out that her father, Gus, who had created his company, seemed always carefree and relaxed despite business problems. On the other hand, her husband Edward would often return home, as she described it, "worn out, unable to eat, unable to sleep."[36] It was as if the brutality the first generation had to condone to make the stockyards yield their fortunes was perceived by the second and third generations as dirty work for which they did not have the same passion.

Nevertheless, meatpacking was in the progeny's bones and controlled every Swift and Morris life, even those who shunned the smelly, bloody stockyards. Edward's younger brother, Ira, wanted no part of what was to him a disgusting business. His revulsion at the slaughtering process was incomprehensible to his father, Nels. After all, in the late nineteenth century, "every young man wanted to work in the yards; it was the Chicago thing to do," Muriel would recall.[37] No match for his father, Ira was finally forced to join the family business, but his brother Edward better understood his sibling's horror and would later help him to escape the slaughterhouse.

Muriel's brothers Nelson and Edward, trained to work at Morris and Company, were told weekly by their father that they would one day take over the business. While the girls were spared, they would be trained for another type of duty, that of society debutante, followed by society matron. When Muriel was born, her older brothers and sister, engaged in various activities in their large home, barely noticed the howling baby. But the cry was certainly heard by her mother, Helen. Reclining on a couch in her boudoir a short time after giving birth, Helen said she was "inclined to agree" with her own mother, who was visiting, when the older woman said Helen had a lovely family now, and that four children were enough.[38] Whether Edward felt the same is unknown.

Toward the end of the nineteenth century, muckrakers and others began to threaten that if the rich did not contribute meaningfully with fair wages and social reforms, "the poor would rise up and take what was rightfully theirs," and Chicago became the scene of terrifying riots and violent strikes. Soon, social critics would describe the Gilded Age's "self-made man" as a man of straw, decried for the wealth and hard business practices for which he had previously been revered.[39] As riches had once been concomitant with morality, by the turn of the century, the upper classes were feeling the sting of society's condemnation.

Despite the many challenges he faced in his business—including the U.S. government's seemingly never-ending investigation of the National Packing Company monopoly—Edward Morris continued to follow the example set by his father, Nels: work hard each day to make Morris and Company the best and most profitable meatpacking operation in Chicago, the country, and the world.

While the public did not follow the government's investigation of the meatpacking industry closely, its attention was nonetheless riveted by bestselling books describing the filthy stockyards, the beef barons' illegal and unethical monopoly, and their seeming lack of concern for human life. In his 1905 novel, *The Greatest Trust in the World,* Charles Edward Russell wrote that it was unconscionable for an industry to hold a nation hostage to fixed prices. Upton Sinclair's *The Jungle* was a poetic and descriptive indictment of the stockyards. For years the battle waged, monopoly on one side, government investigators and critics on the other. In the meantime, Edward Morris and his fellow packers secured their fortunes. Regardless of the professional lives they led, what linked the Swifts and the Morrises most significantly was their offspring. Muriel's own life of leadership and innovation would reflect attributes of both families, and her radically different beliefs and ideals would send her across the world to follow paths her parents and grandparents could not have imagined.

CHAPTER 2

HAPPY, FOR THE MOST PART

When Muriel was three, the family moved to Grand Boulevard, still on Chicago's South Side, but farther from the stockyards and closer to the elegant Kenwood section. In their magnificent new house, despite Edward Morris's work habits and Helen Swift Morris's grandeur, both parents were hospitable to their children's friends. "We had many parties, and could invite children just to come over and play and drink hot chocolate with us in the afternoons," Muriel would recall. Muriel grew up in awe of her parents, who she thought glamorous and "strikingly handsome and attractive."[1] Helen was recalled by some as the most beautiful woman they had ever seen. Muriel's mother was busy with charity work and social events while her father was almost always working, including Saturdays and Sunday mornings, so Muriel spent most of her early childhood years rarely seeing her parents.

After bearing her children, Helen largely turned over the task of rearing them to nursemaids, governesses, cooks, and other staff. In addition to the demanding routines of a socialite's life, Helen faced fearsome challenges as her husband Edward confronted serious obstacles in the course of earning his millions, as violent workers' strikes, government probes, and censure by muckrakers seemed to be ever present. Meanwhile, Helen was defining her place in Chicago society, a time-consuming, energy-draining assignment. In many ways, she was typical of her class: Chicago society was led by wealthy club women like Helen, who typically raised their children in a Victorian manner, importing the rules and codes of nineteenth-century etiquette from abroad. The children were meant to reflect their mother's own regal personage. Always well groomed and beautifully dressed and quiet and well-spoken, young Muriel and her siblings, in spite of the stockyards that funded their lifestyle, were the product of the Gilded Age.

Predictably, in keeping with the era, Helen did not enjoy a close or warm relationship with any of children, including her youngest daughter, Muriel. Named Helen Muriel and called Helen throughout childhood, she would insist on using Muriel as her name from age 16 on. She was tended to mainly by her nurse, Mollie, and protected by her family's great wealth, knowing nothing of the rough-and-tumble background of the stockyards. Every need was met by a phalanx of 12 servants, particularly Mollie, who was by her side day and night, the one unchanging factor in her universe. Mollie loved Muriel like a daughter.

Even Helen's good-morning and good-night kisses were given rather formally. As a consequence, on the rare occasion when Helen took Muriel on her lap, both mother and child were uncomfortable. The emotional distance between them intensified when Muriel was naughty; her mother would lock her in a guest room with no books to read or toys to distract her. Muriel would recall not minding the punishment as much as she hated her mother's verbal excoriations: "The way she talked to us about how terrible whatever we had done was…made me feel like a worm or worse than a worm something very terrible."[2]

From her perspective, Helen believed she was teaching her children discipline and how to overcome adversity. Muriel did eventually absorb these lessons, but, to a little girl, Helen's excessive rigidity seemed unloving. Helen would accept no difference of opinion or any viewpoint other than her own. Afraid of confiding in her mother for fear of being reproached, Muriel kept her own counsel, confiding only in Mollie.

With her "round gentle face, honest gray-blue eyes, and ready grin," as Muriel would describe her, Mollie was the person Muriel loved most. She dressed and bathed Muriel and her older sister, Ruth, fed them supper on trays, and accompanied them everywhere, even sleeping in their room. She had worked for the Morris family since Nelson was born, and now she recounted her well-worn stories again, regaling the little girls with tales of growing up in a large Irish family on the Iowa prairie. "She was one of the kindest and best people I have ever known [and] I loved her more than anyone else I knew, from the time I can remember," Muriel would write.[3]

Muriel's father was even more remote than her mother. Edward Morris was tall and handsome with black hair and dark eyes—but was also high-strung and overly sensitive, according to his wife. He also was rarely home. Preoccupied with business, he was "always busy, often worried, and seldom laughed," as his youngest child would remember.[4] When he was around, however, Muriel recalled some warm acts of kindness. He scratched the soles of her new shoes so she wouldn't slip, and he sent her flowers on Valentine's Day, Easter, and whenever she was ill. He presented her with gold pieces after meetings of his company's directors. But she didn't know him very well because he was almost always working, and when she saw him, even at their regular breakfasts together at 7:00 A.M., they didn't talk much.[5] When she was little, though, if she was still awake, Muriel would wait for his homecoming and run into his arms and sit on his lap. Some Saturdays he worked a half day so the family could lunch together. On other days, Edward took his two daughters with him to work where they would play with pencils and paper in his office.

Despite her parents' insistence on honesty, strict morals, and stoic acceptance, Muriel was rarely punished and only spanked a single time. Once, she had somehow hurt her sister Ruth, and her father told Muriel that she would now learn what it meant to feel pain. "He laid me on the couch, took my clothes down, and spanked my behind," Muriel would recount. Although she was humiliated and furious, Muriel recalled that she had defiantly cried out, "I like it; do it again!" In another instance, about to be spanked a second time, she threatened: "If you ever spank me again, I'll run away from home and I'll never, never come back."[6] She was not hit again.

Her siblings played a large part in Muriel's youth, their presence and involvement often substituting for that of her parents. Her oldest brother, Nelson, was her good fairy, slipping presents under her pillow every week if she behaved. One time, she awakened and lifted her pillow but found no gift: "I tried to deny my disappointment, to be brave as we were always taught to be," she later recalled. "Then...I saw that he had left his gift on the floor beside the bed—a pair of roller skates, the thing I was most longing for!"[7] Nelson was also the family magician, entertaining Muriel and her friends with conjuring tricks that always ended by his pulling a white rabbit out of an empty top hat, then presenting the rabbit with a flourish to a delighted child. Nelson's magic props were kept in a large chest in a room that Muriel and her siblings called the secret dungeon, located in the mansion's tower. Only Nelson could open the iron lock on the chest with his special key.[8]

Muriel's other brother, Edward Jr., had a different personality, one that was less to her liking. Livelier and inclined to tease, Edward often sadistically tickled Muriel. Though she did not mind his verbal rejoinders, the tickling was painful and her automatic laughter, a response she could not control, only encouraged him. However, she stoically told no one, and the tickling continued until she was in her late teens.[9] Keeping her problems to herself was typical for Muriel as a child, portending her adult tendency to repress inner feelings, even when she was with people she loved and trusted.

Though Ruth was three and a half years older and closest in age to Muriel, the two sisters rarely got along. Muriel resented the greater autonomy allowed Ruth while the older girl envied the younger one for her height and agility;

Muriel could ride a bike and skate just about as well as Ruth, in spite of the difference in their ages. This rivalry, maintained throughout their lives, was one reason, or so Muriel claimed, that she developed a sense of justice and injustice at an early age.

But even with her competitiveness with Ruth, Muriel grew up happy for the most part, indulged without knowing it. Helen, though formal in dress and manner, nevertheless encouraged sports and other physical activities, and every November allowed a "toboggan" to be constructed in the back yard that in winter became a sledding hill. Another section of the grounds was flooded in winter for ice-skating. The house, with its towers, parapets (a perfect hiding spot from which to throw snowballs at passersby, then duck down), and turrets, was ideal for playing games. There were also a billiards room, bowling alley, conservatory, two playrooms, and a study for the children. The family owned an assortment of cars, carts, carriages, sleighs, and a bobsled, all housed in the enormous barn, which also held farm animals—horses, cows, and rabbits.

In 1903, when Muriel was two, her grandfather Gus Swift died. He was 63, a tall but stooped white-haired man, still vigorous and determined, who had, according to his daughter Helen, the face of "a scholar or a poet, or an artist...a man who might see visions and dream dreams."[10] But unlike Helen, the world would remember Gus Swift as a shrewd businessman, who at the time of his death had created an empire worth more $600 million in today's dollars.[11] With Gus's death, two years after that of Philip Armour, the only original beef baron still in business was Nels Morris.

The next year, Muriel's family traveled to Europe with both Mollie and Nellie, a maid, accompanying them to help with the children. For Muriel, the journey was magical, as she would later recall despite being only three at the time. She loved everything: the motion of the ship, and the smell of the sea, the friendly German captain, the lively music on deck, and afternoon lemonades and cookies. Docking at Liverpool, the family traveled by train, then hansom cab to London's Savoy Hotel, spending several weeks in the city that Muriel would always love. As she would write as an adult on a visit to her favorite place, "[T]he feel and smell of the city are the same, and on a rainy evening the recurring magic of that first glimpse of London can move me to tears."[12]

After that, the family went on to Holland, where the children were left with Mollie and Nellie. Other than the Irish ditties Nellie sang to her and Ruth, there had been no music at home. In a seaside resort one night, from her hotel window, the little girl saw lights at sea and heard beautiful music played by an unseen band. She would always remember the feeling of ecstasy that came over her, forever associating bliss with both music and beaches.[13]

Not long after the family returned to Chicago, Nelson, who was 14, became ill with typhoid. Muriel kept watch over her beloved brother from the hallway, becoming more and more anxious as nurses bustled in and out of his room. He recovered and that Christmas, Muriel and Nelson sat together in the cozy study with its fireplace that was necessary for Santa Claus's much-anticipated Christmas Eve visit. Muriel left him a plate of bread with butter and sugar and later recalled that "Santa's acceptance of our hospitality gave me almost as much pleasure as his gifts."[14]

On New Year's Eve 1906, Edward and Helen Morris hosted a grand soiree and Muriel and her sister were promised they would be taken downstairs at midnight "to share the strawberries, hear the bells and whistles, and wish everyone a happy New Year"—strawberries were a rare, out-of-season treat— Muriel would remember. Awaiting the magical hour, Muriel and Nelson talked about December 31, 1906, turning into January 1, 1907. The year after that, Nelson explained to his five-year-old sister, would be 1908, then 1909, and so on, correcting Muriel when she assumed that "nineteen-o-ten" would follow. Muriel, entranced, always remembered that Nelson "was so patient and lucid and loving that I was able to understand." In the warm room, smelling deliciously of the blue spruce Christmas tree, Muriel for the first time grasped an abstract idea, a moment of understanding that was thrilling. She would recall New Year's Eve 1906 as a dividing point "between the trusting little girl who still believed in Santa Claus, and...the child who has discovered...thinking, questioning, exploring."[15]

The joy of these young years came to an abrupt halt. Books were the source of the trouble, and, although she could not understand much of what was said at home, Muriel knew that her parents were upset over two that continued to get lots of attention long after they were published: *The Greatest Trust in the World* and *The Jungle*.

In addition, with her brothers and sister in school, Muriel was often lonely. She did have occasional outings with her mother but they consisted of dreaded fittings and sittings—at the dressmaker and photographer—or boring drives in the automobile. Helen insisted on piano lessons for Muriel as well as instruction in dancing, horseback riding (side saddle, of course), good grooming, and deportment, and on fine custom-made clothes that required the maximum hours of tedious visits to the dressmaker. Unfortunately, Muriel particularly disliked "fussy clothes," the proper petticoats and stockings along with other elaborate accoutrements that were part of the daily costume of a wealthy Victorian-era girl.

Occasionally Helen would try to take over Muriel's care in order to teach her important lessons about life. Once, Muriel was lying down in the blue guest room—either as punishment or for a rest—when her mother walked in and asked, as Muriel recalled, "Muriel, would you lend me five dollars?" The child had money of her own, a weekly allowance, Christmas gifts, gold pieces from her father, Santa Claus's stocking gifts, and some saved nickels given to her by Foxy Grandpa Morris. She had been taught to value and save money, but also to be generous. When she heard her mother's request, the child was uncertain as to the correct response and said, "I don't know." Her mother's retort was quick and sharp: "Well, then I'll ask Edward; he's always willing to help me," Muriel remembered.[16]

Muriel would recall crying for a long time, feeling ashamed, but also angry: "If I had been sure Mother would not disapprove of my taking the money from my savings, I would not have hesitated. I wished I could explain this to her, but I could never talk to her about my troubles. Now, sobbing on the bed, I was longing to say 'I'll lend it to you' but she had disappeared," she recalled.[17] In later years, Muriel used this childhood experience to explain why she was never able to deny any request for financial aid, or any other kind of help.

While Helen sought to teach Muriel about the value and proper use of money, the girl was acquiring from Mollie an even more deeply seated lesson about money: the lives of the rich and the poor were very different. Because her time was taken up as surrogate mother for Muriel and Ruth, Mollie boarded her own daughters with a woman named Mrs. Joy. Muriel sometimes accompanied Mollie on visits to her daughters. Since she expected to see poverty when she visited Mrs. Joy and Mollie's daughters, she was shocked on her first visit to see Mrs. Joy's comfortable apartment, complete with piano and all the middle-class trimmings. She cried out in amazement, to Mollie's embarrassment, "This isn't so bad!" Muriel would remember Mollie whispering to her, "You mustn't say that. You'll hurt Mrs. Joy's feelings."[18]

Mollie and Nellie often talked to Muriel about the discrepancy between very rich people, like her family, and average ones like Mrs. Joy. Once, when Muriel mentioned that other children seemed to like her, Nellie quashed that notion by telling her the other girls only acted friendly towards her because she was so rich. Muriel felt awful: Did this mean that her friends liked her simply because she was richer than they? This difference, reiterated in many of the books she read, especially those by her beloved Charles Dickens, haunted her. Once Nellie told her about her voyage to America in steerage, when she was nourished only on potato peels and watery soup. Those who traveled in steerage were cold and hungry for the duration of their journey, Nellie said, and Muriel understood—or thought she did. However, the child remained confused about people like Mrs. Joy with her piano and comfortable home. They were not wealthy, nor were they poor: Where did they fit into Mollie and Nellie's portrait of the classes?

Nellie, particularly, filled Muriel's young mind with ideas about injustice. It was in the air when Nellie sang songs from her homeland such as, "Did you hear the news that's going round? The shamrock is forbid to grow on Irish ground." Or "They're hanging men and women for the wearing of the Green." Muriel asked about the Green and the Orange, and Nellie tried to explain. Muriel came away from their talks with a belief that "terrible things happened to poor people, and also to people who wanted their liberty."[19]

Considering her family's business, it was paradoxical that Muriel hated wearing animal skins, including her ponyskin coat and the sealskin coat she was forced to wear on Sundays. The sealskin was particularly onerous, not only because it meant an animal had been killed, but because it caused her to stand out from the other girls in school; few of them owned fur coats. Of course, Muriel dared not voice these feelings to her mother, and she dressed as she was told to.

Summers at Green Lake, Wisconsin, had become a family tradition by the turn of the century. For Muriel, those summers would be her happiest times, where she and Ruth rode horseback with their father and where her mother relaxed in the outdoors. The family had first summered at this western resort in 1896, three decades after wealthy families had made it popular.[20] Muriel's family lived at Grey Rock, the original house built by a Civil War hero, Brigadier General Mason Braymon, in 1873. Two decades later, in 1899, Muriel's parents bought the property and erected an even larger house for their summer residence.[21]

Each summer, for as long as she could remember, Muriel eagerly anticipated the trip to Green Lake. The long carriage drive to the station was followed by a five-hour train ride where the children could order whatever they wanted in the dining car and then nap comfortably in their compartment. Finally, they arrived at Green Lake where Mr. Biddle met the family in his horse-drawn carriage, with its door at the rear, benches along the sides, and oil lamps for the one-hour night drive to Grey Rock. Muriel felt closer to her mother at Grey Rock, and she recalled hearing Helen laugh out loud there, a rare occurrence. Muriel had her own pony cart, which had been given to her by the famous British conductor Thomas Beecham, a family acquaintance, and Helen allowed her to drive it on the grounds.[22]

Grey Rock meant picnics and boat rides on their 50-foot launch, *The Ruth*, whose crew was composed of "natives, shrewd and, sometimes, witty," as Helen would write.[23] Picnics consisted of fried fish cooked over a wood fire with bacon, salt pork, and potatoes, washed down with icy bottles of sarsaparilla and root beer, and followed by fruit, watermelon, and cake. If she misbehaved at Grey Rock, Muriel's punishment was not being allowed to swim, a great deprivation because she was a "greedy swimmer" who loved the water.[24]

The large white wooden country-style house at Grey Rock should have been a purely pleasant place for Muriel with its wide verandahs and sleeping porches, but she continued to manifest an inner discomfort through night terrors and tantrums, which had been going on since her earliest years. And it was at Grey Rock that she developed an odd and serious phobia of moths and butterflies, apparently connected to the ease with which they were killed, that would mar her life for many years. It had begun innocently enough on a warm summer day when she was five:

> [A friend] Hansl and I walked back up the shaded, sloping lawn to our big white house...On the screen door we saw an enormous dark moth. Hansl, who had a folded newspaper in her hand, raised her arm and brought the paper down on the moth, which literally disintegrated before our eyes. "Crushed to powder"...A shudder of horror ran through me...From that moment I could not bear to see a moth or a butterfly; to have one touch me sent me into "hysterics."[25]

Even at Green Lake, the minor abnormal behavior she had manifested for some time continued—made worse now by the new moth and butterfly phobia, the flying insects all but unavoidable in the country. Because she often had nightmares, if her mother wished her "sweet dreams" at night, she would whisper to herself, "If I have any." She also displayed some obsessive tics and other compulsive behaviors such as nail biting. Helen unsuccessfully tried to make her stop this habit, finally forcing her to have a weekly manicure, during which Muriel shrieked in terror at the nail file: she could not bear the sensation of having her nails filed and remained that way all her life. Helen did not acknowledge that her daughter had some emotional problems. She accounted for the night terrors by saying that Muriel was "overtired." The word for emotional disorders in that day was "nervous" and although Muriel heard it whispered in connection with her problems, Helen forbade it. "[I]t was something to be ashamed of; in any case, a child could not be nervous," Helen maintained, as Muriel would recall.[26]

Muriel also threw temper tantrums that, once begun, took on a life of their own and could not be stopped. From an early age, if she felt that she were about to become hysterical, Muriel would warn Mollie that she was going to have a fit, and would throw herself down on the floor, kicking and screaming. If Mollie felt Muriel was about to experience what she called a "conniption fit" in public, all measures would be taken to stop it: Mollie or whoever was with her would try to distract her.[27]

Since Muriel's mother had a difficult time accepting her daughter's problems and did not help her with them, Muriel coped on her own by creating fantasies. Her most cherished fantasy was that she would suddenly come upon a baby boy in the house or out in the garden. This thought came to her on a day when she felt such jealousy toward Ruth that she could no longer bear it. She imagined that she would take advantage of this new baby brother's helplessness to finally learn how boys and girls differed. Eventually, when he did not appear, her fantasy simply dissolved.

Despite Muriel's mild anxieties, the days at Green Lake were idyllic, passing at a perfectly leisurely pace, the summer seeming to stretch ahead forever. It was not until the first frosty mornings in early September that Muriel realized they would soon be returning to Chicago. She relished "gathering the first nuts, watching the maples turn gold and scarlet, seeing the brightness of the stars as night fell early, having a fire in the fire-place, and popping corn," as she would write.[28] Yet this pleasure was shadowed with sadness that her happy summer was ending.

One particular year, however, everything was different. Muriel's paternal grandfather, Nelson Morris, had been ill with arteriosclerosis for months. In late August 1907, Muriel's family rushed home early from Green Lake to go to his bedside. He died in the early morning hours of August 27 in the house he and his wife had moved into a half-century earlier.[29] Nels left a fortune of $30 million (more than $700 million today), which was divided, after a two-month family battle, into five parts. Muriel's grandmother and her father and his three siblings each received $6 million, about $140 million in today's dollars. Muriel's father, Edward, retained complete control of Morris and Company. Nels wrote in his will that he wanted Muriel and his other grandchildren "to become broad, liberal, high minded and independent in character."[30]

Only a month after her grandfather's death, Muriel's life changed again as she started first grade. On a brilliantly sunny September day, Muriel climbed into the pony cart. As Dave the coachman, along with the faithful Mollie, drove her and the new fifth grader, Ruth, to school, Muriel's spirits matched the bright sunshine. She was so happy that she did not even notice that the Spaids' School, a private institution for girls, was run by "thin, elderly spinsterish sisters, whom nobody loved," as Muriel would later describe them. Seeing only that there were many children here for her to play with, Muriel ignored the ugly bare rooms and rarely paid attention to Miss Spaid, or Miss McClure, a woman who lacked patience and equanimity and disciplined her students by pulling their hair.[31] Muriel felt at home in school and was well liked and popular, especially with the boys. After only a short time, her prescient teachers labeled her a mischief-making ringleader. Aware of her family's wealth and prominence, however, the teachers imposed only the lightest punishment on her if she broke the rules, typically keeping her inside during recess.

Within two years, Muriel had a real best friend, Margery. She was an angelic-looking child who ironically knew everything about sexuality, pregnancy, and birth and she soon filled Muriel in on all of these subjects. Muriel corroborated what her new friend told her by looking in her family's enormous dictionary, and also by agreeing to play doctor with Margery, her brother, and his friend.

She soon ended her friendship with the fascinating Margery, though, when she noticed that some of her possessions disappeared whenever Margery visited: books, money, and then her treasured initialed signet ring. Later, when she saw the ring on Margery's dresser, she took it home with her. She never went back, nor did she speak to Margery again. This would be a harbinger of the way Muriel ended relationships as an adult—if they seemed to be harmful to her, she cut them off swiftly, absolutely, and with no discussion. There were many friends after Margery, happily, with whom Muriel put on theatricals, created secret clubs, and played games—the gregarious girl seemed to have boundless energy.

In 1910, at the age of eight, Muriel developed a serious case of measles, which forced her family to postpone a planned trip to Europe. At this time, she also became aware that her father was gravely ill. Edward had Bright's Disease, an acute and chronic kidney inflammation. There was some concern within the family that his health was further compromised by his ongoing business worries and exacerbated by a rising wave of negative publicity due to government lawsuits and books, and articles censuring him and the other meat packers. Muriel herself was ill enough that she had to stay in a darkened room for weeks, her only bit of cheer coming from her brother Nelson's visits, especially one in which he crept in with a bouquet of dozens of balloons.[32]

On December 22, a catastrophic fire broke out at the stockyards. Raging for a week, it devastated Morris and Company, costing the business $1.5 million and taking the lives of more than 40 Chicago firemen. The sky grew black from smoke, and the odor of burning flesh filled the Morris house.[33] Edward returned each night, despairing at the deaths: firemen, workers, and an untold number of animals that were burned alive. That same autumn, adding to Muriel's sense of loss, Nelson left for Harvard, leaving behind a bereft little sister.

But the family was nothing if not resilient. As soon as Helen and Edward were told that Muriel was fully cured, they traveled to New York. The children and nursemaids would follow on the 20th Century Limited to meet them there. On the train, however, Muriel awakened with sharp dagger-like pains in her eyes. A high fever and the unfamiliar environment exaggerated her usual night terrors, and she screamed in agony and fear. Once in New York, she was rushed to the Plaza Hotel where her parents were living and was quickly seen by an ophthalmologist who treated her for an eye infection, applying leeches around the eye to draw out toxins.

Finally, when Muriel recovered, the family set off on their long-postponed trip to Europe. On board the ship, as she looked down on open decks filled with steerage passengers, Muriel at last understood what Nellie had described years ago. From her comfortable first-class vantage, she would recall "all these people sitting…with waves washing over the deck, women in their black shawls, in steerage." Horrified, she asked her mother, "Why do we have fur coats and a nice warm clean deck while the other people are cold and wet?" Helen never answered her daughter. This voyage left Muriel with an image of the unfairness of life, an image that never left her: "I just couldn't get over people being treated so differently just because some of them had money and some of them didn't."[34]

Once in England, the family settled at Oakley Court, an estate on the Thames three miles from Windsor Castle that they had rented for the summer. Eleven gardeners cared for Oakley Court's peach trees, grapevines, strawberry beds, and multiple gardens of lilies, roses, and other blooms; one maid had as her only occupation arranging flowers throughout the house. Muriel managed to find a wild area among the formal gardens and discovered her first primroses, which would remain her favorite flowers for the rest of her life.

The mischievous girl with the intense curiosity about her world also came upon a gardener's young son urinating in a garden bed and hoped "in vain that this would be repeated." To her disappointment, it never was. Muriel's parents were often away—she learned later that her father was consulting with Harley Street physicians about his kidney disease—so Muriel and her siblings were kept busy with outings to zoos, horse shows, and the theater, accompanied by servants, of course. Picnics were particularly memorable for their delicious treats: cold chicken and sandwiches with sardines or cucumbers or apricot jam made with thin brown or white bread.[35] Once during this vacation, the family traveled to Killarney, Ireland, and even at her young age, Muriel appreciated its beauty, blanketed in green.

King Edward VII died on May 6, 1910, while the family was still in England, and Muriel, standing at the window of a draper's shop in a spot her father had paid for, watched the funeral cortege. She would come to associate that stately and dramatic procession with her father's illness that more and more hampered his activity. Before returning to America, the family, including Edward, who was feeling temporarily stronger, stopped in Paris. The places they visited in Europe, as well as her reading of Charles Dickens's *A Child's History of England*, instilled in Muriel a passion for history.[36]

Because she saw her father daily on this trip, Muriel gained a deeper knowledge of his disease, witnessing his suffering as well as her mother's distress over this illness, and she came to view her parents in a different way. Muriel had also seen a larger world outside of Chicago, and had finally witnessed for herself the disparity between rich and poor. It was a lot for an eight-year-old to absorb over a few months. This summer marked the end of Muriel's innocence.

CHAPTER 3

ROOTS OF DISCOVERY

Muriel entered early adolescence with all the concerns and turbulent feelings typical of pre-teenage girls. But her adolescence would become more fraught as two deeply emotional events destabilized her world.

In September 1911, despite Edward Morris's continually worsening condition, the family moved into a new house on Drexel Boulevard in fancy Kenwood, which although upscale, was still on the South Side. Their mansion took up an entire city block. With its regal rooms with ornate plaster ceilings and its brilliant gardens complete with tea house and pergola, it outdid all the houses in the neighborhood. Living in Kenwood, the "Lake Forest of the South Side," had long been a goal of Helen's as its residents were the very wealthiest Chicagoans and the houses were designed by architects like Frank Lloyd Wright and Howard Van Doren Shaw.[1] Living there meant that the stockyards were far away, literally and symbolically.

As soon as the family settled into their new neighborhood, the nine-year-old Muriel transferred to the exclusive Faulkner School. Its more than 200 students ranged from kindergarteners to young women in college preparatory classes. Founded by a University of Chicago graduate whose mission was to prepare her graduates to attend leading American colleges, the academically progressive Faulkner School instilled in its young charges a love of learning.[2] The school would foster in Muriel a lifelong passion for books, libraries, and scholarship.

Also a day school, Faulkner was a huge improvement over the provincial Spaids' School, and Muriel found new friends as well as intellectual stimulation; she quickly took to both. However, she still resented the requisite French, dancing, and piano lessons—all subjects in a wealthy upper-class child's life, and all of no interest whatsoever to her.[3] If Muriel's competitive nature had previously found no outlet because she was unable to best her older siblings, now, in school, she was determined to outdo her new classmates at their studies. She soon rose to the top of her class.

Popular in school, she would later be elected class president for three consecutive terms. Muriel found her duties in this office, administering and arranging class business, so critical in her life that she later blamed her impatience with disorganization on these early-learned skills. On the other hand, her mischievous side was never long hidden. Once, she led her classmates into trouble by convincing them one day that school had been cancelled. They followed her to the park where they played games and gorged on chocolate-marshmallow walnut cookies she had bought. As the sun began to set, Muriel cried, "April fool! There really was school today but I fooled you."[4]

As a result of this little frolic, the school principal punished Muriel and her classmates by not allowing them to participate in a long-scheduled basketball game against a class of older students. Muriel begged that she alone be punished, but the principal would not relent. This was her first experience with what she viewed as injustice meted out by an institution. She never forgot it.[5]

Another mischievous act, although with a serious purpose, was Muriel's own personal suffrage march. At age ten, during the summer of 1912, Muriel read her brother Nelson's textbooks, which kindled in her an interest in civics, government, and political causes. She convinced a group of school friends to borrow their mothers' dresses and join her in a march in support of votes for women. Muriel had always felt it unfair that boys enjoyed more privileges and independence than girls.[6] So one day she and her friends made banners emblazoned with slogans proclaiming a woman's right to vote, dressed as grownups in their mothers' clothing, and marched down exclusive Drexel Boulevard. Of course, Helen and the other parents were horrified.

Muriel shared the thrilling story of her first suffrage march with her charming cousin Constance, the daughter of her father's brother, Ira, and Muriel's closest friend aside from Mollie. Constance was the only one with whom she shared her thoughts and feelings—as much as a private person such as Muriel would ever do. Although only a year older, Constance introduced her younger cousin to topics innocence had kept her from so much as inquiring about. The girls discussed adults who lied and cheated, as well as Constance's life in Europe with her worldly parents.[7] Later, when her uncle was appointed U.S. ambassador to Sweden the summer Muriel was 14, she was invited to join the family in Stockholm. But, somewhat fearful of new environments—a trait she would deliberately rout as she grew older—she refused.

In addition to reading for school, Muriel began taking books out of the public library near her home, and she grew to love the very smell of the quiet, self-contained building. She also spent hours in her family's library, a vast room used by various family members in the evenings but that was often empty by day. The low, open bookshelves, filled with beautifully bound sets of English and American classics, provided Muriel's first exposure to the books that would form her thinking: *Jane Eyre* and other books by the Brontës, Rudyard Kipling, Robert Louis Stevenson—Muriel came to love books so much that she would ask to be excused from dining with her family in order to read while she had her meal on a tray in her room.[8]

This passion of hers was fueled in part by loneliness at home, as Nelson was away at Harvard. But among the college texts he brought home on vacation, Muriel discovered tomes that would actually alter the course of her life, including Ralph Waldo Emerson's *Essays* and the writings of Marcus Aurelius. *Everyday Ethics* by Ella Lyman Cabot became her bible. Ethics was a new topic for her; Muriel suddenly understood that there could be many sides to a single question, even two sides to certain virtues, which in turn could be altered by circumstances. Her mind was opened to not only "the complexities of moral judgments but of life itself." At thirteen, Muriel began to contemplate the major issues of life, like poverty, war, and good and evil, which inevitably led her to consider her family's business with fresh insight.[9]

Muriel, too smart not to notice the questionable source of her family's enormous wealth, must have read the newspaper articles that documented her father's problems, including the government's investigation of the meatpacking monopoly and the threat of possible criminal charges against him; she also must have known of the violent resistance with which her father and the other beef barons met the challenge of labor unions. Her early childhood despair over inequities between rich and poor had been revived by reading Nelson's books, although what she read was all she knew of poverty. She had some idea about what went on "Back of the Yards," where the workers lived, from *The Jungle*, which she read hiding in a closet behind the coats since the book was not allowed in her house. From her family and their wealthy circle, Muriel had heard that poverty was "shameful…that no hard-working person need be poor" but this dictum contradicted what she knew of Mollie and Nellie; they worked tirelessly but never grew wealthier. For the first time, she began to doubt that poverty was shameful, that it was an individual's own fault if he or she was poor.[10]

Muriel still had no firsthand knowledge of her family's business; she had never been to the yards, and no one at home talked about them. Nevertheless, the business occupied most of the men in the family, and soon a third generation began working there—Muriel's brother Edward Jr., who had decided not to attend college, entered the family business full time. Nelson, who had no interest in the business, hoped to graduate from Harvard and study law. He feared that his plans might fall through, however, should his father's illness grow more serious.[11]

Muriel, the precocious student, read about wars in Nelson's books and studied European geography in school. She also realized that the United States was barely half a century past its own Civil War, and this led her to think about war in general—whether it was right to kill in defense of an idea and whether each side thought it was in the right while it was doing the killing. Such contemplation led Muriel to scrutinize, not just glance over, the daily newspaper and her geography books.[12]

Soon Edward Jr. was running the business while Muriel traveled with the rest of the family, and the servants, to Yellowstone National Park in a private Pullman car accompanied by her father's personal physician. At Yellowstone, large horse-drawn carriages transported the entourage from lodge to lodge, and when it was time to return home, their exclusive conveyance was at the ready. Muriel found this journey as distressing in some ways as her earlier voyage to Europe by ship: this time she observed ragged children, many of them Native Americans, approaching the Pullman car at every stop, begging for money and candy. Muriel gave away all that she had: crayons and paints and all her toys, except for one beloved teddy bear.[13]

A short time later, Muriel was allowed to take her first vacation "alone"— she, of course, was accompanied by Mollie—to visit Nelson at Harvard. One of her happiest times, this trip was memorable because of her brother's treatment of his little sister as the woman she was becoming. He introduced her to his friends as well as to historic Boston landmarks. The trip would influence her, some years later, to choose to attend Wellesley College, as it was not far from Boston.[14]

Back in Chicago, she continued to do well in school, enjoying a full social life, which included the activities expected of a girl of her class. Along with her sister Ruth and a few other daughters of South Side society matrons, for instance, Muriel raised more than $1,000 at a charity bazaar hosted by her mother, a member of the Martha Washington Circle, an organization consisting of affluent Chicago women.[15]

Among her many social activities was horseback riding, which she loved. When she debuted at the Chicago Hunt Club, she was lauded for her seat and her looks: "Muriel Morris makes a picture in her white habit with her jet black curls tied back with a bow of scarlet. She should be an expert horsewoman by the time she is a debutante." For years, the *Chicago Tribune* would occasionally decorate its front page with her picture, including one large photo of Muriel driving her pony cart, dressed in a flowing coat with decorative sleeves, her long dark corkscrew curls set off by a large-brimmed hat.[16]

Just before Muriel's twelfth birthday, at six in the morning on November 3, 1913, her father died at the age of 47. His poor health had deteriorated even more as a result of his business and legal problems. After a decade of staving off the government's legal actions, the beef barons had finally been indicted in 1910; in 1911 they stood trial, charged with violating the Sherman Antitrust Act of 1890, a criminal offense. Although all the defendants were acquitted, the trial was grueling and, according to some reports, caused Muriel's father to have a nervous breakdown. Upon his death, he left his family a fortune. In addition to Morris and Company, he was the largest stockholder in several Chicago banks and financial institutions; he also owned other packing companies, as well as shares in various corporations.[17]

With the exception of $315,000 earmarked for charity, including $100,000 for Morris and Company's employee pension fund and $5,000 for the servants, the estate of $20 million ($450 million today) went to Helen and the four children, with the children's inheritance placed in trust. As the result of the fortunes left her by her husband and her father, Helen was now one of the richest women in the world. And, at the age of twelve, Muriel became a millionaire—inheriting approximately $3 million, a sum equivalent to $67 million today. She would receive an annual allowance in increasing amounts until age 35, when the balance of the estate—invested for all those years—would become hers.[18]

In keeping with Jewish tradition, Edward Morris's funeral took place almost immediately, on November 5. Like his father a few years earlier, Edward was buried in the family plot at Rosehill Cemetery. Although Edward had showed little concern for the well-being of his employees during his lifetime, the family held a two-hour reception in the mansion to which company employees were invited.[19]

That Muriel's father's death affected her is not in question. Still, while she left detailed writings about her childhood, she devoted only one sentence to Edward's death in her memoir: "Although I did not deeply grieve for him, I was impressed by the tragedy of early death and by my mother's suffering."[20]

Despite his own hopes, as well as those of his mother that he would become a lawyer, as the eldest son Nelson had to leave Harvard after his father's death to take over the management of Morris and Company. Both he and Edward Jr. also became bankers, a decision they thought wise since the family owned large shares in major banks.[21]

Interestingly, Muriel's father's death solved one mystery for her: She had been wondering about her religion for several years by now, especially since it was a subject never discussed at home. The family had rarely attended church, and neither Edward nor her other Morris relatives went to synagogue. One day, a year before her father's death, two of her closest school friends remarked that they were Jewish and that Muriel was as well. She denied the claim in a neutral way, since she knew nothing either for or against the Jews. But a third girl chimed in, seeming to defend Muriel from an apparent accusation, leading her to think there might be something wrong with being Jewish. Her curiosity was satisfied a year later when, at Edward's death, the newspapers described him as "a freethinker from a Jewish family...married to a Gentile."[22]

After her husband died, Helen wanted to send Muriel and Ruth to a luxurious boarding school in Switzerland, but the assassination of Archduke Franz Ferdinand, the heir to the Austro-Hungarian throne, on June 28, 1914, disrupted her plans. Nelson told his little sister that war might break out, and she began scouring the daily papers for war news. Although the United States would not enter the struggle for almost three years, stories of combat in Europe and the threat of her country's imminent involvement worried the 12-year-old girl. Throughout her high school years, World War I was a distant but constant backdrop, developing in Muriel an aversion to any violence predicated on nationalism, nation building, or tyranny of any sort. It would not be until college, however, that she would begin to speak out on the subject.

Regardless of all the war talk in 1914 and 1915 that concerned her, Muriel continued to pursue her everyday interests, sports and academics, getting elected captain of her high school basketball team and winning numerous horseback riding competitions. She began modeling herself on her favorite teacher, Helen Boice, an unusually well-educated and tolerant woman for the times, and before long, Muriel had decided to become a schoolteacher herself. Boice did not try to indoctrinate her students but instead attempted to convince her young charges to express their own thoughts and opinions. It was that openness that so delighted Muriel, when compared to her childhood of rigid rules and regulations.[23]

In addition to her interest in world affairs, Muriel was also fascinated by national politics, and no subject was more compelling to her than her long-held passion for women's suffrage. When Muriel was 14 years old, 5,000 women marched along Chicago's Michigan Avenue to present their demands to the National Republican Party's committee on resolutions. On June 7, 1916, despite torrential rains and gale winds, a "suffrage army" picketed and protested to claim a place in the national campaign. Voicing the women's demands that the G.O.P. support the Susan B. Anthony constitutional amendment allowing women the right to vote, the charismatic suffrage leader Inez Milholland spoke to the assembled throng, thrilling her listeners.[24]

Accompanied by the always-present Mollie, Muriel was in the audience to hear Milholland. Excited by the great assembly, their chance of success slim but their determination huge, Muriel recalled her own little suffrage march when she was younger and was more determined than ever to work for women's rights. She also idolized Milholland, fascinated by the suffragist's concerns and actions. Milholland had even been in jail in solidarity with striking shirtwaist "girls" employed in New York City sweatshops.[25]

Muriel's fascination with Milholland's politically progressive father, Socialist views, and imprisonment in England, where she had learned the more militant tactics of British suffragists, deeply influenced the young girl. At this same time, she slowly began to realize that her developing belief system was dramatically at odds with that of her family.

Five short months later, the 14-year-old Muriel would suffer another loss, although less significant than that of her father's death. In October 1916, at the urging of the suffrage leader Alice Paul, Inez Milholland, though ill, agreed to take part in Paul's campaign against President Woodrow Wilson, who had refused to add voting rights for women to his platform. Paul planned to use the brilliant but clearly weakening speaker in all 12 states, ending in the Midwest. After Milholland had collapsed several times, even Paul had to concede that the determined young woman was too sick to continue.

Muriel was present when a substitute for Milholland delivered the keynote speech in Chicago on November 7, 1916. Even as the speaker rallied the crowd, doctors were administering blood transfusions to Milholland in a desperate attempt to save her life. It was no use: she died of leukemia on November 24 at the age of thirty. Her death devastated Muriel, who had seen Inez Milholland as one of her role models.[26]

The Chicago Horse Show took place the following month, on December 2, 1916, and took Muriel's mind off Milholland's death. She competed enthusiastically. But the same day that she won her blue ribbons, her photo gracing the front page of the local papers, another story revealed that the Chicago beef industry had again bested the U.S. government, forcing the lifting of an embargo on the shipment of livestock. The powerful meatpackers convinced the government that what ailed their stock was a mild viral disease, stomatitis, not the dreaded hoof-and-mouth disease. Muriel's joy in riding that day was tainted by her sense that the money that sustained her hobby, and that paid for the entire Chicago

Horse Show, came from a questionable business with which she would rather not be associated.[27]

The following autumn, Muriel suffered further familial instability in what seemed the cruelest blow of all: Helen announced that she was remarrying. On the evening of September 4, 1917, at her magisterial home on Drexel Boulevard, Helen shook off the stench of the stockyards by marrying an upper-class Englishman.[28] Her new husband, Francis Neilson, had excellent credentials. Formerly in the theater, but in politics when he met Helen Morris, Neilson was a great-grandson of the Scottish philosopher and historian David Hume, and a cousin of William Gladstone, who had been prime minister during the reign of Queen Victoria. Muriel felt more alienated from her mother than ever. She did not care for Neilson's political views, or for his manner.[29]

Serving in Parliament alongside David Lloyd George and Winston Churchill, Neilson had blamed the First World War on England and the machinations of British statesmen. Along with his romantic view of Teutonic culture and his lifelong sympathy for Germanic tradition, Neilson's views included the notion that an individual could control his own destiny if he behaved a certain way. In 1915, Neilson's views were so unpopular in England that he decamped for America, vacating his seat in Parliament. In America, he met Helen Morris who, soon after their marriage, became his patron, supporting his career as he wrote 60 books and published a short-lived but influential journal of opinion and criticism, *The Freeman*. From their first acquaintance, Muriel considered her stepfather to be a conceited man with an unlikely "mixture of ideas, in some ways extremely radical, radical left, and in other ways, so incredibly bigoted on certain subjects." She noted the anti-Semitism with which Neilson had been associated; along with those of his publishing colleague on *The Freeman*, Albert Jay Nock, Neilson's writings, including those that blame Winston Churchill for World War II, now figure prominently in Holocaust revisionist theories.[30]

Helen's remarriage was followed by yet another calamity: Muriel's beloved brother Nelson was leaving home to join his regiment, the 11th Illinois National Guard, for preparation and training to fight in the Great War.

Nelson's departure for the war and the addition of Francis Neilson to the family cast a long shadow over Muriel's last years at home.

CHAPTER 4

IN A DIFFERENT VOICE

In the fall of 1918, thrilled to finally leave home for college, Muriel headed to Wellesley. Though she had dutifully visited Vassar and Smith the winter before, there was never any real question of her destination. She loved Wellesley for itself, but it also linked her with the female side of her family and gave her a sense of belonging to a tradition: her mother had attended for a year and Ruth was a senior there.[1]

When she arrived on campus that September, two months before her seventeenth birthday, Muriel intended to succeed on her own merits, not on her family's riches. At Wellesley, Muriel decided to harden herself after the soft life she had had as a child—she gave up all luxuries, did not wear a watch, took cold showers, and slept on the floor. She found it difficult to integrate wealth into her life as she developed a value system that was incompatible with that wealth. This dilemma would trouble her for years. During her time at college, she found ingenious ways to spend her money on others anonymously.[2] In a paradox that she would eventually acknowledge, it was her inheritance that supported her future rebellion against her family's values.

On her first day at Wellesley, as she entered Noanett, the dormitory where she would live during her freshman year, Muriel finally felt free—released from the Victorian mores of her mother, the snobbishness of her British stepfather, and the pretensions of her family's ostentatious mansion.[3] Even something as trivial as having others call her Muriel—being able to drop entirely her given name Helen—gave her a new sense of identity.

Just as in high school, she again found that she loved the world of scholarship. At Wellesley, Muriel studied all the subjects she held dearest: history, literature, and philosophy. In part because of her family's lack of interest in spirituality of any sort, she took courses in religion. She also kept a close eye on

politics and world events. As her first semester ended, Americans were trying
to recover from the effects of the First World War—the armistice was signed
on November 11, 1918. Thrilled that the battles were finally over, Muriel, along
with everyone else, hoped that, as President Woodrow Wilson had said, this
was indeed "the war to end all wars."[4]

The rising sophomore returned to Chicago in June 1919 to pursue a new
interest. During her first year at Wellesley, Muriel's political beliefs had begun
to coalesce—pacifism, women's rights, issues of justice versus injustice, anger
at the dichotomy between rich and poor. She was fascinated by the Russian
Revolution at the same time as she was repulsed by the murder and terrorism
that accompanied it. Still, she often felt she had no outlet for her newly forming ideology. Spending that summer in a city where she had lived all her life
would, paradoxically, give her a strong beginning: Muriel did clerical work in
the offices of Morris and Company, which was once again being run by her
brother Nelson, who had returned home from the war.[5]

Muriel's summer foray into her family's business did not go unnoticed:
"Most stories are rags to riches," smirked the *Chicago Tribune*, but in the case
of this "young and popular debutante," it appeared to be the other way around.
For the first time, she experienced the stockyards for herself, having taken the
job "to learn something about the condition of girls who have to work for a living," she would recall. Muriel had been long aware of the plight of these working girls, if only from the publicity over the 1911 Triangle Shirtwaist Factory
fire in New York. Now, at Morris and Company, she became so engrossed in
interacting with these workers, many of whom were her age or younger, that
she was even reluctant to leave for vacation at the beloved Morris compound on
Green Lake, Wisconsin.[6]

Back at college for her sophomore year, Muriel moved into a different
dorm, Pomeroy, or Pom, as it was called. She lived in the dun-colored stone
building for three years, leaving for class each morning aware that learning is
eternal, that the intellect lives forever through what it creates, as she would later
write. At Wellesley in the autumn of 1919, she became friends with women she
would know all her life, including Gladys Lack and Margaret Willard Shepard.
Especially as she became close to Glad, as she was called, Muriel was embarrassed
to find herself envying this young woman who, with no family money, had to
pay her own way. Compared to Glad, Muriel felt like a dependent person.[7]

During spring semester, as women's suffrage continued to capture head-
lines, a local story drew Muriel's attention. On April 15, 1920, the deaths of a
paymaster and a security guard during an armed robbery in South Braintree,
a few miles from Wellesley, led to the arrest of two Italian immigrants, Nicola
Sacco and Bartolomeo Vanzetti. While in custody, the two admitted that they

.were anarchists and had been involved in strikes, political agitation, and anti-war propaganda. With this sensational disclosure, Sacco and Vanzetti became fair game for conservatives and the right wing, as this was the period of the Red Scare. Just after the end of World War I and the Bolshevik Revolution, many Americans came to fear Communism and Socialism. Sacco and Vanzetti's trial the following year would be one of the century's most infamous, pitting their Socialist defense attorney Fred H. Moore against J. Edgar Hoover on his first case as director of a new division in the Justice Department's FBI, the General Intelligence Division.[8]

Like most of her Wellesley classmates, Muriel was serious, academic, and political and had little time for frivolity. Influenced by the college's faculty—who ranged from liberal all the way to radical—Muriel started tilting to the left on national issues such as trade unionism as well as notorious cases such as Sacco and Vanzetti.

During the summer of 1920, after sophomore year, encouraged by the publication of a short essay she had written, she enrolled in writing classes at the Bread Loaf School of English in Middlebury, Vermont, and, on the train there, met a young man named Brooks Phillips with whom she enjoyed what was likely her first flirtation. He was a decade older and a graduate student who taught at Harvard. They did not have a sexual relationship, she would later say, if only because they were bound by college rules about teachers and students not fraternizing. Nevertheless, the pair became close, and remained friends throughout their lives.[9]

In September 1920, despite the grim news about the indictment of Sacco and Vanzetti for murder, Muriel began junior year on a high note: for the first time in American history, women could vote. Congress had passed the Nineteenth Amendment in June 1919, and it was finally ratified on August 18, 1920, by the required 36th state. Muriel felt certain that the death of her heroine Inez Milholland four years earlier had also helped spark the militancy in the movement that led to the passage of this historic amendment. The nearly 19-year-old took this victory personally, remembering the rallies she had attended in Chicago, the charismatic Milholland, as well as her own suffrage march as a girl. Women's voices would be heard in the upcoming November presidential election, which pitted Senator Warren Harding against Ohio Governor James Cox and his vice presidential candidate Franklin Delano Roosevelt.[10]

Forgetting politics briefly, Muriel attended the junior prom on February 11, 1921, dancing to every song from "Humming" and "Palesteena" to "Home Again Blues," according to her dance card. Several months later, in late spring, when the Sacco and Vanzetti trial began, Muriel found herself riveted by it. She drove an old car of her sister Ruth's to the courthouse in Dedham, taking along any friends who were available. Apparently Sacco and Vanzetti had lied when they were first arrested; the authorities claimed that the men's lies proved their criminality and guilt in the Braintree robbery and murder. But, the other side argued, the lying was an understandable effort to hide their radical politics and to protect others during this time of the Red Scare. Muriel, convinced of the latter, sympathized with the immigrants, certain the government was conspiring against them, and despaired when the men were convicted on July 14.[11]

She was outraged at the seeming injustice of this trial, seeing it as a failure of the nation's rule of law. As with women's suffrage, Muriel's politics had become personal. Now, in the case of Sacco and Vanzetti, she found herself once again emotionally involved, on the side of the liberals, aligned against self-proclaimed conservative patriots.

This line in the sand between liberals and conservatives would come to divide Americans in the twentieth century. Personally, politically, and socially, Muriel crossed the line with Sacco and Vanzetti and would move far to the left, eventually becoming a Socialist. She had felt the first stirrings of revolutionary politics while reading about the Bolshevik Revolution. Her early ideas had been supported and influenced by certain radical members of Wellesley's faculty, encouraging her to develop her childhood quandary over justice versus injustice, rich versus poor, into a strong belief system that would inform her actions for the rest of her life.[12]

In an era when young women were refused entry to top male-only universities, women's colleges such as Wellesley provided a place for female intellectuals to develop—and Muriel was taking full advantage of this. She was deeply influenced by a number of her professors, especially one she referred to as AF: Agnes Frances Perkins, an associate professor of rhetoric and composition, had written a revolutionary book positing the notion that women could choose careers other than teaching. Economics professor Emily Greene Balch, whose contract was not renewed by Wellesley because of her outspoken pacifist views, also affected Muriel significantly.[13]

Muriel plunged into the political fray with enthusiasm, quickly becoming a campus leader. Students respected her and paid attention to her positions on disarmament and on America's refusal to ratify the Treaty of Versailles or join the League of Nations. During her junior and senior years, she also proved her intellectual mettle by being named a Durant Scholar, the college's highest academic honor.[14]

On April 2, 1921, Muriel met with representatives from East Coast colleges and universities at Harvard to set up what would be the first intercollegiate liberal organization in America, the Intercollegiate Liberal League (ILL). The group would later be compared to the 1960s Students for a Democratic Society (SDS). Muriel proudly felt that, in her own way, she was following the example of Inez Milholland, who had originated the Socialist Club of Vassar during her own college days. Soon after the ILL's formation, its members elected Muriel president and also changed its name to the National Student Forum. Highly unpopular with traditionalists and conservatives, the group's members were denounced as "Bolshies" or "Reds" by those in the universities and colleges who disagreed with their politics.[15]

That same spring, Muriel was elected president of a separate organization, the Student Forum at Wellesley, for a term to begin in the fall of her senior year. Her reputation as a leftist was bolstered by the speakers she brought to campus, among them four of the twentieth century's most radical thinkers: antiwar activist, socialist, and repeat presidential candidate Norman Thomas; Roger Baldwin, who helped found the American Civil Liberties Union; Harry Laidlaw, the socialist director of the League for Industrial Democracy; and pacifist and socialist Scott Nearing, a founder of the 1960s back-to-the-land movement.[16]

After a summer walking tour in England, Muriel returned to Wellesley for her senior year in the fall of 1921 and really hit her stride. She was elected president of her class and traveled in October to Vassar College in Poughkeepsie, New York, for a large conference of women's colleges on disarmament at which she represented Wellesley. Most of the students attending, Muriel included, believed strongly that peace could only be achieved if nations eliminated their weapons; they resolved that the United States set an example by first limiting arms, with a future goal of complete disarmament.[17]

When Muriel returned from Vassar, she gave a keynote speech at Wellesley's Armistice Day program in which she reported on the conference. Her voice rang out, filled with her strong young enthusiasm for her cause: each Wellesley student should "take a definite stand, and let her voice be heard" on the great issue of nations laying down their arms. At the end of the program, as if to hammer home the message Muriel delivered against carnage, a student read "In Flanders Fields," the poem by John McCrae commemorating the dead of World War I.[18]

Muriel's senior year was marked by a heated debate between Wellesley administration and students over whether students had a responsibility to inform on each other if they witnessed someone breaking a rule. This led to Muriel's first participation in a student protest. After a year of disagreement between the two sides, in May 1922, the administration voted that students had to inform. Muriel and others who had been protesting this all year, disagreed with the administration's final ruling and signed a petition against it. Muriel then nailed it to the door of the Wellesley chapel. Other students were angry but "Muriel was the one who decided to do something about it," a college friend would recall. The college eventually capitulated and voted to end the so-called honor system.[19]

As senior year drew to a close, the accolades and distinctions heaped upon Muriel Morris were almost embarrassing: seniors voted her "most intelligent" and "most educated," while juniors chose her as "most highbrow," and the faculty pronounced her "most intelligent." She received a joking prognosis about what she would do after graduation: "Muriel Morris has been appointed to the office of Assistant Secretary of State. Her new book 'From Cicero to 1932' is having a large sale in diplomatic circles in Washington.'"[20]

Along with 387 other young women, Muriel graduated from Wellesley College on June 20. At the class supper, in addition to the traditional college song and the engagement announcement—newly engaged young women ran around the table displaying their rings—this year's event held a surprise. Certain "prominent members" of the class of 1922 had at their places mock radiograms from two decades into the future, 1942. Each radiogram was deliberately at odds with the characteristic behaviors and beliefs of the young woman who had received it. Muriel, showing that her classmates indeed knew her, would be a censor in 1942, her radiogram stated, with the mission of controlling radio messages issued by the Town Hall in Orfle Bluffs, Iowa.[21]

Immediately after graduation, Muriel felt ready to move ahead—having become "independent of material things," she had already given away, to her friends, the clothing she liked best, and her fur coat and jewelry. She had sold most of her books to a bookstore in Boston and sent the money to needy students at the University of Vienna, whose administration had written to Wellesley's, asking for help. Yet, despite what would have to be viewed, even by Muriel herself, as a most successful college career, she remained shy. "At Wellesley," she said, "I was reticent and didn't talk about myself and my real feelings and desires." This reluctance to share her deepest emotions remained an abiding characteristic: She would always value privacy, a quality that encouraged others to assume a kind of secrecy about her. Only years of psychoanalysis would reveal Muriel fully, even to herself.[22]

CHAPTER 5

SCHOLARS AND LOVERS

After graduation in June 1922, Muriel delayed her plan to become a teacher and instead decided to travel to Italy, a place she had longed to visit ever since she first saw photographs of the country and read of its lushness, warmth, and color. However, Muriel knew that Helen would not permit a trip abroad without structure and purpose, so to ensure her strict mother's approval, she secured admission and a small scholarship to the American School of Classical Studies in Rome.[1]

Avoiding the luxury ocean liners, Muriel and a college friend, Katherine "Kay" Cooke sailed to the Continent on a small boat, as Muriel described it; she paid for Kay's passage, anonymously through Wellesley, as she would also pay for her housing. At Wellesley, Kay had been the one who discouraged Muriel's bashful tendencies, convincing her friend to try out for the debating society in order to overcome her fear of public speaking. Along with the other passengers to Italy, Muriel and Kay ate with the officers, flirting a little, as self-assured young women of the world might. All went well until one night when a slightly tipsy Muriel—already drunk on the idea that she would be halfway around the world from her mother for the first time—raised her glass and cried, "*Abbasso i fascisti!*" (Down with the Fascists!) Noting even in her muddled state the terrified faces of the officers at these words, she had her first inkling of how seriously the Italians took Fascism.[2]

Not only Italy, but all of Europe in 1922 was a continent in economic turmoil, suffering from political "impotence and corruption," and populated by fatigued citizens who were diminished and exhausted from the toll of more than 20 million dead and wounded and 42 million mobilized in the war just ended.[3] In the wake of this horrific war, the 1917 Russian Revolution, and the 1918 flu pandemic, Europe was weary, embattled, and all but bankrupt. With the political, social, and cultural old ways practically obliterated, the decade of the twenties would see new dictatorships in Russia and in Italy, signs of the rise of two more, in Spain and Germany, and would culminate in the Wall Street Crash of 1929 and the Great Depression.

The reshaped political map of Europe, especially the dissolution of the Habsburg Empire into separate nation states that now suffered additional financial burdens, created shifting alliances and added fears and anxieties. Stalin, Mussolini, Franco, and Hitler all rose to power during this post–World War I period as desperate citizens turned to these dictators in the hope that they would lead them out of this very dark period into the light.

Knowing little of the European political climate, on arriving in Rome Muriel dutifully registered in the American School but never attended classes. She used the library, attended school-organized expeditions, and participated enthusiastically in social events. Rooming with a Roman family, she soon met 20-year-old Oliviero de Fabritiis, a conductor at the Teatro Nazionale in Rome, who became her lover, likely her first.[4]

Without a doubt, this year in Italy marked Muriel's progression from girl to woman as she learned to make her way in a foreign country on her own with no real support from anyone but a few friends. As she enjoyed her new feelings of independence and maturity, she saw every day as an adventure. On October 29, she watched as Benito Mussolini's Blackshirts marched into Rome. Almost immediately, King Victor Emmanuel, in an attempt to avoid bloodshed, appointed Mussolini as prime minister. Within two years, Mussolini would create a totalitarian state and name himself dictator, thus beginning Italy's inexorable march toward entente with Hitler and the Axis in the Second World War.[5]

Still unaware of the politics around her, after eight months of parties and socializing in Rome, Muriel grew more serious and, after much thought, decided to pursue an advanced degree at Oxford University, knowing that her mother could not possibly object: Oxford fit in with Helen's upper-class aspirations as well as with her husband's British heritage. In truth, Muriel had fallen in love with the picturesque medieval town of Oxford when she had visited after her junior year in college, vowing to return someday. Oxford University offered an intellectually challenging graduate program—it was also far from Chicago and her mother. Further, women-only graduate schools in England and in America resembled girls' boarding schools and after her year of freedom in Italy, this was not at all appealing to Muriel. Oxford, with its predominantly male population, made more sense.

When Muriel matriculated at Oxford on October 13, 1923, registering as Helen Muriel Morris with a BA from Wellesley, there existed four residential colleges for women at the university. Nevertheless, she chose the non-residential Society of Oxford Home Students for women in order to maintain her independence. The society was perfect for a student like her—someone who was older than most undergraduates, from abroad, and did not want to live on campus. The Society had no physical location but was an "administrative arrangement without central facilities that enabled women to study with Oxford tutors."[6]

Home Students enjoyed a large degree of autonomy, residing in boardinghouses of their own choice within the town of Oxford, their landladies thoroughly vetted by the university's administration. They also did not adhere to set class schedules; they could study and attend lectures under the supervision of a tutor in their field and a second academic who had general charge of them. Inevitably, there were still many regulations that Muriel and other women in the Home Society had to follow. Some she viewed as silly, such as the one allowing women to attend lectures only if they agreed not to socialize with the men in class.[7]

In addition, Oxford women in 1923 had to follow a strict set of rules concerning chaperones and curfew, and several regarding dress and deportment. Once, the Home Students' principal chastised Muriel for walking on the High Street without a hat, a serious misdemeanor that could lead, he said, to her being mistaken for the "other kind of woman"—not a lady. "Well, if that's the only difference, that's okay," was Muriel's response.[8]

Nor did she like curfews. On one occasion, she returned a day late to Oxford from a vacation to Italy with two Wellesley friends. Her tardiness turned out to be a good thing because their scheduled train had been in a wreck, with several passengers killed. When Muriel got back to the university and was censured for being late, she responded that at least she hadn't died in the crash.[9]

Under the supervision of her tutor, the noted author and poet the Reverend Maurice Roy Ridley and her overseeing tutor, Christina Violet Butler, Muriel spent more than two years attending lectures and doing independent studies, one of nine Home Students pursuing a B. Litt., or bachelor's degree in literature, considered a research degree.[10]

Since the Oxford year had three terms, there were two midyear recesses and a long summer vacation. Muriel spent these breaks touring Europe, either on her own or with Wellesley friends whose expenses she often paid anonymously, as she had Kay's. The first year, she and a friend traveled by cargo ship up the Norwegian coast, stopping at towns along the way. Muriel and her closest friend from Wellesley, Gladys Lack—now also at Oxford—spent six weeks navigating the hills and towns of Greece, mostly on mule back, except for one snowbound week in Delphi. There, Muriel, Glad, and a dozen other American tourists sat around a single tiny stove, tore their paperback books into batches of twenty or so pages and passed them around in a circle, each person reading, then waiting to receive the next twenty pages of the novel or whatever was available to read.[11]

One summer, Muriel invited Nellie and Mollie to join her, all expenses paid, for a few weeks in Ireland. She traveled to Rome and Sicily, too, and, in 1925, visited Berlin for the first time; in February of that year, she attended her sister Ruth's wedding in Paris to Dr. Harry Bakwin, a professor of medicine, whom Ruth had met while studying at Cornell Medical School. She had just completed postdoctoral work in Vienna where, as part of her educational requirements, she underwent psychoanalysis—impressively, with Anna Freud. Even as an American medical student, Ruth was required to understand the relatively new field and to experience it, hence her brief analysis with Sigmund Freud's daughter. Ruth disliked her short interaction with psychoanalysis and judged it to be of no value after Anna Freud told her young analysand that she disapproved of Harry Bakwin.[12]

Psychoanalysis had been introduced to Americans in 1909 when Freud presented an introductory course about his theories at Clark University in Massachusetts. Freud's *Interpretation of Dreams*, published in the last year of the nineteenth century, would hold the twentieth century in its grip, as the Viennese neurologist had created an innovative and complex theory of subconscious and unconscious reasons for human actions that he had been developing for two decades. He would say that his appearance in America was "the first official recognition of our endeavors," and welcomed the recognition he received there.[13]

At the beginning of her third year at Oxford, in the fall of 1925, Muriel was ready to present her thesis on the life of Mary Shelley. She had researched the subject for months at the Bodleian Library in Oxford and at the British Library in London. Shelley, author of *Frankenstein* and a believer in free love, was someone Muriel admired: an independent intellectual woman who led an unconventional life—the kind of life Muriel had realized she wanted for herself. Now in her early twenties, she believed she had found a perfect place for herself at Oxford—relative freedom, intellectual stimulation, not too much supervision—but she had misjudged the extent of the institution's bias against women.

Her tutors, Ridley and Butler, along with one other interlocutor, had judged the thesis, and Muriel, unsatisfactory. They didn't think her topic suitable, and Muriel found herself in conflict with a stifling social order that Shelley herself would have rebelled against. During Muriel's oral defense of her thesis, replete with the suicides and suicide threats that dotted the landscape of Mary Shelley's life, the Reverend Mr. Ridley, Miss Butler, and the third questioner, an Oxford don, challenged her, saying that nowhere in her thesis had she stated that she condemned suicide. Muriel responded that she did not, and that such a condemnation would be "out of place" in her thesis. Miss Butler said, "But surely you know suicide is a sin."[14]

Muriel found herself defending her own morals and values rather than her research paper. When she received notice that her tutors would not accept the work, she asked them for guidance on scholarship and style and offered to rewrite it. They responded that it was no use—Muriel would not receive a degree.[15] After a lifetime of academic achievement, this failure was a great blow for the scholar who had been named most intelligent and most studious. But, in a skillful psychological about-face, Muriel managed to deflect her anger at and frustration with Oxford's forbidding self-righteousness. Escaping the pain of rejection, she pursued a different interest—sex, and men.

While at the British Museum in September 1925, Muriel had run into an acquaintance, Harold Abramson, a good-looking 28-year-old man whom she had first met in Ithaca, New York, while visiting her sister at medical school. Ruth had taken the teenage girl on a double date; Ruth's date had been Harold. That day in the British Museum, Harold, eager to renew his acquaintance with Ruth's beautiful raven-haired sister, stopped her and reintroduced himself. Muriel's sculptured face, creamy skin, and deep brown eyes immediately drew him. He was in London, he told her, doing advanced studies after his recent graduation from Columbia University's College of Physicians and Surgeons.[16]

The couple soon began a passionate love affair and, a short time later, disheartened by the rejection of her thesis and emboldened by her strong attraction toward her new beau, Muriel decided she would never return to Oxford. Although Muriel had hoped to keep their relationship only sexual, Harold began to insist on marriage. Two months shy of her twenty-fourth birthday at the time, she felt very much alone in England and did not want to give up their affair, which she was enjoying. Further, she entertained doubts about the institution of marriage itself. Eventually, Harold prevailed and Muriel gave in, even though she knew that he was the wrong man for her. Harold and his most reluctant bride exchanged vows on November 5, 1925, at the Registrar's office in the District of St. Giles in London.[17]

Almost immediately after the ceremony, Muriel regretted the union that, she felt, had occurred against her will. Earlier she had insisted that Harold promise not to oppose a divorce if she ever decided she wanted one, and he was so eager to marry her that he assented. Muriel later said that had a good friend been nearby at the time, she probably could have been talked out of the wedding. Or, she might have added, if she and her mother had related on a more

intimate level, things might have turned out differently for Helen Swift Neilson
was a witness that day at her youngest child's nuptials.

But both women acted in character: Helen, not knowing how her daughter
really felt, said nothing to stop the wedding, and Muriel, afraid to speak her
mind, went ahead with it. As it turned out, Muriel's instinct proved right: her
union with Harold Abramson was a disaster from the beginning as he began
to criticize and find fault with her almost as soon as they were married. As
their marriage unraveled, Harold blamed Muriel and urged her to seek psychoanalysis, later commenting, "Oh, we know that Muriel really belongs in a
sanitarium."[18] Though in no way agreeing that she was at fault for the failed
relationship, Muriel nevertheless believed that she might be an appropriate
candidate for psychoanalysis for other reasons: she had retained vestiges of her
childhood tics and phobias.

In Muriel's single recorded conversation about Harold, she described him
as "vain, sadistic, impulsive, with paranoid traits." Otherwise, she failed to
acknowledge her early marriage or even to speak Harold Abramson's name:
it was as if it had never happened. She even tried to avoid thinking about this
period in her life, "pass[ing] over most of the events and my emotions of the
1920s ..."[19]

After only a few months of marriage, Harold, with his wife's knowledge,
wrote to the father of psychoanalysis seeking an appointment for her. Both
Muriel and her physician husband knew of Freud's work in Vienna, but Freud
wrote back that he was not then taking on new patients. Nevertheless, as a result
of his effort to correct Muriel's behavior—though only for the purpose of convincing her to stay with him—it was Harold Abramson who, however uninten-
tionally, pushed Muriel onto the path toward her destiny.

CHAPTER 6

VIENNA:
ON THE OEDIPAL BED

After Freud had turned down Harold's request, Muriel was determined to go to Vienna and seek out the great man herself. Harold insisted on accompanying her and so, a scant six months after her ill-fated wedding, Muriel arrived in Vienna on a beautiful May afternoon in 1926, the air filled with the scent of lilac, her sullen husband at her side.[1]

In the 1920s, Vienna, the cosmopolitan and sophisticated Austrian capital and the cradle of psychoanalysis, was also the backdrop for two opposing political parties, the Social Democrats and the Christian Socialists, who were locked in a battle for control of the nation. A third group, the National Socialists, or Nazi Party, was not large enough at this point to have much of an effect. Until recently, under the Social Democratic Party, Vienna had been a mainly progressive island in the middle of a provincial country, the First Austrian Republic, created at the end of World War I. But, by 1926, Austria had been reduced to a tiny Alpine state with a broken economy and a starving populace: a weak nation with uncertain frontiers.[2]

Pleased to be out of London where her life with Harold had been on a downward spiral, Muriel believed that she could begin anew in Vienna, despite her husband's presence. In an optimistic mood, she decided to try and engage Sigmund Freud herself; she hoped he could cure neuroses remaining from her childhood. Muriel wrote her own letter this time, asking if he would take her on as a patient.[3] That it would have been more prudent to send this inquiry before she moved to Vienna seemed to escape her notice.

Paradoxically, in light of her disdain for her husband, it was Harold's belief in Freud that had instigated Muriel's desire to undergo psychoanalysis. Though

Harold had urged her on for his own purposes, Muriel herself became convinced not only that psychoanalysis would enable her to end her marriage, but also that understanding Freud's theories would make her a better educator, a career goal she had first considered back in high school, when she admired, almost idolized, Miss Helen Boice.[4]

Muriel was aware of her sister's negative opinion of Freud's science of the mind. However, she felt her own personality made her an excellent candidate for analysis. After all, she tended to avoid confrontation, she already realized; and she was inappropriately secretive about her feelings, especially about anything unpleasant. She even found herself telling others that her father had been "in business"—omitting that his enterprise was meatpacking.[5]

Perhaps Muriel had more insight into her psyche than she knew, even before psychoanalysis. In summing up Mary Shelley in her Oxford thesis, she could just as well have been describing herself: Shelley, Muriel wrote, had "intellectual and moral courage, but in most matters of emotion she had her share of timidity." Maintaining "a certain cautiousness in all her relationships...she never embarked upon any emotional adventure without a return ticket in her pocket."[6]

Muriel was deeply disappointed when Professor Freud turned her down a second time in May 1926 almost immediately after she had penned her request to become his patient. Already ill with the throat and mouth cancer that would eventually kill him, Freud could not take on new patients, but he wrote Muriel suggesting an alternative: the brilliant young American psychoanalyst Dr. Ruth Mack, his protégé. Dr. Mack was also from Chicago, the daughter of a renowned liberal jurist and philanthropist and, like Muriel, she had sought help from Freud to escape a difficult marriage. She had analysis with the professor—as Freud was called—and eventually entered the field, becoming his disciple, mediating for him between American analysts in Vienna and his sacred inner group of European analysts, the esteemed Vienna Psychoanalytic Society. Dr. Mack, despite being young and American, had won a special place in Freud's heart, even receiving from him a gold ring inlaid with an inscribed glass intaglio or carving—a gift he presented only to those analysts to whom he felt especially close.[7]

Treatment by a woman from her hometown appealed to Muriel: there would be no language barrier and, because of Dr. Mack's liberal background, she was sure that they would find intellectual common ground. While Muriel still harbored some doubts about the efficacy of psychoanalysis and felt nervous about committing herself to a process that might take as long as six months or a year, given the prohibitions in those days against divorce, she decided to give it a chance, if only as a way to end her painful marriage. Needing the imprimatur of an expert to allow her to feel comfortable and not guilty about divorcing Harold, she contacted Dr. Mack.

After only three sessions, Dr. Mack impressed Muriel with her common-sense approach to the psychoanalytic process, which depended on the so-called talking cure. The cure famously allowed a patient to say whatever came to mind, including dreams, memories, and slips of the tongue—all word play—aimed at discovering repressed emotions in the unconscious.

But at this time, Muriel was most concerned with her marriage, not with her unconscious. When she told Dr. Mack that she no longer wanted to live with her husband, the analyst agreed with her instantly, saying that it would be better for Muriel to be on her own. Even after Muriel learned that analysis would last longer than she had imagined, up to several years, she had no qualms about continuing with her commitment. Not only did she believe it would help her secure a divorce and make her a better educator, she also felt a kinship with Dr. Mack, who held political views similar to Muriel's on issues ranging from the Sacco and Vanzetti case to the cat-and-mouse games of Austrian politics in which leftist Social Democrats and conservative Christian Socialists toyed with each other rather than engaging in all-out battle.

Freudian analysts often asked favorite patients to accompany them on vacation in order to avoid breaks in the analytic process and, after her first few exploratory sessions in Vienna, in June 1926, Muriel found herself invited to New York City to continue her analysis with Dr. Mack in earnest. She hurried back to London to pack her belongings—and to bid farewell to Harold, who she hoped never to see again. She sailed to America at the end of May. From the ship, Muriel, a bit anxious, wrote Dr. Mack, who had not yet left Vienna, seeking reassurance that her analyst truly understood her unchangeable conviction about her marriage: "I'm serious about analysis, but I want you to know right now that my mind is made up. I will never go back to my husband."[8]

During a brief visit to her family in Chicago, Muriel took a deep breath and announced to her mother that she was divorcing her husband and undergoing psychoanalysis. Helen, who, Muriel suddenly realized, appeared unhappy herself, made no objections, saying instead that she too had considered consulting a psychiatrist. On the other hand, Muriel's brother Edward dismissed her analysis, saying: "What do you want that stuff for?" His response, in spite of her mother's apparent support, only strengthened Muriel's resolve not to share her private life with her family.[9] Perhaps male censure meant more to her at that time of her life than female approval.

In New York, Muriel settled in an apartment on Waverly Place in Greenwich Village, her time only partially taken up with daily analytic sessions with Dr.

Mack, whose office was uptown. Muriel developed a lively social life in the Village, where she met more creative, unconventional, and unpredictable people than she had ever known. She renewed her friendship with Betty Sanford, whom she knew from Wellesley, and Betty's husband, lawyer and professor Karl Llewellyn. They introduced her to a circle of artists, writers, and musicians, including a couple who soon became good friends of Muriel's, the Russian sculptor Sergei Konenkov, a handsome man of 50, and his lovely blond, blue-eyed wife, 30-year-old Margarita. Konenkov and Margarita brought out the joyful side of Muriel as they laughed and sang and shared happy times together that summer. The three would remain friends for life. Muriel also enjoyed a number of flirtations and trysts with men at the many parties she attended, but she lied about these liaisons to Dr. Mack. The analyst had suggested strongly that Muriel abstain from sex. In Dr. Mack's opinion, any overt expression of sex in casual affairs would detract from Muriel's analysis. Instead of engaging in sex, the analyst suggested that Muriel talk about it during her sessions. Being dishonest in analysis made Muriel feel guilty—Dr. Mack had gradually taken on the role of her strict mother—but she was also enjoying herself sexually for the first time since those early days with Harold, and she was unwilling to give up her erotic self again.[10]

By the end of the summer, however, Muriel experienced the type of psychoanalytic breakthrough that she would later read about in the professor's textbooks. When she and Dr. Mack sailed back to Europe, they kept up daily sessions, using, in lieu of a couch, the bed in the analyst's stateroom—the bed where Dr. Mack and her husband slept each night. As Muriel would later recount, when she lay down to talk on Dr. Mack's bed, it would become a substitute or, in Freudian terms, a displacement for the Oedipal bed—the parental bed, and therefore forbidden and so very exciting. "So there on the Oedipal bed, the dam burst," and Muriel finally told Dr. Mack that she had a secret that was blocking her analysis: she had not given up sex.

Rather than censuring Muriel, Dr. Mack said, "Well, I made a mistake that I imposed a rule on you…as though I were your mother."[11] After that confession, the block was dissolved, and Muriel's analysis progressed. She even overcame some of her most longstanding neuroses, including the moth and butterfly phobia.

However, Muriel had one more problem with Dr. Mack, The analyst constantly urged her patient to live a more luxurious lifestyle that would be in keeping with what she could afford. The analyst considered her patient's rejection of luxury—which Muriel viewed as a symbol of capitalism—to be part of her neurosis, with Muriel arguing that it was actually a healthy choice.[12] She chose to live more like her friends Glad and Margaret, who did not own furs and jewels, traveled tourist class, and were middle-class. Over time, however, Muriel decided that she could maintain her Socialist beliefs while still living a more comfortable existence—that the two were not necessarily at odds. In fact, she later discovered that her friends thought her stingy when she did not spend money freely since they knew about her inheritance. Although it would take years for Muriel to come to terms with her money—she would eventually live well while avoiding the extravagant displays that she disliked—for now, she could at least make certain that no one around her wanted for anything.

Upon her return to Vienna from New York in the fall of 1926, Muriel rented an apartment and hired someone to help with housekeeping, particularly to maintain the constant coal fires needed for warmth. Her income continued to grow—her brother Nelson oversaw its investment for her—and in December, she received a tax return of $535, more than $6,000 today. (The following year, her return was $632, almost $8,000.)[13]

Finances notwithstanding, Muriel led a rather quiet and somewhat lonely life that first year in Vienna. In addition to her analytic hour every day but Sunday, she took piano lessons and apprenticed to a bookbinder two or three afternoons a week. She read, and she walked in the Vienna Woods and saw a lot of her close Wellesley friend Margaret Willard Shepard, who also was in Vienna that year. The two of them took in concerts, often several in a week. Despite the music and the loveliness of the surrounding countryside, Muriel found Vienna to be a rather sad place, with noticeable poverty and hunger—even starvation in some rural areas—a legacy from the Great War.[14]

Another result of the war was the tense complexity of Austrian politics as Muriel saw it for the first time. Returning to her old habit of scouring the newspapers, she read everything written by G. E. R. Gedye, the eastern European correspondent for the *New York Times*. His articles made it clear that the shaky government formed at the end of the war in 1918 included opposing political parties that were now at each other's throats. Three parties dominated politics between the two world wars, their radical differences reflecting the divisions in Austrian society: the pan-German nationalists (National Socialists or Nazis), the Catholics and Christian Socialists (the Blacks), and the Social Democrats (the Reds). To further complicate matters, as Muriel read, each group had countless internal divisions and breakaway parties. Of the three parties, the two most visible at the time of Muriel's settling in Vienna were the Social Democrats and the Christian Socialists, but the one that would soon become all-powerful was the still puny Austrian Nazi Party, which held that Austria and Germany were one nation and aimed for *Anschluss*, or annexation, with Germany.[15]

Adolf Hitler, who had lived in Linz, Austria, until his 1913 emigration to Germany, had belonged to the nascent Austrian Nazi Party. In 1926, it was still quite overshadowed by the Austrian Christian Socialist Party. The Christian

Socialists—who stood for conservatism, the sanctity of Roman Catholicism, and an authoritarian form of government—were led by charismatic strategist Monsignor Ignaz Seipel (called "Cardinal Without Mercy" by his enemies and "Austria's Richelieu" by his friends). Seipel spewed anti-Semitic rhetoric—for example, that Jews and Socialists were destroying Austrian traditions—which helped the Christian Socialists grow in strength and size. Along with the paramilitary fascist group, the *Heimwehr*, whose rural members were financed by Austrian industrialists, the Christian Socialists formed an Austrofascist movement that laid the groundwork for the 1938 German *Anschluss*.[16]

During Muriel's first three years in Vienna, while the Christian Socialists took a leadership role in government—Seipel was chancellor from 1926 to 1929—Muriel sided with the Social Democrats, whose beliefs were more in line with hers. The Reds had enacted sizable social reforms when they had the majority in Parliament and had undertaken huge construction projects that were paid for by a tax on the wealthy.[17]

In the late 1920s and early 1930s, the innovative Viennese Reds built hospitals, schools, swimming pools, kindergartens, cultural and educational institutions, and huge housing projects, all to benefit the workers of the city. They also revamped labor laws to include paid vacations, unemployment benefits, enfranchisement of women, and restrictions on child labor. They had their own form of Marxism—Austro-Marxism—that combined revolutionary rhetoric with a strong democratic and reform element. At the time of Muriel's arrival in Vienna, the longtime leader of the party was Dr. Otto Bauer, who was described by journalist Gedye as the "brains" and "spiritual leader" of the party, providing the workers of Vienna with a "scientific education in socialism and the doctrines of the class war" since he had taken over the party's leadership in 1918.[18]

The Reds' army, the *Schutzbund* or people's militia, was comprised of young, enthusiastic Socialists who carried only light arms and had even lighter financial backing. During the mid-1920s, the left-wing *Schutzbund* and the right-wing *Heimwehr* conducted weekend maneuvers and marches that led to frequent bloody clashes. The *Heimwehr* always won, thanks to their superior weaponry, military-trained leaders, and wealthy backers.[19]

At this time, Vienna also represented a convergence of politics and psychoanalysis. For example, one of Sigmund Freud's extensive psychoanalytical reports was on a patient he called "Dora"—Ida Bauer, the sister of Dr. Otto Bauer, one of the professor's most famous cases. She was a highly neurotic woman who had been sexually abused by a friend of her father's. Her brother had neuroses as well: he was a "tortured, indecisive" and passive man who constantly procrastinated. Unfortunately, Bauer's psychological problems contributed to some major difficulties for the Social Democratic party.[20]

Although she had heard of "Dora," Muriel knew nothing of Otto Bauer's connection with the case when, in the spring of 1927, she asked Dr. Mack to introduce her to Professor Freud. Now that she was invested in her own psychoanalysis, she wanted to meet the person whose theories were affecting her so deeply. She was soon invited to tea at the Freud family's summer cottage in the Vienna Woods. Meeting the great man and feeling shy, she barely spoke to him, but she always remembered his face, especially his eyes, from which, as she recalled, "a fiery life shone."[21]

Shortly after this tea party, in June 1927, Dr. Mack again invited Muriel to spend July and August in New York City to keep up daily sessions while the therapist was "on vacation." Muriel lived in Greenwich Village again, reuniting with some of the friends she had met in 1926. Unlike the relative peace she had experienced the previous year, this summer would see the rise of violence, not only in her adopted country but in America as well over the Sacco and Vanzetti case.[22] First, Austria went through a "Bloody Friday" on July 15, when paramilitary forces and angry workers clashed in the streets of Vienna, precipitated by the acquittal of right-wing gunmen who had earlier shot into a crowd of workers. The workers of Vienna then called a three-day strike and refused to end it despite appeals from Social Democratic leaders. They mobbed the streets and burned the Palace of Justice to the ground, killing several people.[23] One man recalled what happened next:

So all the workers of Vienna, without any notification, they stopped. They left their jobs, they left streetcars standing on the streets. Some went home, got their wives and families, and walked in protest to the palace of justice. They had no weapons....hr All of a sudden we heard shouts and screaming. There was a big glass house behind us for tropical plants. They struck it and shards of glass came down. We hid under a bench...lay down and looked out. We saw police come out of vans with rifles, shooting.... Others came on horseback, swinging sabers and hitting people...I felt my dreams were shattered.[24]

Although the *Heimwehr*, aided by Austrian police, killed many of the striking workers, it was clear that the extent of this bloodbath was also in part due to the poor guidance, tactical errors, and delays of Otto Bauer and the other Social Democratic leaders. Bloody Friday made it clear "in this first blow struck by reaction at the Austrian Socialists, the first breach made in the wall of Red Vienna," that only the party with the best-armed militia could gain control of Austria. And it would not be the Reds. Even the enthusiastic Reds' youth group,

Die Rote Fahne (the Red Flag) or the active *Schutzbund* could not save the Social
Democrats: beginning in 1926, *Schutzbund* arms caches were systematically
raided by Fascist government forces and police, until the group was basically
neutered.[25]

Meanwhile, Muriel, still in America and in analysis with Dr. Mack, learned
not long after she heard about Austria's Bloody Friday that Sacco and Vanzetti
had been executed on August 23, 1927, in Boston. Riots erupted in major
American cities and internationally in response to the executions. Talking with
Dr. Mack, who felt the same way she did about violence, she would always link
together the two brutal events of the summer of 1927 as painful examples of
how corrupt power almost always triumphed over those who were in the right
but less powerful.[26]

When she returned to Vienna that fall, Muriel decided to hire a cook to
help her maid, choosing a woman who had worked for Dorothy Burlingham,
an American expatriate and heir to the Tiffany fortune, then being treated by
Sigmund Freud. Burlingham had grown so close to the famous professor and to
his daughter Anna that she and her children had moved into the Freud household, where she would remain for the rest of her life. Hiring servants was not
the only domestic change Muriel wanted to make: she was still trying to divorce
Harold, despite his continued resistance. Although they had not lived together
for more than a year, he refused to accede to her request that they legally part,
most likely because he felt it was not her place to make such a demand. She even
included him in a meeting with Dr. Mack, but the session was both uncomfortable and unsuccessful, as he blamed Muriel for their problems, even suggesting
that she be institutionalized.

She tried to focus her attention on matters outside her marriage, turning to
the larger world and politics. During her second year in Vienna, beginning in
the autumn of 1927, Muriel continued to faithfully read Gedye and other journalists, and also maintained her pattern of the previous year, reading, walking,
and attending as many concerts as she could. She also kept up her piano lessons
and in early 1928, met a handsome Englishman, Julian Gardiner, a musician, at
her piano teacher's studio. He was single, available, and attracted to the beautiful young American. Not yet divorced, Muriel nevertheless began an affair with
Gardiner.[27]

Their relationship flourished, but in the summer of 1928 Muriel took a rare vacation from analysis—Dr. Mack was busy with her own new romance—to go on
a two-month sightseeing tour through the north of England with Margaret
Willard Shepard. Early on in the trip, the women met a young Welsh inventor
and artist named Richard Hughes, who was, according to Muriel, "the most

beautiful young man" she had ever seen. He had dark hair and eyes, and wore exotic Russian-looking shirts and shorts, his bare legs in sandals, and Muriel found him wildly appealing. Soon, the three of them took off together, with Muriel driving and Richard sitting between the two young women. Some nights they slept outside, and other nights stayed at inns, in one room because Richard had no money. After only a short time, both Muriel and her friend were infatuated with the young Welshman. It soon became evident, however, that Muriel was the one he wanted. Margaret discreetly left them and went on alone, and the couple continued their tour, ending up in the home of a fisherman and his family where they spent more time together. The charming Richard spoke beautifully in a particularly resonant voice, and even sang, accompanying himself on his lute. Muriel fell madly in love with him.[28]

The night before they were due to go back to England, Richard said, "I would like this to last forever," Muriel, to her great surprise, said she did also. He had swept her off her feet. Then Richard asked her to marry him.

Though she had never imagined that she would marry again, Muriel was transformed by her love for him, and said yes—although she was still legally married to Harold. She immediately returned to Vienna to end her affair with Julian, a breakup that the gentle man accepted peacefully. Then she went off again, on a hiking trip with Richard. At once, she noticed that he seemed to have cooled in his feelings toward her. According to Muriel, Richard was "gypsy-like, free, independent," and she assumed he was having second thoughts about marriage. "Look," she said to him with difficulty, "I think you don't really want to marry me, do you?"

"No, I don't," he answered. She ended it before he could, by saying, "Well, we better break it off."[29]

Although she would later say that she knew the marriage would likely not have worked—Richard was an ardent Welsh nationalist who wanted to live in a little Welsh village, which was not a life that appealed to Muriel—she showed a rare ambivalence over this breakup. Perhaps, she said, the relationship might have worked out if she had told Richard at the time that she was leaving to spend a year in America with Dr. Mack. This would have allowed their love to mature and solidify. But she said nothing, and although there would be many other men after Richard, she never stopped wondering if, on that hiking trip in the summer of 1928, she had lost the love of her life. "I think," Muriel would say in retrospect, "that we always remained a little in love with each other." Instead, they stayed friends forever.[30]

While recovering from her bruised heart, Muriel set out again for New York in the fall of 1928, this time intending to stay for almost a year. Her analyst had remarried—she was Dr. Brunswick now—and was pregnant. Because she wanted her child to be born in America, she and her husband, Mark, along with Muriel, returned to Manhattan. There, it turned out, Harold was also in residence. Often drunk, he carried a gun, unusual behavior for him, but nevertheless frightening for Muriel who, although aware of the risks, continued to pressure him for a divorce. Finally, she decided to hire lawyers to take over where she had failed. The attorneys soon secured Harold's signature on divorce papers and by the spring of 1929, Muriel was finally free.[31]

That June, tired of both New York and analysis, Muriel was eager to return to Vienna. She believed that her analysis of the past three years had been useful but now it seemed to have run its course. She had seen her analyst for 55 minutes six or seven times a week, with a rare Sunday off and only one long vacation after the first two years. Such an extreme schedule had isolated Muriel from family and friends—her life centered upon her analytic hour. It was grueling, both a chore and a duty, but she had forced herself to continue, attributing her perseverance, she later said, to a persistent and determined character that seldom stopped anything once she had begun.[32] She hesitated, however, about telling Dr. Brunswick that she wanted to stop analysis.

Then, on June 29, as the session ended in Dr. Brunswick's Manhattan office, the analyst and her patient shook hands, as they always did. But this time was different. The doctor turned to Muriel and said, "Goodbye."

"Do you mean it's the end? My analysis is over?" Muriel asked and Dr. Brunswick said, "Yes." Both knew that Muriel had not solved all her problems—even though she was now divorced and had overcome the moth and butterfly phobia—so the future could easily hold a return to analysis. But for now, it was over and to formalize the end, her analyst presented Muriel with a first edition of Freud's recently published *Lay Analysis*. It was a gift Muriel cherished; it marked her connection not only to Dr. Brunswick but also to Sigmund Freud.[33]

Preparing to return to Austria, Muriel was not aware of the details of the escalating chaos there: American newspapers didn't give much ink to problems in small European nations. Unaware of Fascism's vise squeezing the nation to its limits, Muriel set sail for the Continent, her destination Vienna, that romantic city she'd learned to love, a city where anything could happen.

CHAPTER 7

REDS VS. BLACKS

Back in Vienna and finished, she believed, with the all-consuming psycho-analysis, Muriel found herself seduced by other gods in its stead: Mozart, Haydn, Schubert, and *Kaffee mit Schlag*, coffee with whipped cream on top, which exemplified *Gemütlichkeit*, the coziness and geniality of her adopted country. She could also spend more time on the Russian lessons she had begun taking from Sergei Pankejeff, Freud's "Wolf-Man," who was also a patient of Dr. Brunswick's. The Wolf-Man, who first became a patient of Freud's in 1910 (the father of psychoanalysis gave this Russian aristocrat the name by which he would be known because of his dreams of wolves) spent the remainder of his life in and out of psychoanalysis. This "most famous patient of the most famous of healers," as Freud biographer Peter Gay would write, would forever after enjoy his prominence in the world of mental health. But in Vienna, with Russian lessons followed by tea and conversation about literature, art, and, of course, Freud, Muriel and the Wolf-Man began what would turn out to be a lifelong friendship.[1]

Managing to overlook the political skirmishes going on around the city, Muriel escaped often to the verdant Vienna Woods. She was so attracted to the countryside around Vienna that she commissioned a young architect, Felix Augenfeld, called Auge, to build her a cottage in Sulz, a tiny village just out-side the city. Auge also designed Anna Freud's house in the Vienna Woods and Freud's back-friendly hand-shaped chair.[2]

Muriel's cabin, called the Blockhaus, had been built to her specifications, with large windows through which could be seen a field of grass dotted with wildflowers. In the evening, the only sound to be heard through the open win-dows was the singing of cicadas. It was a lovely refuge: "Lamplit ... the Blockhaus glowed like the interior of a cedar box," Stephen Spender would write.[3]

While Muriel was enjoying her new home, the government of Austria continued to crumble as internecine battles raged; the Reds' power and influence fell, and the Blacks' Fascism grew more oppressive. At the same time, reflecting the privations of the worldwide Great Depression, the Austrian economy was in a dire situation. The 1929 financial crisis that led to the weakening of Central European currencies began in Vienna with the failure of the number two bank in Austria, the Bodencreditanstalt. Meanwhile, the largest bank, the Creditanstalt, continued operating dangerously, "as if the Habsburg Empire had not been broken up."[4]

In these frightening times as "the bottom fell out" for many Austrians, some of them turned to the Nazi Party, which, in contrast to the other contenders, was revitalized by the Great Depression. On the surface, the Nazis promised hope to the "half-educated jobless" as journalist Gedye wrote, by turning their resentment against capitalism into acrimony against the minority of capitalists who were Jewish.[5]

Though one could not be a resident of Vienna without taking sides politically, Muriel was determined to use the insights of her analysis to work on her own life for a while. Trying to ignore the growing fear all around her, she resumed her love affair with the easygoing Julian Gardiner, who had waited for her and now wanted to marry her. Although she still was not enamored of the institution of marriage, she was no longer opposed to a legal union, if only because now, in her late twenties, she was eager to become a mother. The moment was right, as she didn't want to become too old to safely bear children. But, as she would later admit, Muriel's sudden interest in parenthood, which she viewed as a monumental event, came more from her desire to experience life fully than from a love of children. Even at age 17, she had wanted to become a mother, but not a wife. "With the help of a young lawyer friend, I worked out some crazy, complicated scheme by which I might secretly have an illegitimate child and then legally adopt my own child to give it legitimacy," she would recall.[6]

She made up her mind to marry Julian, stipulating that should she ever want a divorce, he would not oppose her. It was not unlike the agreement she had made with Harold, only this time she felt certain that, in contrast to her first husband, Julian would keep his word. Julian would make a good father, she believed, and, as soon as she committed to this marriage, she never wavered. This reflected a trait that Muriel had expressed from her childhood days and her reading of *Everyday Ethics*: Once her mind was made up, barring an emergency, she would not change it. With the exception of her passionate affair with Richard Hughes, she rarely allowed herself to have second thoughts, and this strong need to be rational and to hold firmly to a decision without allowing any ambivalence dominated her behavior as an adult.[7]

Focused on marriage and motherhood, Muriel thought of little else, although there was little romance on her part: she was sexually attracted to Julian but felt no love for him. On a warm late spring day, May 20, 1930, with her brother Nelson as the witness, she and Julian married. The wedding license describes her as a divorced American student with no listed religion and Julian as a Protestant musician from England.[8]

Before she married Julian, Muriel had maintained a lifestyle typical of her era, in which single upper-class women experimented freely with sex—first one lover, then another. While her love life had been complicated for some time, it soon became much more stable as Muriel and Julian settled in at her apartment at No. 1 Frankgasse in the Ninth District, with occasional visits to her cottage in Sulz. It wasn't long before Muriel became pregnant. On March 24, 1931, she gave birth to a daughter, Constance Mary, named after Muriel's favorite cousin. Muriel found herself delighted with her baby, but not much interested in her husband. She realized that, just as with Harold, while she had never really loved Julian, he loved her very much. They had been married only a short time when she began thinking about divorce.[9] Later, Muriel would say,

> Probably partly because I was satisfied in my desire to have a child, I kept thinking some day I am going to meet the man that I'll really want to marry and then everything will blow up.[10]

In May of that same year, as the Creditanstalt failed, destroying what was left of the country's economy, Muriel was consumed with two aspects of her personal life: her love for Connie and her distress over her marriage. When the baby was eight months old, Muriel took her across the Atlantic to Canada, a country where she knew no one, so she could think things over. She returned in a matter of weeks, having made up her mind to divorce Julian. The young musician was so accommodating that he agreed to everything, including what must have been a humiliating arrangement for a "faked adultery," complete with hotel room, prostitute, and photographer in order to establish grounds for divorce. He moved out of Muriel's apartment on December 5, 1931.[11]

Although Muriel remained financially unaffected by the Depression because her trust fund, overseen by Nelson, was safely secured in American and Swiss banks, she nevertheless couldn't help seeing how seriously the economic downturn had injured the people of Austria. Still, however, her main focus during this time remained on herself. She was remorseful and guilty at how she had treated the good-natured Julian, and contacted Ruth Mack Brunswick again: she needed additional psychoanalysis, Muriel told her, and Dr. Brunswick, who was back in Vienna, agreed to treat her at once.

This round of analysis would be different, Muriel was certain, since she was no longer a novice analysand. She began her sessions eagerly, hoping not only to clarify her feelings but to understand more about the analytic process she was undergoing. For some time she had been considering the idea of studying psychoanalysis, both because she loved learning and also because she had thoughts of becoming a psychoanalyst herself. Now she asked Dr. Brunswick to recommend an analyst who would be willing to teach her Freudian theory. The doctor suggested Dr. Robert Waelder, a psychoanalyst closely aligned with Sigmund Freud, Anna Freud, and the Vienna Psychoanalytic Society, so Muriel began seeing him weekly for an hour and a half to discuss Freud's most famous cases, as well as the work of other important contributors to the field. Always a fast learner, Muriel absorbed everything, coming to understand, at least on a novice's level, the concept and the application of Freudian theory. Such knowledge not only fed her desire for more information, but also helped her in her own analysis because she understood the process better, as she was now a student of psychoanalysis.[12]

Her attention was soon deflected from her academic pursuits when, on May 20, 1932, Austrian Chancellor Engelbert Dollfuss staged a breathtaking coup. He quickly created what was essentially a new government controlled by the Fascist Christian Socialists, with order maintained by the Fascist *Heimwehr*, using his one-vote majority in Parliament and completely ignoring the Social Democrats. Muriel, now responsible for a child, began to worry that perhaps Austria was no longer safe for her and Connie. But her analysis was going well, and she was enjoying learning again—for the first time since Oxford—so she pushed aside her concerns and decided to stay.

Between her own analysis and the hours of tutorials with Dr. Waelder, Muriel began to rely more heavily than before on her cook, her housemaid, and a nurse-governess, Grace, who had been trained by Anna Freud at her famous kindergarten in Vienna where teachers used psychoanalytic principles with their young charges.[13]

Feeling that Connie was well cared for, Muriel increased her private lessons, studying with two august specialists whose primary work was the psychoanalysis of adolescents, and attending a special class they taught in English for American students of psychoanalysis.[14]

She also managed to fit in a quick trip to Moscow in the summer of 1932, accompanied by a young Oxford student, Shiela Grant Duff, and two of Shiela's friends because she was interested in Communism and would remain fascinated with it until Stalin's purges began in 1934. Shiela would recount that Muriel's flat in Vienna was for many former Oxford students a place to drop in for a late supper and a glass of wine and that one night, Muriel offered to take Shiela and two young men friends of hers to the Soviet Union at her expense. Shiela and her friends gladly agreed. They all set out on their trip to Moscow from the Warsaw train station, where their "sophisticated and immaculate benefactress," as Shiela would later write, stepped out of her first-class Wagon-lit car from Paris, where she had traveled initially, to join them for the train to Russia. Shiela and her companions had traveled third class to Warsaw and were quite disheveled in comparison, she wrote. Once in Moscow, they visited Soviet museums, the opera, tombs, and also a workers' farm, a nursery kitchen, a prison, a court and a textile factory.[15]

Back in Vienna, Muriel found herself thinking seriously about the possibility of becoming a psychoanalyst. She had always been interested in people's minds and emotions but had never thought of a career other than teaching. Now, she "found there could be a much more direct means to the same end of understanding people and working with them towards happier and more harmonious lives."[16] If she became a psychoanalyst, she could work with educators and students in addition to having a private practice. In her mind she went back and forth, one day sure she should put all her efforts into becoming an analyst, the next concluding that teaching suited her better—a rare example of some indecision.

In September 1932, the first serious sign of German Nazi interference in Austria occurred in Vienna as Dr. Joseph Goebbels addressed a gathering of the Austrian Nazi Party. Only 15,000 citizens showed up, though Goebbels had expected 100,000, but this appearance in the country's capital by Hitler's close colleague nevertheless strengthened the Austrian-German Nazi relationship. A month later, the Austrian Nazis clashed with the Social Democrats' *Schutzbund* in Vienna, bringing to power a former Fascist *Heimwehr* leader, Major Emil Fey. The swiftness of the Fascists' assumption of total leadership made the impassioned language of the Social Democrats about revolutionary tactics leading to a new world seem like bravado. Their talk was a poor match for the Fascists' action.[17]

Meanwhile, Muriel decided to stay the course of her studies instead of involving herself in the politics of the day. In November, her decision about her career made, she switched to the Department of Medicine at the University of Vienna, having earlier enrolled in the History Department to take a few courses. Although requirements for admission to medical school were not stringent— Muriel had the requisite college degree and knowledge of Latin and was one of more than a thousand students entering that year—she hired a tutor, Alexander Rogowski, to help her in science courses. It was as if she was afraid of not being at the top of her class. Rogowski was a young Jewish student who never forgot Muriel: "She stood out. She looked different. She behaved different. And she wore pants."[18]

Muriel was a reluctant physician-to-be, for science didn't particularly interest her. Nevertheless, she was pragmatic and immediately reconciled herself to the role medical science would play in her life. She knew that she would need a medical degree to practice as an analyst in America. She would always believe, however, that one should not have to be a doctor of medicine in order to be an analyst: one's own psychoanalysis, plus a rigorous course in theory, should be the only requirements. Nonetheless, she committed herself to becoming an M. D., what she would call "the seven years of dearth" because there was no room in her schedule for anything but science—no room for the philosophy, arts, history, and literature that she loved. Much later, and to her surprise, she would come to find physics and chemistry "thrilling and valuable," almost as much as her beloved humanities.[19]

At the University of Vienna, nearly a third of her fellow medical students were women. They were treated well; Jews were not. Nazi harassment of Jewish students was becoming worse by 1932 and, probably because Freud was Jewish, Freudian theory was barely mentioned at the school. It was as though he didn't even exist. At the university, Jews were often brutally attacked by Fascists. In the medical school, there were even two departments of anatomy, one's politics dictating one's enrollment: Jewish and Socialist students went to lectures by Professor Julius Tandler, and the Nazis attended those by Professor Hoffstaetter, a Christian Socialist. These groups would physically split up as they entered the anatomy building, the large double staircase on the right for Jewish students, the one on the left for students who were Nazis or Nazi sympathizers. Quite often Tandler's students were assaulted with sticks as they tried to exit his lecture hall, and so were forced to climb out the building's windows to avoid the beatings. On occasion, Fascist and pro-Nazi students would post signs on the anatomy building's front columns declaring "Juden Eintritt Verboten"—entry forbidden to Jews. Yet Jewish students continued to attend, as did Muriel.[20]

Obviously, Muriel witnessed the violent anti-Jewish sentiment at the university. But leaving the university would mean relocating to study elsewhere. After years of analysis, she didn't want to leave Dr. Brunswick or the process that was helping her so much. Intent on achieving her goal this time, feeling guilty about the abuse of the Jewish students, but determined to graduate and become a psychoanalyst, she closed her eyes to the conditions in school, and focused instead on her conviction that her life was finally on the right course.[21] But in a little more than a year, when the violence against Jews and others deemed undesirable by the government would reach newly horrific levels, she would hold a personal stake in Vienna's politics, and leaving the city would no longer be an option for her.

CHAPTER 8

BLOOD IN THE STREETS

The first three months of 1933 proved arduous for Muriel. She tried to arrange her schedule to accommodate both medical school and time with Connie, who was now nearly two; all the while she was distracted by the visibly rising wave of Fascism in both Austria and Germany that provided an ominous backdrop to her life. On January 30 in Berlin, Adolf Hitler had been sworn in as chancellor of Germany, and Muriel's thoughts turned to her own city, to those who spoke out against this development. Even as she contemplated their courage, as she would later write, the news about Hitler emboldened the still small Austrian Nazi Party to raid a Jewish neighborhood, smashing shop windows and beating Jews.[1]

Even schoolchildren in Vienna were affected. Boys and girls had to wear lapel pins inscribed "Seid einig!" ("Be United!"), and had to come to attention, shouting "Österreich" while raising two fingers in imitation of the *"Heil Hitler!"* salute. Children were forbidden to criticize the government and were encouraged to join a national youth organization—but, in contrast to Germany's wildly popular Hitler Youth,[2] not many did.

Then, on March 8, Austria took a fast swing to the right, becoming a Fascist dictatorship almost overnight as Chancellor Engelbert Dollfuss executed yet another swift action to prevent Parliament from meeting—effectively ending Austrian democracy. This move was no surprise to the Social Democrats. The procrastinators in the leadership, especially Otto Bauer, had done nothing to stave it off, and their ambivalence helped to pave the road to their own, and Austria's, destruction.[3]

Increasingly nervous about the political turmoil surrounding her, Muriel tried to maintain as normal a life as possible for herself and her daughter, organizing her class schedule so she could spend time with Connie without neglecting her studies. Connie went to pre-kindergarten for two hours in the morning, then took a long walk in the park with her new nurse-governess, Gerda—Grace's replacement and also a teacher-trainee from Anna Freud's kindergarten. Muriel took a very early morning pathology course so she could return home by eight to have breakfast with Connie. Generally, they had lunch and supper together and she read to the girl every night: *The Twilight of Magic, The Wind in the Willows, Alice in Wonderland, The Secret Garden,* and *Peter Rabbit.* Two days a week, when Gerda was off duty, Muriel took Connie to the little house in the Vienna Woods where they holed up like rabbits themselves, spending every minute together. Despite this, Connie doesn't remember seeing much of her mother when she was very young: Later in life, she even told Muriel that she wished she hadn't studied medicine while Connie was little.[4]

From her own perspective, however, Muriel was doing well, even if she was tense and worried about what was happening in Austria. Balancing childcare with school, she still managed to shoehorn in her daily analytic hour with Dr. Brunswick. Medical school continued to be less than satisfying, though, and she was studying only enough to pass her exams. In addition to the few courses that held her interest—psychiatry, neurology, gynecology, and obstetrics—she did develop a new passion: surgery. She found her surgery instructor exciting because he allowed students to perform minor operations immediately, even if they had never before held scalpel or needle, and so Muriel again found herself moved by a dynamic teacher. For a short period, she found herself so enthusiastic about surgery that, during the summer, she worked as a student assistant at a hospital, where she was allowed to administer anesthesia and perform simple surgeries.[5]

On her way to and from school and in the university building itself, Muriel saw daily skirmishes between Jewish and Nazi students. She was disheartened by the inertia she perceived in the Social Democratic Party, whose members' achievements—uniting the workers and constructing enormous housing projects, and other workers' amenities such as hospitals and nurseries—she had so admired. The party seemed to be doing almost nothing to oppose the Nazis and the newly Fascist government. She was becoming disenchanted with her adopted city, especially after Dollfuss enacted laws reinstating the death penalty, censorship, and ruling by decree, and she even began to think about leaving Vienna. To her amazement, the majority of Austrians appeared to support Dollfuss and his new reliance on Italy's Mussolini as his country's last best hope against any encroaching threat from Germany. Meanwhile, Germany continued to re-arm, growing stronger, it seemed, by the day.[6]

Muriel would come to care more about politics than about her psyche at this time: the political had again become personal, and her ideology and her emotions were closely entwined. She would even have been willing to give up analysis had Dr. Brunswick held political views that differed from hers. Luckily, both women felt the same about the Fascists. Where once they would discuss theater or other cultural events, now they spent most of Muriel's analytic hour talking about the unfolding political drama—they could speak of nothing else. One disaster followed another: on March 23, 1933, the German Reichstag passed the Enabling Act which allowed Chancellor Hitler to establish a dictatorship. Only a day earlier, Germany had established its first concentration camp, in a suburb of Munich called Dachau.[7]

Muriel watched as the effects of Hitler's election began to ravage her beloved Vienna: Social Democrats were rounded up and sent to detention camps or were murdered. The Austrian Nazi Party quickly absorbed the Pan-Germans—those Austrians who wanted unity for the German-speaking nations—and accelerated its acts of violence, actions that not only went unpunished but led to a "glorification of crime."[8]

So distressed was Dr. Brunswick that while on a trip to Czechoslovakia on March 28, she sent an impassioned cablegram to an American friend, the Vienna-born Harvard-educated jurist Felix Frankfurter who would become a U.S. Supreme Court Justice in 1939:

> Sending this cable from Czechoslovakia because enormously growing Nazi sentiment Vienna makes such communication ill advised. Personal interviews with Jewish and also Social Democratic refugees from Germany reveal unbelievable widespread brutalities continuing at present moment despite denials. We greatly fear efforts to whitewash possibly successful due to complete terrorization of victims and their relatives and fear of threatened reprisals. Victims' intimidation and governments adroit methods and concealment of persecution so great that we doubt feasibility of ascertaining true facts through official channels.
>
> Strong probability same situation developing in Austria unless wide public opinion mobilized now. Perhaps also official pressure. Press censorship such that we are ignorant of America's information and activities hence cabling to give you firsthand impressions. Communication with me on this matter advisable only through American Legion Vienna. Guarded use of my name because of Viennese friends.[9]

When Dr. Brunswick wrote this cablegram, her politics were clear but she was suffering from an addiction to paregoric, a form of opium, probably originating from treatment of an earlier gastrointestinal illness.

Though Muriel didn't know it at the time, Dr. Brunswick's judgment may well have been impaired by what would turn out to be a fatal dependence. That the political situation in Vienna was turning into a nightmare, however, was indisputable. During the early summer of 1933 the *Heimwehr* became openly affiliated with the Nazi Party, conducting terrorist raids in Vienna. Muriel continued to try to ignore the Fascist crime wave, focusing on her looming medical school examinations, particularly one for which she felt unprepared, in physics, always difficult but made even harder for her because, like all classes at the University of Vienna, it was taught in German. Seeking a tutor, Muriel contacted a young physicist recommended to her by Dr. Brunswick named Franz Urbach. Urbach agreed to tutor Muriel three times a week, warning her that she should not take her physics exam because at that point, she would likely fail. After the lessons began and she was finally learning the material, Muriel found that she delighted in the mathematics, as well as the graceful manner in which Urbach taught, "opening new vistas and understanding." After only three weeks, however, Muriel interrupted the sessions so she could escape briefly from Vienna's oppressiveness. Possibly tempted by the thought that she could just live in America for a while, she took Connie to New York City for the summer.[10]

Again, Muriel stayed in Greenwich Village, which she had come to love. This time, however, with a two-year-old in tow, her social life was more low-key. She saw the Konenkovs, of course, and the artist sculpted a bust of Connie, a piece that perfectly captured the blue-eyed, dark-haired girl.[11] At summer's end, setting sail on an ocean liner for Europe, Muriel realized with a start that instead of the pleasure she had always felt when returning to Vienna, she now dreaded seeing its cobblestoned streets and gray stone buildings. Nevertheless, she had made a commitment to medical school and, in the tradition of *Everyday Ethics*, she felt she had to follow through. She and Connie, the girl with her sculpted likeness proudly in tow, went back to Europe, where they would remain for the next six years.

Immediately upon her arrival in the autumn of 1933, Muriel found Vienna rife with German-orchestrated terrorism, the Austrian Nazis running wild: bombings, propaganda dropped from planes, executions of "traitors," and an unsuccessful attempt on Austrian Chancellor Dollfuss's life by a young Nazi, all in the space of a few weeks. Sensitive to the endangered Jews and Socialists in the city, Muriel nevertheless didn't see how she, an American student with a young child, could help. Troubled but determined to follow the course she'd set for herself, she continued going to classes and tutoring sessions, caring for Connie, and meeting with Dr. Brunswick. With a shiver, she read that Hitler's totalitarian state was galvanizing its citizenry with propaganda measures such as its adoption a few months earlier, in May 1933, of the Nazi anthem, the

"Horst-Wessel-Lied," which extolled the virtues of totalitarianism, as a second German national anthem. Surely she should do something—but what?[12]

Then, in early February 1934, Chancellor Dollfuss took the final step: he declared all labor unions illegal, and he dissolved and outlawed the Social Democratic Party. On Monday, February 12, in an instant, everything changed.

While she was at Dr. Brunswick's office in the Eighteenth District, near the apartment buildings where many Socialists and workers lived, Muriel heard the blasts of mortar fire, howitzers, and machine guns. In a state of near shock, she witnessed men, women, and children being shot in the street. A few hours earlier, after government forces and the *Heimwehr* had turned their artillery on the Linz workers' club, the outlawed labor unions of Vienna responded with a general strike. That strike was the excuse for Chancellor Dollfuss to order his troops to mow down any Social Democrats, *Schutzbunder*, or striking workers they could find. Muriel watched the subsequent slaughter from the office window—"one of the most bloodthirsty, unwarranted, inexcusable employments of armed force against helpless women and children in all history," according to newspaper publisher Frank Knox.[13]

A few blocks from the office, the members of the *Schutzbund* were all but disarmed, but were making a brave last stand, hunkering down to fight in apartment buildings where they had cached arms—some sites were already emptied of guns after being compromised by traitors. But there were not enough *Schutzbunder*, pitifully few weapons, and no direction from the outlawed Social Democratic leaders. Muriel saw Vienna police, armed with the *Heimwehr*'s heavy artillery, run down workers, shooting them with the machine guns that they had stationed on street corners. They also bombarded workers in their homes, the remarkable housing complexes built years earlier by the Social Democrats of which it had been said, "Long after we are gone, these stones will speak for us and for Socialism."[14] Now guns blasted gaping holes in the concrete, targeting the families huddled inside.

Turning to Dr. Brunswick, Muriel announced she was leaving immediately to be with Connie. "I am going to have my chauffeur drive you home right now," the analyst said.[15] In the car, Muriel passed bodies lying in the street, either dead or wounded, but she couldn't tend to the victims. She had to get to her child.

This day would come to be called "der 12. Feber" or the Twelfth of February, marking both the true end of the Social Democratic Party and the beginning of Germany's planned takeover of Austria. This day also decided Muriel's new commitment to political involvement, whatever the cost. After what she had witnessed, simply going to school and taking care of her daughter was no longer possible. "I identified with these people though I didn't know them. They'd created such a beautiful city...to help the poor," she would later say.[16]

The fighting that so galvanized Muriel would last nearly a week, with the *Schutzbund* suffering more than 1,000 casualties. Hundreds of wounded hid in Vienna's sewers or ran for the border, through the woods and over mountain passes. Four thousand socialists and workers were arrested. It was neither a civil war nor a Socialist revolution. It was a Fascist insurgency. Nor was it an equal fight: the workers were no match for the combined power of police, paramilitary, and government forces. Phil Rosner, then only 17, remembered fighting his way with his fellow *Schutzbunder* into the Karl-Marx-Hof, a housing project built under the Social Democrats. Inside, he saw people lying wounded or dead on the floor. Positioning mattresses and furniture in front of the windows as a shield against bullets and flying glass, Rosner and his comrades held off the Fascists for a week until they ran out of ammunition and food and their short-wave radio was destroyed by machine-gun bullets.[17]

The Scottish writer Lady Naomi Mitchison wrote of the dead left in the street for days, of prisoners beaten to reveal locations of weapons, and of neighbors who betrayed neighbors. The arrests ripped families apart. A child during "der 12. Feber," Gus Papanek would later recall the day his father Ernst, a *Schutzbunder* and Socialist labor leader, bid farewell to his family after the battle was lost and he had to leave Austria. Ernst mentioned to his young son that the mayor of Vienna had just been arrested, and Papanek remembered feeling that this meant the end. If the mayor, a charismatic and powerful man, could be arrested, then the world he had grown up in had just been overturned.[18]

Muriel could no longer stand aside. Hitler's looming ascendancy, Germany's re-arming, Austrian xenophobia—the storm had built relentlessly, pulling her into its maelstrom, and she made her decision to act. She was certain that no one would suspect her of being anything other than a disinterested wealthy expatriate. She would recall thinking,

I was an American, what the Italians called "the crazy English." No one thought that an American medical student was likely to be mixed up with anything like this.[19]

Before long, people came to know her as someone they could come to for help: she was seen as outside the fray; she was sympathetic and, most importantly, she had money. At first, she was a bit confused because she did not always know the people who came to ask her for money to hide, to care for the wounded, and to aid the escape of others. Muriel turned to her acquaintances in

Vienna for direction. The journalist Gedye along with Hugh Gaitskell, British Socialist and member of the Labor Party, both sided with the Social Democrats and, despising Austria's Fascist government, willingly advised Muriel. Together, they and other English men and women began to quietly provide help to the endangered Socialists in hiding.[20]

Muriel was forced to make some changes in her life. Only a month before "der 12. Feber," she had told her landlord that she was leaving Vienna in the summer and would have no need for her apartment after May 1934. She had fully intended to transfer to an American medical school. "I thought I would learn more," she would later say.[21] But now that she was remaining in Vienna, she would need a new place to live.

"I am not going to leave," she told Gedye, Gaitskill, and other like-minded friends. "I am going to stay and see what happens and do what I can…. As an American I could do a lot." Although thousands of Austrians emigrated immediately after the February bloodbath, most to Paris, the majority remained, encouraged by a new optimism about the Social Democrats. The party was still alive, though underground, and seemed to be only waiting for someone to reorganize it and reestablish democracy. Some aid was provided to the embattled Socialists from abroad by the Quakers and the European Socialist parties, particularly the British Labour Party and the American Jewish Joint Distribution Committee.[22]

Nonetheless, even among these Socialist colleagues, there had been a breakdown in communication: people simply did not know how to contact each other. Those who were alive were on the run, danger always one step behind them. Despite the "desperate impression of broken morale," now that she had decided to act, Muriel remained hopeful that those Socialists who were still in Vienna, and not too badly injured, would pull together at some point. On the other hand, she was discouraged to find that many Viennese were deluded about anti-Semitism; though an obvious reality of city life, it was denied by most residents. As more and more restrictions were placed not only on Jews and Socialists but even on some Christian leaders, and Germany's re-arming was ignored, Muriel thought she finally understood. The people of Vienna were in denial, to use a Freudian term. This was perfectly summed up in one man's memory of those days: "It could not happen here—the golden Viennese heart could never be so mean."[23]

Muriel's first covert action was to establish her apartment (the one she would soon have to vacate) as a place to hide people. There she also held secret meetings of Leopold and Ilse Kulczar's Funke (Spark) group, named after Lenin's underground newspaper, *Iskra* (The Spark). The Kulczars were intelligent and savvy left-wing Socialists—a label that also identified her, Muriel now realized, bemused. The meetings were risky, since everyone faced arrest if they were discovered.[24]

After two months of such frightening clandestine activities, along with the constant violence on the city's streets, Muriel decided she needed to get out of the city for a time and, in April, went on vacation. With Connie and Gerda, she settled in a *pensione* in Mlini, five miles from Dubrovnik, on the coast of Yugoslavia. The Adriatic Sea, the beach, and the quiet little town would, she hoped, provide her with a much-needed escape from the desperation of Vienna. But that would not be the case. Craving peace and quiet, she found passion instead—and with it, an experience that would change her forever.

CHAPTER 9

LOVE IN TIME OF WAR

The spring of 1934 did nothing less than transform Muriel. Two momentous events occurred at the same time, one thrusting her even more into the world that seemed to be exploding around her, while the other removed her from it.

Muriel sat on the beach at Mlini, soaking in the sea and the sunshine. Accompanying her were Connie, Connie's nurse Gerda, and a companion, Furth Ullman, "a rather steely fawn-eyed young man who passed as her cousin (actually he was her lover)," as the British poet Stephen Spender would say.[1]

Staying in the same pension, a stone farmhouse not far from the water with a view of the ocean and the rocky shoreline, were Spender and his lover, Tony Hyndman. Muriel's impression of the tall, boyishly handsome young writer was of a "graceful animal." On the beach that first day when he saw her, Stephen simply watched Muriel, taken by her beauty—"black hair and eyes, a clear complexion slightly tanned but not expressionless" with signs of her humanity: tension around her mouth, a "little scar of a suffering" on her lips. Infatuated, he deemed Muriel's beauty irresistible, a combination of the "classicism of the Renaissance with the freedom of the New World."[2]

> [She] recalled a portrait of Leda by Leonardo. She had the same dark eyes, oval face, and smilingly attentive expression. Her hair framed her face, and if it had been plaited and braided into tresses would have had a snake-like sinuous quality, as in the drawings of Leda.[3]

As they talked, they grew more and more mesmerized by each other, the feeling deepening into an attraction that was, for Stephen, like the proverbial thunderbolt: his previous lovers had all been men. They spoke intimately, with

Muriel telling of her two failed marriages as well as her quest to find the one man she could completely love, while he admitted that no woman had ever appealed to him before now. Before they could decide upon their next step, within a day or two, Muriel had to continue on the already planned boat trip with Furth Ullman, traveling to Greece while Connie stayed with Gerda at Mlini. Before she left Mlini, Muriel made plans to see Stephen in Vienna where he and Tony planned to seek medical help for Tony's inflamed and possibly infected appendix. Then, after two weeks with Ullman, Muriel rejoined Connie and Gerda; by early May they had returned to Vienna.[4]

Back home, Muriel was soon in touch with small groups of Socialists, as well as with Hugh Gaitskell and Frederick Elwyn Jones, young Englishmen who would later become influential in British politics, Gaitskell in the House of Commons and in several Cabinet positions, Jones as a Labour member of Parliament and counsel at the Nuremberg Trials. Gaitskell and Jones helped establish communications among the scattered Socialists, set up relief efforts through the British trade unions, and managed to send reports out to the world about the truth of the February bloodbath.[5] Gedye's articles, too, continued to flow from Vienna to the rest of the world, telling the story of what had *really* happened in Austria.

Not long after her return to Vienna, Muriel heard from Stephen Spender, asking if he and Tony could stay with her. Tony needed surgery for appendicitis, a diagnosis he had received from a physician in Dubrovnik.[6] Muriel, thrilled at the prospect of seeing Stephen again, agreed, probably having ended her liaison with Furth Ullman in anticipation of seeing Stephen. During the weeks before Stephen and Tony arrived, she went on with her life: classes in the morning, lunch with Connie, and her analytic hour—and her nascent efforts to help the Austrians.

A few days after Muriel received Stephen's request, the Austrian government ordered the release of several Austrian Nazis from the Woellersdorf detention camp, where they had been imprisoned as punishment for a reign of terror including bombings and riots in Vienna. But, upon their release, these miscreants returned immediately to their old ways, setting off bombs in crowded areas of the city, apparently on instructions from Munich.[7]

When Stephen and Tony arrived in Vienna, with its tense atmosphere, Muriel quickly took them to visit her house in the woods. They stayed overnight, the three of them sleeping outside under the stars with Muriel lying between the two men. Tony fell asleep but she was restless—until she felt Stephen's hand exploring her thighs and her rest of her body. She did nothing, allowing Stephen the opportunity to feel every part of her. He later admitted that it was strange that the two of them didn't walk into the woods to do what they both clearly wanted. Instead, they stayed there, next to Tony, for the rest of the night.[8]

But the delay was temporary. While Tony was in the hospital recovering from his surgery, Muriel took Stephen to the cabin again. Embarrassed, he told her he had never been in love with or even attracted to a woman. Muriel, about whom Stephen said to a friend that she "lived 'entirely for love,'"[9] soon relaxed him, and seduced him. The young poet, ecstatic with this new experience, celebrated their union:

> There was a wood
> Habitat of foxes and fleshy burrows
> Where I learnt to uncast my childhood, and not alone,
> I learnt, not alone. There were four hands, four eyes,
> A third mouth of the dark to kiss. Two people
> And a third not either; and both double, yet different.
> I entered with myself. I left with a woman.[10]

Now Muriel added something new to her already crowded routine—a passionate affair with Stephen. In the evenings, after Connie was asleep, Muriel and Stephen would spend the night at the cabin. They would visit Tony, still recuperating in the hospital, during the day, but nights were for love. Stephen's long poem, "Vienna," about meeting Muriel in a time of war, described simultaneous "intense, personal and emotional"[11] experiences: the Fascist overthrow of Austrian democracy, and a transformative love affair.

For Muriel, too, her new activism in Austrian politics came at the same time as her ardor for the captivating young poet. Both Muriel and Stephen believed their love was a treasured gift; "for in a world where humanity was trampled on publicly, private affection was also undermined," he would write.[12]

Nevertheless, unable to break from Tony, Stephen continued that relationship too, despite his feelings for Muriel: he remained committed to Tony and felt he could never leave him. This "'ambivalence' forever kept unsleeping watch between us, like a sword," Stephen wrote. Yet, it was precisely Stephen's sexual confusion and his ties to Tony that gave his relationship with Muriel "the texture of catastrophe," creating more excitement than they could ever have imagined.[13]

When she was not with Stephen, Muriel tried to keep her priorities in order: she spent as much time as possible with Connie, she kept up with medical school, maintained her analytic hour, and saw her "cell," the small Funke group that used her apartment for their secret meetings. Only a dozen people were in the cell, part of the strategy of the newly reorganizing Social Democratic Party—or, as it was now called, the Revolutionary Socialists. It ran on the principle that the less an individual knew, the fewer people she could name, therefore the safer the underground operations.[14]

Muriel's affair with Stephen flourished, despite her time-consuming underground meetings. They would rendezvous as often as possible at her cottage in the Vienna Woods, spending long hours in each other's arms. Back in her Vienna apartment, Stephen wrote or read while waiting for Muriel to return from school. There, inspired by "her face like cold marble under her fur cap,"[15] he wrote the love poem, "Ice."

> She came in from the snowing air
> Where icicle-hung Architecture
> Strung white fleece round the Baroque square.
> I saw her face freeze in her fur,
> Then my lips ran to her with fire
> From the chimney corner of the room
> Where I had waited in my chair.
> I kissed their heat against her skin
> And watched the red make the white bloom,
> While, at my care, her smiling eyes
> Shone with the brilliance of the ice
> Outside, whose dazzling they brought in.
> That day, until this, I forgot.
> How is it now I so remember
> Who, when she came indoors, saw not
> The passion of her white December.[16]

In the midst of all this, just when she believed she could not accommodate one more demand on her time, Muriel received an intriguing visitor who was vouched for by someone she trusted. Tall, handsome, charming, and intelligent, the man was English, and he fascinated Muriel. They talked for hours, the man never giving his name. Then he handed her an oversized envelope and asked her to deliver it to a comrade the next day. It was to be, he explained, a clandestine handover complete with codes that had to be done exactly right so that neither Muriel nor her contact would be caught. Convinced that she would be helping the cause of freedom and opposing Austrofascism, Muriel agreed. But once he left, nervous at the weight of the envelope, she carefully unsealed it and discovered not only thousands of schillings but a large batch of underground Communist literature. Deeply annoyed that she had been tricked into delivering Communist propaganda, Muriel nevertheless kept her promise and made the drop, with little complication or fanfare. But she felt used and, although she would not know his name for more than three decades, her intuition about his duplicity was correct: she had indeed been used, and by a master: Kim Philby.[17]

Philby had arrived in Vienna that spring of 1934, his mission to work with leftists, such as Stephen and Muriel, in the Socialist struggle. In Vienna, perhaps even in Muriel's apartment, passing her that envelope and assigning her to hand it on, he discovered the excitement of fighting Fascism, and by association, Hitler, if only as a bit player. Not long after enticing Muriel into being his courier, Philby returned to England. By summer, he had become a member of the Cambridge Five, a famed group of British agents working for the Soviets, perhaps the most storied double agents ever.[18]

Meanwhile, having no idea of Philby's identity, Muriel put the incident out of her mind; her affair with Stephen seemed to take precedence over almost everything else in spite of her efforts to maintain a balanced life. In late June, the threesome celebrated Tony's birthday at a party given by Muriel. Though it had its pleasures, it was, predictably, tense as well because of the love triangle that none of them could relinquish.[19] For Muriel, the wonderful relationship with Stephen was complicated by Tony's constant presence—after all, the two men were staying with her—and Stephen's inability to choose between her and Tony.

Her love life soon took second stage, however, when, on June 25, 1934, Chancellor Dollfuss was assassinated, shot in the throat by a group of Austrian Nazis. In the city with Stephen that day, Muriel witnessed, as she had on the "der 12. Feber" and its aftermath, stands of machine guns set up on street corners. The killers had reportedly been encouraged in this new violence by the German regime, but the attempted overthrow ultimately failed as it was premature: Germany was not yet strong enough to take Austria. Within hours after Dollfuss's murder, another Christian Socialist, Dr. Kurt von Schuschnigg, had become chancellor.[20]

A month later, with Austria's Fascist government secure for the moment, the courts sentenced Dollfuss's assassins to death for their crime, and they were hanged within three hours. As they were about to die, the men shouted, *"Heil Hitler!"*[21]

Muriel and Stephen wanted to escape from the lunacy, at least for a few weeks, so Muriel took a vacation in Juan-les-Pins on the French Riviera where she, Connie, and Gerda stayed with friends, and she had time to study and relax. Stephen went off to do some writing. By the end of August, rested, ready to take on the responsibilities waiting for her in Vienna, she stopped in Lucerne on her way home to attend the International Psychoanalytic Congress, and reunite with her good friend Gladys Lack, who would return with her to Vienna. At the congress, uncertain of her role among all the accomplished professional analysts, Muriel felt completely out of place. Her insecurity was particularly vexing because she was acquainted with some of the participants whose children

Connie played with.[22] Determined but miserable, Muriel managed to get along, in part because one of the analysts, Grete Bibring, guided the shy young analyst-to-be through the event.

Back in Vienna, Muriel had to move out of her apartment. Eager to be reunited with Stephen, who was still out of town, she moved into the only apartment she had been able to find, on Rummelhardtgasse in the Ninth District, an upscale neighborhood. Though the apartment was conveniently located across from the hospital and the medical school, its size was inadequate: with only two small bedrooms, one each for Connie and Gerda, Muriel would have to sleep on a daybed in the living room. Not only was it too small for secret meetings, it wouldn't suffice for studying either. She knew that Connie, then three, would try to talk to her and she wasn't willing to tell her child to leave her alone.[23]

Luckily, only a few weeks later, Muriel heard from her architect friend Auge who had learned that she needed a place to hide people who had to be sheltered from the Fascists: he could make available to her a small studio apartment. Thrilled, Muriel took this second apartment, at No. 2 Lammgasse, not far from the Rummelhardtgasse. It was ideal for her purposes since the concierge was at the back of the building and couldn't see anyone leaving or entering. She planned to use it for hiding people and holding clandestine meetings, along with studying and, of course, for trysts with Stephen.[24]

Gladys helped Muriel settle into both apartments and then, in September, when Stephen finally returned, with Tony, they all squeezed into the apartment on the Rummelhardtgasse. Muriel had more free time at this point because her analyst was still away on summer vacation and school had not yet begun. She met often at her apartment or at the house in the woods with the six or seven members of the Central Committee of the Funke, who had, before her recent trip to France, asked her to join them permanently.

Muriel took Stephen to some of her meetings in spite of the fact that his presence exacerbated the already tense atmosphere of the gatherings. Members went by their code names—Muriel's was Mary—giving them anonymity and a unity that came, as Stephen wrote, from "exile, persecution and anxiety." The group's members lived haunted lives, and they felt hunted even when they weren't. There was also some rivalry between a group of former Social Democratic leaders who had fled to Czechoslovakia after the February violence, and Vienna's Revolutionary Socialists, comprised of newer Social Democrats.[25]

Finally, as Muriel eventually came to learn from dealing with the Kulczars, just because people risked their lives for democracy didn't mean they were immune to baser instincts—at least one of the group acted like a petty criminal and poached off others and sometimes even stole money. Muriel provided much of the funding for this group, and she was distressed to learn later of Leopold Kulczar's irregular bookkeeping methods and his tendency to withhold money for his own personal use.[26]

At one meeting, this time in the Kulczars' apartment, Muriel, the only non-Austrian present at the encounter, met with Otto Leichter, Karl Hans Sailer, Manfred Ackermann, and other prominent Socialists whom she would come to know well as they worked together in the months ahead. One man, code named "Weiser" (his real name, she would later learn, was Joseph Buttinger) stood out to her—because of his attractive appearance and because of an energetic quality that Muriel was quick to notice. He had curly blond hair, kind blue-gray eyes, an honest face, and although he was well built, he was not tall, about five feet, five inches. Weiser, the head of the Socialist Party of Austria in St. Veit an der Glan in the country, had been called to Vienna to contribute his political know-how to building a new illegal organization, and possibly to head that organization.[27]

Once out of the meeting, Muriel returned home to Stephen, who was impatiently waiting for her: her summer tan made her more beautiful than ever, and he found her irresistible. They continued their torrid love affair, and on September 14, Stephen wrote to his friend the novelist Christopher Isherwood:

> By the way, almost I hate to tell you, but I have been having quite a lot of normal sex lately. The effect is funny, because I find boys much more attractive, in fact I am rather more than usually susceptible, but actually, I find the actual sex act with women more satisfactory, more terrible, more disgusting, and, in fact, more everything. To me it is much more of an experience, I think and that is all there is to it.[28]

When Stephen left Vienna with Tony at the very end of September, Muriel and he agreed to write often. Only days later, she wrote in response to his first letter, "Darling, I was so happy to have your letter today—and I'm glad you miss me because I am missing you very much. Vienna is very different without you." They agreed to rendezvous back in the city in January, Stephen promising to arrive without Tony this time and Muriel guaranteeing "lovely days and nights."[29]

Although Stephen referred to his time with Muriel as "a kind of lived poetry," for Muriel, it was more earthly and earthy than that: she cherished Stephen's "youth and health and energy." Before their planned reunion in January, Muriel was busy connecting all the many strands of her life, including the meetings with the Funke committee. They met every two or three weeks, usually at her cabin in the Sulz woods. She was careful about the meetings, telling her Sulz caretakers to expect that she would have many guests because she planned to entertain often.[30]

She also held some meetings in her apartment where Weiser, or Joe, was present. He still worked in the provinces, and since he only traveled to Vienna for these meetings, took great care about his comings and goings to avoid the attention of the police. He began to contact Muriel ahead of time to make sure the coast was clear, carefully following the rules of conspiracy, never making an unexpected move.

In December, Muriel and Connie had a wonderful holiday with a young medical school friend, Harold Kutz, whom Muriel had run into on the stairs of her apartment building; the two students knew each other from their days of dissecting corpses. Muriel was alone for Christmas with her daughter and she spontaneously asked Harold to join them for Christmas Eve tree trimming. He accepted and, after the tree decoration, they had dinner, then put Connie to bed.[31] Years later, Harold would come to play an important role in both of their lives.

Stephen returned to Vienna in January, having written a story in which Muriel was a character, an "etherealized Jamesian" version of herself. At this point, Muriel still loved him, and because she knew that his attachment to Tony was more obligation than anything else, she and Stephen seemed ready to marry. But it wasn't that simple: "What we faced was the knowledge that there might be a real inability on my part to choose," Stephen would write.[32] That the couple cared deeply about each other was clear, as was Muriel's willingness to marry again. But he never asked her, and the opportunity was lost. As Stephen prepared to depart, planning to return to Vienna and to Muriel in April, their romance was ending, though neither of them knew it. Within only a few weeks, Muriel would belong, body and soul, to another man.

CHAPTER 10

CLEAR AND DECIDED

In spite of other demands on her time and affection, Muriel stayed in contact with Stephen throughout the early winter of 1934–1935. But their affair was ending. Stephen was clueless, even trying unsuccessfully to arrange for Christopher Isherwood to meet the woman he loved. Muriel's love for Stephen had already changed. She had become interested in another man, the young Socialist Joe Buttinger, whom she had first noticed at that September 1934 meeting of the Funke group. She learned that Joe had arrived in Vienna after spending four months in jail in the Austrian district of Carinthia. Given early release on the condition that he leave the area and never return, he nevertheless attempted to stay in his village, where he had been a Social Democratic activist for about eight years. But it was no use: after a short time, Joe realized he could not accomplish anything there politically because the region was just too small. With the police everywhere and with his identity well known, he decided to accept an invitation he had just received from Muriel's Funke group in Vienna. Reluctantly leaving friends and work as well as Gisela Rauter, his lover of the past few years, Joe headed to Vienna. The metropolis would provide him with anonymity.[1]

Although Muriel saw Joe briefly and intermittently at the fall and winter meetings of the resistance group, they had not yet become well acquainted. Joe was extremely cautious, even paranoid, about keeping his presence in Vienna a secret and talked very little. Before long, however, his natural political acumen came to the fore and he became a leader in the small group, as others came to recognize his unique abilities. In addition to his passionate belief in Socialism and Marxist theory, he differed from other Socialists in that he could respect methods and goals different from his own, making him that rarest kind of politician—flexible and willing to entertain the ideas of others.[2]

In January 1935, after nearly a year of the government's treatment of the Austrian Left as outlaws without rights, a series of raids sent the top leadership of the Social Democrats to prison, including Manfred Ackermann, who had been chairman of the new resistance group, the Revolutionary Socialists. Then, at a Friday, January 22, meeting of former and current Social Democratic party leaders in Brno, Czechoslovakia, where Otto Bauer and other former leaders were living in self-imposed exile, a spy infiltrated and later revealed names, leading to even more arrests.[3]

By the next day, almost everyone who had attended that meeting was in jail, with the exception of Joe. And his escape had been narrow: He had crossed over into Czechoslovakia to attend the meeting but, always careful, he had in his possession a letter that provided him with an excuse for being out of Austria, ostensibly from a company manager offering him a job interview. When a policeman came for Joe in his rented room at six o'clock the morning after the meeting, Joe chatted in a friendly, relaxed manner, presented his letter, and said he was in the country to get work. Finally, finding nothing overtly incriminating, the officer started toward the door. "Auf Wiedersehen, see you again," said Joe, but the officer replied, as if tipping him off, "It won't be very good for you if you see me again."[4]

Joe knew he meant that if he stayed where he was, he would soon join his comrades in jail. He grabbed his knapsack and ran out, hearing later that within half an hour the police did return for him. He returned to Vienna but had nowhere to stay. When Muriel was asked by friends if he could stay temporarily at her cabin in the Vienna Woods, she agreed without hesitation.

Excited about hosting Joe in spite of the danger, Muriel set about preparing the house. She pumped water, got the fireplace ready, and set out food she had brought with her. Joe arrived, having waited until dark to walk from the bus stop half a mile away. When he entered Muriel's cozy little house, they shook hands but his were so cold from walking without gloves that Muriel instinctively tried to warm them in her own. She immediately felt an "erotic spark"—the attractive "stocky and broad, round-headed, flat-nosed, light-haired" Joe, with his "clear blue eyes, smiling lips and cleft chin,"—as Stephen would later describe him— had had a different life from that of any man she had ever known.[5]

They ate in front of the fire and talked. Joe had had a very difficult childhood, full of losses, and his irrepressible optimism astonished Muriel. She felt like crying as he told his story of an insecure youth, marked by unemployment, grim poverty, and even starvation. His father suffered a mental breakdown after serving in the Austrian army during World War I and remained hospitalized until his death. Hungry and poor, Joe renounced the Catholic Church—he had been an altar boy—said farewell to his mother and sisters and brothers, and left home for what would turn out to be grueling work on a farm. Eventually, he moved farther away and found a job at a glass factory where he became involved in union politics and eventually in Socialism.[6] He became an area leader, heading a Socialist youth group and working in a children's center for several years.

At the end of his dramatic story, Joe said to Muriel, "You see, I've always been lucky."[7] He was so good natured about his hard life that Muriel found herself smitten, in a way she had never been before. He spent the night in her cabin and, in the morning, when Herr Winter, who had formerly been the local town's Socialist mayor, came to deliver a load of wood, Muriel introduced him, making it clear that Joe was there at her invitation and had nothing to hide.

She bought him new clothes, as Joe's current clothing proclaimed too loudly exactly what he was—a man on the run, rather than a visitor spending a weekend in the country.[8] On the main shopping street in the city, the Mariahilferstrasse, Muriel bought a knickerbocker suit, commonly worn in Austria, plus long wool socks, a shirt and sweater, and boots. Returning with her gifts to the cabin, she again spent the night keeping watch, but left very early the next morning for a class.

For some weeks during that winter of 1935, Joe—who had been named chairman of the Revolutionary Socialists now that the previous leaders Manfred Ackermann and Karl Hans Sailer were in prison—moved around, sometimes staying at Muriel's house, other times sleeping at different friends' apartments. Then things fell apart. A friend's home was raided and the man was arrested. Joe was not there that day; in fact, he had had a series of lucky escapes during this time. In another case, a woman arranged a hiding place for Joe and two friends. The next day, she was herself arrested and jailed. He stayed in that hiding spot until early morning when he left to catch a train to Salzburg; ten minutes later, at six o'clock, the police showed up and arrested his hosts.

These were difficult months for Muriel as her newfound commitment to the Socialists was tenuous as a result of the party's own instability. Although the Socialists and the Communists differed ideologically, the two groups became mixed up as many Socialists joined the Communist Party, and the police, who didn't care about party affiliations, arrested leftists of any persuasion, sending them all to prisons or detention camps.[9]

Meanwhile the Socialists in Vienna and in Brno were in rare agreement: at a meeting on February 17, 1935, they agreed that the new underground organization, the Revolutionary Socialists (RS), would have different aims from those of the old party: it would resist the Fascist government, try to return workers and Socialists to their pre-February 1934 level of security, and help those who wanted to leave the country. Its new leader, Joe Buttinger, would concentrate on distributing news of the underground to every district in Vienna, as well as smuggling in the newspaper of the Social Democratic Party, which was published in Brno. The RS would also support the illegal trade unions that were forming.[10]

Muriel thought it would be difficult and even unrealistic for the Revolutionary Socialists to confront the Fascists, but she nevertheless felt compelled to join them. She had made her decision to stay on in Vienna to engage in the resistance, and she put all her efforts into this struggle—along with caring for her daughter, going to lectures, and keeping up with her analysis, although she reduced the seven hours a week to five. Somehow, she managed it all, and even found time for love.

It happened as an indirect result of Joe's third narrow escape. On the night of March 11, he was to stay at the home of Karl Hartl, a colleague in the resistance who was also a friend of Muriel's. Near Hartl's apartment building, Joe saw someone standing in a doorway and felt a premonition. He called Muriel. Could she put him up? It would only be one night, he said, for he would leave for Linz the next day to confer with Karl Frank of the German resistance group Neu Beginnen, which had been created by disenchanted Communists after Hitler came to power. "We don't know a thing about Germany," Joe had told Muriel, "and yet all depends on what will happen there."[11]

After she agreed to shelter him for the night, she went downstairs to check that it was clear and to bring him upstairs. That night they sat up talking and decided that it would be safer for Joe if he lived only with her, either there, at the Lammgasse apartment, or in her cabin in the woods. They agreed to tell no one of this decision, not even their Revolutionary Socialist colleagues. The next morning, after she heard that the police had showed up at Hartl's apartment, Muriel's faith in Joe's good luck strengthened, and she no longer scoffed when he said, at the end of every story he told about himself, "For me everything ends well."[12]

As Muriel and Joe had agreed, Joe spent the next two nights at Muriel's cabin and, knowing he was there, she left Connie at home with Gerda and joined him. Very quickly the spark she had felt earlier became a flame, fueled by long dinners and intimate conversations in a room lit by candlelight and a fireplace. They became lovers on March 13, 1935, noted by Muriel as the date her "marriage with Joe really began." Joyful that she had finally met the man she was certain she could be happy with, Muriel felt her happiness somewhat diminished by one thing—she would have to tell Stephen. She wrote him quickly, nervously, that she was passionately in love with Joe and that they were engaged. Although she and Joe had not yet discussed marriage, she told Stephen this so he would understand the seriousness of her new affair. But, she wrote, he should continue to visit her in Vienna. She hoped they would always remain friends. Stephen, realizing they "were not made for one another," remained rueful[13]:

> I did not satisfy her; and from my point of view, she was too clear, too decided, too much in possession of all the threads of her life, too confident in what she knew, too little mystified by what she did not know.[14]

A year later, he wrote the even more regretful "If It Were Not Too Late!" about his loss of Muriel's love:

> If it were not too late!
> If I could mould my thought
> To the curved form of that woman
> with gleaming eyes, raven hair,
> Lips drawn too tight like a scar,
> Eye sockets shadowed with migraines
> Memory of earlier loves and wars
> And her smile learned with being so human.[15]

But even as Muriel was gently if unequivocally letting Stephen know that their relationship was over, Joe was lying to *his* other lover, Gisela. In a telling indication of Joe's attitude toward sex, he did not reveal the truth about the two women in his life to either one. Such lies contradicted his abstemious behavior as a dedicated Socialist, wherein he followed the party's Quaker-like discipline, drinking and smoking little and never spending extravagantly.[16] His dealings with women, however, would be quite another matter now and for years to come.

Joe continued to see Gisela whenever she came to Vienna, keeping his affair with Muriel a secret. Joe didn't think he needed to tell Gisela that he was in love with someone else. Eventually, Muriel learned about Gisela, when the younger woman showed up at the Lammgasse apartment, unaware that her hostess was Joe's lover as well. Muriel offered her food and invited her to stay. Joe's behavior was less than admirable:

> During the two nights Gisela stayed in Vienna, I slept with her as if nothing had happened. And then I was inconsiderate enough to confess it to Muriel, and reported to her that I had left Gisela with the impression that our relationship would continue, because I was too cowardly to tell her the truth.[17]

He continued to see Gisela whenever he was out of the city on business, or on vacation—even on trips with Muriel.[18] Things would remain this way, for the most part, for the rest of Muriel and Joe's lives together. Though they were from such radically different backgrounds, both Joe and Muriel shared a reluctance to be committed solely to one mate. In the spring of 1935, in the midst of their resistance work, it became clear that Joe expected to continue his relationship with Gisela, despite his love for Muriel. Muriel was able to assuage her hurt feelings and acknowledge to herself that she too might want freedom in times ahead.

Whatever its origins, she developed a tolerance toward Joe and Gisela that she would exercise toward his many other similar sexual indiscretions in the future. And, making up her mind to accept Joe as he was, she never deviated, often explaining him with these mild words: "Well, Joe likes women."[19]

In contrast to Joe's duplicity, when Stephen arrived in Vienna, Muriel greeted him warmly and openly. Accepting her decision to choose Joe, Stephen's loyalty to his dear Muriel allowed for a deep, loving friendship that would endure. Muriel's ability to handle these cosmopolitan situations, perhaps more typical of an older, more sophisticated woman, reflected how much she had gained from her years of analysis, but also her innate ability to intuit other people's needs and desires.[20]

Joe's strength was political: he brought energy and commitment to all that he did, whether it was making speeches, writing, or organizing. Finely attuned to nuances, the reality that he—a poor, uneducated peasant—had been chosen to lead the Revolutionary Socialists during this dangerous and historic period was a continual surprise to him. He would never fully understand the way intellectuals and politicians had accepted him as one of their own.

As Muriel spent more and more time with Joe working for the illegal Revolutionary Socialists, she grew closer to its leader both sexually and emotionally, and she came to a decision. Feeling vulnerable because of the illegality of her alliance with the party, and with Joe, Muriel thought up a safer and more prudent course of action for herself. She also believed it would, in the long run, benefit the RS and its leader as well.

She dropped out of the day-to-day workings of the party.

It was a decision not made lightly, but rather as part of her increasing understanding of just how dangerous this work was, and how much was at stake not only for her, but also for her young daughter. She risked arrest each time she went to an illegal meeting, each time she smuggled papers and money across the border to or from the Socialists in Brno. She risked even more each time she secured false documents for a Jew or a Socialist who wanted to flee Austria. Although Muriel enjoyed a certain measure of immunity as an American and had never been suspected by the clerico-fascist tyrants in charge of the police and government, she was nevertheless taking on a lot, especially considering Connie: after all, Muriel was a single mother and had no one to share her responsibility for her daughter.

Toward the end of March, Muriel announced that she would no longer attend meetings or maintain any overt political contacts in Vienna, telling everyone that she needed more time to study and to care for Connie. But it was all a cover.

She had decided to dedicate herself to keeping Joe safely out of sight for as long as it took, for as long as there was a resistance. With the party underground, resisting the Fascist government illegally, she hid Joe, keeping the secret from everyone. But she remained connected with the chairman of the Revolutionary Socialists and the other groups of comrades throughout Vienna and Austria, as well as the group in Brno, and she believed this would be the greatest contribution she could make to the cause of freedom and democracy.

From 1935 on, while Joe remained hidden for three years, Muriel moved around freely, a seemingly uninvolved non-political medical student. It was during these years that Muriel became "the most hidden of all outlaws," and the resistance against Fascism and the struggle for Socialism became her life's work. Her most critical job was serving as the main link between Vienna and Brno. She traveled often, crossing into Czechoslovakia on one of her two passports: She had an American passport as well as a British one from her marriage to Julian, and such a wealth of documents enabled her to make frequent trips without arousing suspicion. Because of her cover as a wealthy American student, she was never stopped, or questioned, although she never made a single one of these trips without feeling practically smothered by anxiety and fear. She often carried photographs into Czechoslovakia, waited while they were incorporated into false passports, and then smuggled the passports back into Austria, hiding them in a corset she had purchased for that purpose.[21]

Muriel's typically busy routine became even more crammed now that she was Joe's only link to the outside world. She rose every morning at 5:30, and went to buy rolls and milk, checking to see if "the air was clean."[22] If it was safe, Joe would go out. Muriel's early morning class began soon afterward and, following class, she returned home for breakfast with Connie. During the day, she had her analytic hour, studied, and carried messages.

At night, after a very full day, Muriel returned to the Lammgasse apartment and waited for Joe. It was always late. She had to stay awake until he called from a pay phone to ask her, in code, if the coast was clear; then she went down to the street to let him into the building. Her unceasing vigilance was no doubt responsible for Joe's freedom and contributed to the continued existence of the Revolutionary Socialists.

In addition to all this, Muriel provided the American consulate with guarantees and helped secure affidavits of support and other papers needed by those seeking to escape. Sometimes she used her apartment to hide people, often giving money to those who asked for it, to help them either to survive or to escape from the country.

Muriel could do all this because, in today's parlance, she was superb at compartmentalizing. She was able to transform herself from student to caring mother to resistance worker to lover.[23] She had apparently learned the trick of doing one thing at a time, with complete and total concentration, and so she could keep everything in her life going.

One thing still worried her, however. Aware that she was not spending enough time with Connie, she fretted about the effects on a four-year-old of having a mother with a secret life that demanded most of her energy. Seeking help where she always had before, Muriel sent Connie to see the psychoanalyst Berta Bornstein. Dr. Bornstein, whom she affectionately called "Bertele," was Muriel's closest friend among the analysts. During their sessions, Connie and Dr. Bornstein had tea, and the analyst knitted and the girl drew.[24]

But, even with her friend Bertele, Muriel kept her underground life to herself. And Muriel hated lying to Connie, wondering if her daughter might have been able to tell that she was keeping secrets from her. In addition to being bright, the girl's inquisitiveness was legendary: Stephen Spender and Tony Hyndman had dubbed her *Miss Warum, Wie So*: Miss Why and How Come. Muriel's quandary was whether to tell Connie that she could never talk about Joe, or Herr Josef as Connie called him. After all, the three spent considerable time together, including weekends in Sulz. But the child never asked who he was, what he did, or where he lived—she did not seem to want to know anything about Herr Josef, not even his full name. Finally, after months of agonizing over this, Muriel came to a conclusion: on some level, the child must have known that Joe's presence, his very existence, was a secret she should never discuss. Even so, still concerned about the duties of a single parent, Muriel kept Connie in analysis for three full years—apparently with no enthusiasm on Connie's part. Although she wouldn't challenge her mother, the child did not enjoy her sessions with Berta Bornstein.[25]

Meanwhile, the Revolutionary Socialists and their leader took up more and more of Muriel's time and compounded her worries. As the group became more secretive and had more code names and underground couriers, the public knew less and less about them and their work, leading to Muriel's other concern: How could they truly affect the government and put a stop to Hitler's plans for Austria if they worked completely in the dark? As good Socialists, they tried to figure this out, some taking the long perspective on this political work, and others the short. Muriel remained convinced that the inevitable end of Fascism would take a very long time, possibly twelve or thirteen years, and would involve great sacrifices and many deaths.[26]

While other comrades believed in the short perspective—they were certain the conflict between democracy and Fascism would be over quickly—those such as Muriel and Joe, Otto Bauer, and the other leaders in Brno, were in it for the long haul. Thus, for them, the utmost secrecy was required. None of them could afford to be arrested since this small group felt it was the only bulwark remaining between the Austrian people and total tyranny.

The Revolutionary Socialists needed huge sums of money, both to help the families of comrades who were in jail or who had fled, and also to help support Socialists who had lost their jobs and had no incomes. Funds had to be found to feed and clothe them and to provide them with pocket money to ensure that they could disappear quickly if necessary. Muriel contributed her own money, but the RS also enlisted aid from abroad, from American Quakers and from Socialists in the British Labour Party. Financial support also came from the Socialist International and its secretary Friedrich Adler to write and print the workers' newspaper in Brno, which was then smuggled, sometimes by Muriel, back into Austria.[27]

In late spring of 1935, Muriel again welcomed Stephen to Vienna, but because of her hectic life he found her rarely available, and the visit was unsatisfying to her former lover. Whenever she traveled to Paris and London for political reasons, generously leaving her apartments and house available to Stephen and Tony,[28] Stephen felt shortchanged. An empty apartment and a house in the woods without Muriel were not what he wanted. He departed from Vienna feeling that perhaps they should have married, that maybe he had indeed missed the boat with her.

A month later, on July 1, Muriel and Joe left Vienna for the summer, her goal to escape the unremitting pressure of living a secret life, and his to meet with comrades in other cities. Muriel agreed with her friend G. E. R. Gedye's assessment that those on the left in Vienna were "free game for *Heimwehr* and the largely Nazified police," and she found the strain difficult, to say the least.[29] The intensified bombings at train stations, railway lines, and other locations in the city by Austrian Nazis had made daily life increasingly grim and dangerous.

As the couple traveled through Europe that summer, they mixed business and pleasure in their own ways. Muriel went off to see Stephen at Innsbruck, but she was shaken at his obvious sadness when she left: "I shall not see her again for about a year, I am afraid," he wrote. Joe, traveling on a forged Czech passport, met with leading Socialists in the Labor and Socialist International, including Otto Bauer and Leopold Kulczar in Brno, Karl Frank in Prague, Friedrich Adler in Brussels, and others in London and Paris.[30]

Muriel also spent a week in London visiting her mother and stepfather, who were staying at the Savoy. She rented a room at a less expensive and busier hotel: Joe would soon be meeting her and she wanted a place where he would not be so noticeable. Explaining that she wanted her London friends to be comfortable visiting her—Helen was used to Muriel's "threadbare friends" and her preference for avoiding first-class travel—she had no trouble getting her mother to accept her refusal to stay at the Savoy. But there was another reason for Muriel's choice of a different hotel: she still found Helen's disapproval intimidating and knew she could not admit that she and Joe lived together. Helen's Victorian standards would not permit cohabitation.

When Joe arrived, he and Muriel spent several days together in London, and she met his younger brother, Loisl, who had recently emigrated to England. After saying farewell to her mother without introducing her to Joe, Muriel and Joe went on a short trip to Ploumanac'h, a tiny resort in Brittany. It was after that trip that Joe supposedly returned to Paris on business, while Muriel met Connie and Gerda in Lussin Piccolo, a Croatian town on the Adriatic. Instead, her lover was off to rendezvous with Gisela, whom he took to a small town in France, introducing her to everyone as his girlfriend, as Muriel would learn much later.[31]

Near the end of that summer, Muriel and Joe reunited in the Swiss Alps at a resort called Andermatt, 800 kilometers from Vienna. For Muriel, it was a respite before returning to her many responsibilities; Joe kept his two weeks with Gisela to himself.

Back in Vienna, Muriel saw that anti-Semitism was on the rise, "rife and virulent," varying from the racism of the Austrian Nazis to the more "polite and socially acceptable exclusiveness" of the middle and upper classes.[32] The city seemed so suddenly overtly anti-Semitic that Muriel had a difficult time maneuvering calmly through her typical day, at medical school, on the street, in the shops. And with the rise in Vienna of Fascism, as an anti-Fascist, Muriel placed herself in the gravest danger—despite her cover. She had been raised as a Protestant, but the truth was something she never thought about—that she was actually half Jewish.

In the news stories of the day, she saw England and France dismiss the seriousness of the rise of Fascism, almost as if the government officials in those countries thought the Nazis would come around after a while. To her, it was clear: it would take much more than hope to defeat this encroaching menace. While citizens of democratic nations seemed naively unaware of the change in the atmosphere, Muriel and others of similar mind felt true horror and despair at the onward march of boots to an incessant drumbeat that gained momentum and strength with the passing weeks and months.

The woman from the stockyards believed strongly that only by her individual efforts, in partnership with Joe and other anti-Fascists, might Nazism "be defeated, and world war averted."[33] During the mid-to-late 1930s, despite her overwhelming sense of dread and anxiety about the political situation, as well as in her personal life where she often felt that she was neglecting something—Connie or her studies—she soldiered on, certain that she was doing nothing less than trying to save the world.

CHAPTER 11

IN HIDING, IN LOVE

Muriel hid Joe throughout the fall of 1935, usually in her apartment on the Lammgasse or in the cabin but sometimes at the Rummelhardtgasse apartment after she expanded it: she had rented an adjacent flat and had a doorway cut through, thus giving her place two exits for a quick getaway.

Muriel's affiliation with the Revolutionary Socialists and her romance with its chairman continued as the group worked to prepare for what both Muriel and Joe felt was a certainty: Germany would soon move aggressively against Austria, with a profound and deadly effect. Muriel also felt certain there would be a sudden and urgent need for money and papers to help Jews and others flee Austria when that time came.

But she often found herself frustrated because of all the other responsibilities that stood in the way of her commitment to the Resistance, which had become her all-consuming passion. At least she was able to help Joe with his work: writing and disseminating broadsheets to the Socialists and workers of Vienna, funneling money in to help support those who had lost their jobs, and maintaining contact with the group in Brno.

Muriel had been in good standing with all the Socialists, both in Vienna and in Brno, before she dropped out of the daily work of the resistance to protect Joe. She had come to know the others in the organization, especially the Leichters, a family with whom she would have close contact for the next few years. Otto Leichter had been coeditor of the Social Democratic newspaper, the *Arbeiter-Zeitung*, prior to 1934, and his wife, Käthe, studied and wrote about pay inequality between men and women and acted as secretary for Otto Bauer. The Leichters had fled to Zurich after the February 1934 bloodshed. By late 1935, however, along with a number of Social Democrats, the Leichter family had moved back to Vienna, living underground as Revolutionary Socialists.

But the Leichters' gamble, that they could hide in the suburbs of Vienna without being noticed by the police, failed, and a short time later, Otto and Käthe Leichter were arrested.[1]

Horrified at the arrests of the Leichters and other comrades, Muriel found herself in a state of constant anxiety about the events unfolding around her. Hoping to calm herself, she associated only with friends who had the same leftist viewpoints, including her analyst and the journalists and writers she knew well. Certainly Stephen had been liberal and progressive, and so were the journalist G. E. R. Gedye and the people she knew from the Funke group, and her new friends, Karl and Anna Frank, the organizers of Neu Beginnen, the left-wing German anti-Fascist group. But in many situations, such as in her classes, she wasn't certain about the political views of other people she came in contact with. As a result, she kept her thoughts to herself and rarely talked to her medical school colleagues.

Despite her fears, she never doubted that she had made the right choice when she decided to stay in Vienna and aid the resistance. She finally understood what her nurse Mollie and the maid Nellie had been saying about people dying for freedom. Now, all these years later, she was reminded of Nellie's song—"Oh, Paddy dear, oh did you hear, they're hanging men and women for the wearing of the Green"—and thought that she too was willing to give her life for her cause. Every day, members of the resistance were arrested and taken to prison or to detention camps. Although anxious about her own safety as well as Connie's, Muriel was more convinced than ever that she had to remain in Vienna.

> I just felt this is what I want to do. I can do something that is useful and necessary for some human beings, and I can do something for an idea or a cause that I believe in…[2]

She held fast to her beliefs as the news from neighboring Fascist dictatorships grew worse. On October 3, 1935, Mussolini invaded Abyssinia in direct violation of the Covenant of the League of Nations. On November 21, the French ambassador in Berlin reported to Paris that Hitler would soon make a move to occupy the Rhineland. The ambassador's prescient warning was ignored as the democracies continued to deny the full extent of the evil emanating from Germany. Muriel agreed with the ambassador and felt sure that the Rhineland would be Hitler's first target and that Austria would soon follow.

The constant fear of being discovered continued to be a source of intense stress for Muriel, so she again escaped her anxieties by leaving the country. She and Joe spent Christmas week relaxing on the small Yugoslavian island of Hvar in the Adriatic Sea, but then quickly returned to the fight. Back in Vienna, it seemed as if things were static as everyone awaited Hitler's next move. A few people were changing their lives in response to Hitler, though: Muriel heard from Stephen that he and Tony had joined the Communist Party.[3] And in Vienna, the Revolutionary Socialists continued their attempts to destabilize the Fascist Austrian government.

Muriel saw the skies over her adopted home darkening. The Austrian Chancellor Kurt von Schuschnigg had made appeasement overtures to Hitler and, as a result, the Austrian Nazis now moved from being an illegal party to becoming almost legal and generally accepted by most of their countrymen and women.[4] The Nazis stepped up their train and terminal bombings and violent demonstrations in the outlying areas of the city. Their punishment? A slap on the wrist from a sympathetic government. The Nazis' impunity emboldened them, and each week also brought more acts of violent anti-Semitism. Meanwhile, as Muriel read in the daily papers, France and Britain were still ignoring conditions in Austria and appeared to treat Hitler as a temporary aberration.

The Revolutionary Socialists were increasingly threatened by government crackdowns as the powerful police rounded up leftists and members of the resistance daily, and the courts handed out outrageous sentences, such as five years' hard labor for circulating an illegal newspaper with allegedly treasonable content.[5] Throughout 1936, police took into custody people who were active in the Revolutionary Socialists or who were in the wrong place at the wrong time. A typical arrest began with a name. In March, it was Phil Rosner's. He had been a member of *Wehrsport,* the youth group of the *Schutzbund,* and was on the staff of the clandestine publication *Die Rote Fahne,* the Red Flag.[6]

We had a new courier. She would collect stencils and papers...to bring into the place where we had the mimeograph machine. But she got in a traffic accident...She fell off the bicycle and her briefcase fell off and the stencil and stuff fell out. Two policemen came to help her and found it. She was new, and she had a list with our real names on it. It took them six weeks to find me.[7]

Rosner was arrested by the Austrian secret police. They held him for nine months, trying to get him to name names. Convicted of "treason," he was sentenced to five years in prison.

Joe and the others devised systems to counter the Fascist government and to keep the Revolutionary Socialists functioning. First, there was division of responsibilities, which meant that the group's members, in separate units according to their function, did not know each other's true identities and so could not bring the whole organization toppling down if any one person was arrested. These units included youth groups, an education department, socialist workers' help organizations, and a group that printed Socialist pamphlets.[8]

Second, Muriel and Joe were careful to never once let down their guard. Through Muriel, Joe was indirectly in touch with only one member of the Revolutionary Socialists, a woman named Leopoldine Moll, code named "Lore." She worked in a lending library, the Bukum Bookshop, and she passed Joe's messages—delivered to her by Muriel—on to Otto Bauer and the group in Brno by writing them in invisible ink between the lines of letters she sent to her father and other relatives in Czechoslovakia.[9] Her family members forwarded her letters to Bauer, and he wrote back to Joe, also in invisible ink, with the letters being sent to Lore at the Bukum Bookshop. Muriel came in and picked up books that had Bauer's letters concealed in them. It was a complicated system but it worked for nearly three years until Lore was arrested. If any information was too dangerous to be written down, or if it needed immediate transmission, Muriel took the train to Brno to relay the news in person.

It was a nerve-wracking business. Although Muriel was fairly certain she was not being watched, and her cover continued to hold up, she nevertheless always felt a frisson of fear as she neared the border. For Joe's part, he only felt safe when he was among American and English visitors, for example at the Salzburg Festival in the summer, with Muriel at his side.

During 1936, Joe spent more and more time at the Rummelhardtgasse flat—in addition to its two exits, he could always jump out a window to the street since the apartment was on the second floor. Whenever he thought he was being watched, though, he left the city, traveling on his illegal Czech passport. If anything seemed to be at all unusual, Muriel investigated.

Because of these seemingly excessive precautions, no matter how many operatives were arrested, Joe was safe for the three years that Muriel hid him, and the Revolutionary Socialists continued to function.

Muriel had long identified with her lovely adopted city Vienna, whose citizens defined themselves as Viennese first, Socialist second, and Austrian third, and the Socialist values connected with it. And now, after living there for a decade, Muriel felt more than ever that Vienna was her home—and it was under attack.[10] Muriel tried to fortify that home; when Gerda left to get married in the spring of 1936, Muriel quickly asked Anna Freud to recommend a replacement. Another young teacher-trainee, Fini Wodak, soon arrived and would remain as a part of Muriel's family for many years. And Muriel continued sending Connie to Dr. Bornstein simply because she felt the times were too troubling, and she wanted the analyst's input and advice.

Because Joe and the Revolutionary Socialists took up so much of her time, Muriel had streamlined her other responsibilities, but found that hard as she tried, she could not rush medical school. One had to attend for at least five years and pass twelve final exams. Eager as she was to graduate, Muriel knew that she still had at least another year or two of studies.

Then, in a crushing blow against freedom and a sign that the Nazis were rapidly gaining power, on March 7, 1936, German troops invaded the Rhineland, violating the terms of the 1919 Treaty of Versailles, which had dictated that the Rhineland would remain demilitarized. With one move, Hitler's actions had left democracy in Europe gravely threatened, but France and England continued to do nothing. This was their opportunity to put the brakes on Hitler, but "they let the chance slip by."[11] Hitler immediately began remilitarizing the Rhineland, a clear prelude to war.

Austrian Chancellor Schuschnigg continued to appease Hitler. The Austro-German agreement of July 11, 1936, appeared to promise independence to Austria but secretly granted freedom to every Austrian Nazi then in prison. Releasing these Nazis inside the borders of Austria was effectively letting in a ticking time bomb. Meanwhile, in addition to local Nazis, Hitler had infiltrated Austria with his own agents, such as the German ambassador Franz von Papen, to weaken Austria from the inside.

In July 1936 the Spanish Civil War erupted. Hitler and Mussolini both supported Francisco Franco, thus creating even more pressure in Europe as these three Fascist dictators united. Muriel took Connie and Fini to Salzburg to meet Joe for a brief respite from the chaos on his return from a quick trip to Brno. At this point, traveling outside the country was not difficult for anyone, especially not for Muriel with her American passport. But Joe could not be seen in Vienna, where he might be picked up by the police. Since Muriel and Joe almost never went out together in Vienna, the Salzburg vacation was a new experience. The presence of the man she loved, dressed in grey flannels and a tweed blazer to fit in with the many tourists, made Muriel ebullient. Surrounded by people she loved—Gladys was there, as were Tony and Stephen, and even her medical-school friend Harold Harvey (he had changed his last name from Kutz) Muriel felt happier and more relaxed than she had in a long while. There must have been talk of war but Muriel, so relieved to be out of danger, ignored it.

In this carefree, congenial atmosphere we were all full of life and laughter. I remember, perhaps mistakenly, the weather as fine. I know we walked and swam and made excursions to the lakes and mountains. Every evening we would listen to superb music and after that we'd sit talking in a café or a wine cellar, often until late.[12]

Newly energized, back in Vienna after the week in Salzburg, Muriel was ready to take on whatever she had to. She spent more time at her medical studies as she took a brief internship in obstetrics where she had to live at the hospital, in dormitories with other women students, to be on hand for deliveries. She found this a novel and gratifying experience—with its bittersweet side, too, since she couldn't reveal anything about her secret existence to her new friends, the other medical students. Muriel enjoyed her internship and from it developed a lifelong interest in obstetrics.

After that, although she continued her coursework, she spent more and more time delivering coded messages and letters and underground papers for the Revolutionary Socialists in secret, not allowing the news from Berlin to distract or frighten her. In early 1937, Muriel finally shook Dr. Brunswick's hand for the last time, ending more than six years of analysis.[13]

That spring, Muriel took Connie to spend a week with her mother, Helen, in Paris. It was a real family reunion because her brother Nelson also was there, though he soon left them to return to the United States on the dirigible *Hindenberg*, an experimental way to cross the Atlantic (airplanes would not be routinely used until 1939). Nelson shook off his mother's warnings about the dangers of airships as he left her, Muriel, and Connie with a smile to board the ship on May 3. Three days later, on May 6, as the *Hindenberg* was about to land in New Jersey, it caught fire and, within seconds, was totally aflame. When the fire first broke out, Nelson and a friend traveling with him jumped. Nelson made it, but his friend did not clear the ship so Nelson went back into the burning debris three times to try to save his companion. He failed. The burns he suffered and the trauma of the crash so shocked Nelson that it took him a year to recover.[14]

Despite being terribly disturbed by her brother's brush with death, Muriel soldiered on, spending a short time with her sister Ruth, a pediatrician, who dropped in during the summer. When Ruth asked if she could leave her three youngest children with Muriel for a week, she agreed, and Ruth, her husband, Harry Bakwin, both successful pediatricians, and their oldest son went off on a driving tour of Yugoslavia in search of art works. Harry and Ruth, like Helen, were serious art collectors.[15]

Muriel had a different preoccupation. The summer of 1937 became more tense by the hour as more and more Austrian Socialists were arrested each day. As one adolescent boy, Henry Leichter, would write when his parents, Otto and Käthe, were taken away, "1937 was the last summer of my family."[16]

In the fall of that year Mussolini visited Berlin at Hitler's invitation and, impressed with Hitler's presence, oratory, and ability to command the attention of a huge crowd of one million, "returned to Rome convinced that his future lay at the side of Hitler."[17]

In the midst of this grim news, Muriel finally reached the end of medical school, having successfully completed the ten required semesters. She now had only to pass her final exams in order to graduate, and she began to plot out a study routine for the arduous tests ahead. At the same time, she was dismayed to learn that Joe and Otto Bauer were squabbling: Joe insisted that Chancellor Schuschnigg "would rather surrender to the Nazis than call the socialist workers to the defense of the regime,"[18] while Bauer accused Joe of being pessimistic.

This dissension among Austrian political leaders did not go unnoticed by Hitler, and he would put it to good use when he moved against Austria. By November 5, 1937, as Joe and Otto continued their argument, their contretemps became symbolic of a rift growing throughout the country among various factions. Meanwhile, in Berlin "the die was cast [and] Hitler had communicated his irrevocable decision to go to war."[19] Austria was headed toward its downfall.

A Socialist leader named Robert Danneberg, acting as a mediator, insisted that Joe go to Brno to make peace with Otto Bauer in order to minimize the factionalism among Social Democrats.[20] Muriel agreed. She hoped that Joe and Bauer could unite to face what was certain to be a difficult period ahead. Meanwhile, she went into the hospital for minor surgery, leaving Connie in Fini's capable hands while Joe was arguing philosophy in Brno.

Out of the hospital after three days, Muriel got some very bad news. When Joe returned, gloomy and moody from his talks with Bauer, Muriel told him that when she had been at the lending library, she had discovered that her contact Lore was absent, but no one knew why. The next morning, Muriel had called the library, asking for Lore by her real name. When she was told the woman was again not in, Muriel said, "Will she be in on Monday?" The person on the phone told her, "We don't know."[21]

When Joe heard this, he hastened to Lore's apartment. He would know in an instant if she had been arrested because they had arranged that if she were ever taken away, she would remove her doormat. Joe climbed the stairs and saw that the doormat was gone. For the next two weeks, Muriel and Joe avoided each other, assuming that since Lore had been arrested, Muriel was likely being watched.

Muriel soon learned that Lore's arrest was only the beginning. A systematic and careful police investigation had unearthed most of the Revolutionary Socialists' leaders so that during the last days of November and the beginning of December 1937, almost all of them, in Vienna as well as in other regions of Austria, had been arrested. Only Joe and two other men were still free.[22]

Muriel, who now remained in contact with Joe only under the most stringent safety precautions, was terrified as she left for Brno on December 10 to
see Otto Bauer. Sitting on the train for an hour and a half, she pretended to
read from a medical textbook. In the margins of the textbook, she had written Joe's report to Bauer on the Revolutionary Socialists in coded notes. When
she arrived in Brno, Bauer told her that he thought Joe should leave Austria
immediately.

She took this message back to Vienna, and Joe left at once for Switzerland.
A week or so later, Muriel and Connie joined him there so they could at least
spend Christmas together. Muriel had to return to Vienna for her studies after
the brief holiday, but Joe thought it best that he stay in Switzerland since much
of their work was now at a standstill.[23]

In February 1938, Muriel reunited with her lover in Paris for a few days.
When they returned to Vienna in mid-month, they learned that most of their
Socialist friends had been released from jail. This was hopeful, but there was bad
news, too: Schuschnigg and Hitler had just met at Berchtesgaden—the *Führer*'s
retreat in the Bavarian Alps, not far from beautiful Salzburg, where Muriel had
enjoyed so many happy summer vacations. They had signed an agreement that
was "Austria's death warrant."[24] For Austria, this meeting was the beginning of
the end, marking the start of a month of uncertainty and fear for many as the
country braced for a German invasion.

Muriel, too, now entered a new world: Despite the risk, Joe took her around
and introduced her to any leading Socialists she didn't already know. They were
all aware that the days of an independent Austria were numbered, that most of
them would soon be either on the run or arrested.[25] Only Muriel had a chance
of remaining free, and her freedom would be critical to the cause. In the months
ahead, in the Nazi onslaught that now seemed inevitable, she could save lives
and, in her own small way, try to keep democracy alive.

Chapter 12

INVASION

The groundwork for the *Anschluss,* Hitler's invasion of Austria, had begun years earlier, but for Muriel it was the month immediately preceding the German incursion that was excruciating. She feared that those she loved most, as well as the many comrades and friends to whom she had grown close during her twelve years in Vienna, were all in danger.

But she was in a minority. Right up to the day that Hitler invaded Austria, most Austrians held onto their faith in their nation's legal system, believing that everything would ultimately work out. Despite evidence that the Nazis, rooted in Austria "almost as early as in Germany,"[1] had taken hold fully and by 1938 were operating openly on the street, many Austrians continued to be optimistic.

Not Muriel, of course. She was a realist. Back from Paris, in the Rummelhardtgasse apartment with Connie and Fini, it was clear from what they had heard on the street that Austria's days were numbered. As Joe went around to all his fellow Revolutionary Socialists urging them to leave the country immediately, Muriel tried to convince her Jewish friends to flee as well.

Since Muriel now had even less time at home than usual, Connie felt more neglected than ever. Although Muriel had for years devoted what is today called "quality time" to her daughter, it was not enough. From infancy on, Connie had been cared for by a series of governesses. In later life, she would call these young women "manipulative," with many rules that cramped her freedom, such as forcing her to take a daily nap even at the age of seven.[2] But at the time, her only complaint was simply that she missed her mother. When Muriel took care of her, she was 100 percent there, reading stories at night, talking with her daughter. But Connie was only too aware of the parts of her mother's life that didn't include her, so she often felt left out and unhappy:

> I had a rotten childhood. I would rather die than go through it again.[3]

Connie would later point out that she "was not offered a choice about whether [she] was prepared to make a sacrifice" so that her mother could work in the resistance.[4] Clearly the gain of some Austrians was Connie's loss. Nevertheless, she loved and admired her mother. As the "four weeks' agony"[5] continued, Connie would be even lonelier as Muriel threw herself into her resistance work.

On February 24, Schuschnigg, in a surprising about-face, declared defiantly that his country "would never voluntarily give up its independence." At the same time, for support against Nazi Germany, he turned to the Austrian workers, a population he had heretofore ignored and, worse, suppressed. There was no choice. The workers, led by Joe and other Socialist leaders, rallied, asking the Austrian people to back an independent Austria. On March 4, the Socialists publicly agreed to aid Schuschnigg despite his past acts. The workers and the RS all knew that an Austria under Adolf Hitler would be the worst possible fate for the nation.[6]

Until the *Anschluss*, the Revolutionary Socialists had managed to survive, even after the debacle of February 1934, with Joe at their head and Muriel backing him, and had made some progress with unions, factories, and other workers' groups, joining forces with the powerful clandestine Socialist Free Trade Unions. The growing Nazi threat added to the Revolutionary Socialists' clarity of purpose. But by early March 1938, despite the glimmer of harmony between workers and the RS and Schuschnigg, it was too late. Neither the RS nor any other Austrian group had the numbers, the power, or the strength to withstand the Nazis. As the threat of armed German intervention came closer, "the RS simply yielded to events."[7]

In early March, in preparation for what lay ahead, Muriel had ordered a large sum of money from her bank in the Netherlands, where she kept most of her funds because of the instability of Austrian currency. Then she sat and waited for the money, knowing that she would only be able to help people if she had quantities of cash on hand.

On Wednesday, March 9, Schuschnigg announced that he would ask the country to vote in a referendum, to be held in four days, in which Austrians would choose between two dictatorships, his or Hitler's.[8] In the wake of this announcement, many Socialists converged on the Café Meteor, their usual meeting place, to talk over this latest news. They thought that the referendum boded well for them since Schuschnigg could not win without the support of the Left.

Having heard about Schuschnigg's plan to hold a vote, an enraged Hitler had begun to mobilize his troops at once, moving to occupy Austria immediately.[9] In his support, Austrian Nazis rioted in Vienna and other cities.

Thursday night, March 10, even more political activists showed up at the café, with Manfred Ackermann representing the Revolutionary Socialists. Already in jeopardy because he was Jewish, Ackermann was the first person Muriel would help to freedom a few days later. Joe didn't get involved in these discussions because he and Muriel had decided that party members should avoid illegal meetings that could be infiltrated by the Gestapo—and Joe was following his own advice.

As the other Socialists talked that night, many said they would not publicly support their old enemy, Schuschnigg, even if he claimed he required their help to hold off Hitler. Although the beleaguered Austrian chancellor had claimed to want the backing of the Left, the truth was that he would quickly sell out labor if Hitler granted him more time. But Schuschnigg failed to recognize that Hitler no longer needed him—if indeed he ever had. Most thought that Schuschnigg would back down in the face of force. In addition, none of the RS members believed that Schuschnigg's plan had a chance—"Things were clearly all going the other way."[10]

At some point during that tense week, Connie rescued Joe from his ambivalence over how to deal with Schuschnigg's referendum. "It's very simple," the precocious seven-year-old told him. "You don't want to vote for Hitler; you can't vote for yourself; so there's nothing you can do but vote for Schuschnigg." Accepting Connie's "simple" solution, Joe wrote what would be the last manifesto of Austria's Revolutionary Socialists, urging workers to vote "yes" in Sunday's referendum. This was not the time to retaliate against Austrian Fascists for what they had done to workers in 1934. This was the time to reject Hitler: "Next Sunday, we must manifest our burning hatred of Hitler-Fascism."[11] Although the flyer would be widely distributed, it would have no effect at all as events were hurtling forward.

Muriel had spent days anxiously awaiting the delivery of her money and making plans for the time when she would be on her own. She fully expected Joe and other Socialist leaders to abandon the city when Hitler marched in. The money finally arrived on Friday, March 11, just as Austria ceased to exist as an independent nation. Pressured by Nazis inside his administration as well as in Germany, a weakened Chancellor Schuschnigg seemed inclined to resign. All day long, the actors in this drama played on with Hitler being more demanding, Schuschnigg being more conciliatory. Finally, at 5:30 in the afternoon, the "stubborn, upright" Austrian president Wilhelm Miklas accepted Schuschnigg's resignation. But he refused to name German Nazi Arthur Seyss-Inquart as Schuschnigg's successor.[12]

Miklas's brave position came to naught when, later that afternoon, Austrian Nazis took control of government buildings and of the streets, and Seyss-Inquart became chancellor. At 7:30 that evening, Schuschnigg gave his famous "Farewell, Austria" speech, which was broadcast over the radio. Because German armies were already on the march and German tanks and airplanes were also on their way to Austria, he said he would surrender peacefully to avoid bloodshed: "…we have yielded to force…God protect Austria."[13]

Muriel missed the speech because she was putting Connie to bed: it was Fini's day off, and the child had a bad cold. Muriel had spent the evening in the apartment trying to destroy incriminating literature linking her to the illegal Revolutionary Socialists while she waited for Joe, who had hurriedly gone off to Brno to consult with Otto Bauer. The old-line Socialist leader would remain unrealistic to the end. As evidence of either gullibility or naiveté, Otto Bauer's last words to Joe at that meeting were: "Hitler must know that the western powers would not allow a German military intervention against Austria."[14] Constantly watching for Joe at the window, Muriel fed Connie supper and listened to the clamorous shouting in the streets. Finally the child fell asleep, and Muriel turned out her light. Then the phone rang; it was Dr. Bornstein calling with a cryptic message, urging Muriel to send Connie away from Vienna.

After the call, Muriel rushed to the window and saw streets crowded with swaggering Austrian Nazis brandishing swastikas and singing the "Horst-Wessel-Lied," voices hoarse from jubilant shouting. The *Anschluss* was a reality, there was no way for Muriel to hope otherwise, and Joe would have to bolt. Her daughter too, just as Dr. Bornstein had warned, would have to be sent somewhere safe from the looming danger.

The hours between nightfall on Friday and sunrise on Saturday, the night that would usher in seven years of Nazi tyranny, felt like the longest of Muriel's life. As she waited, Muriel decided how she would persuade Joe to leave the country at once; she expected him to resist. Back in Vienna later that night, Joe found his way home blocked by raving crowds. When he finally arrived, the couple discussed the situation. She would remain, Muriel said, and she would be safe, she insisted, because as an American medical student, she was in no danger. But the future of the Revolutionary Socialists rested on his shoulders and, since he was sure to be arrested, he had a responsibility to save himself.

"Well, I don't know," Joe said.

"Remember, that it was decided by both of us and by all your friends that you *must* leave at once," she responded.[15]

"I know, but I have some things to do first," Joe argued. "I've got to go around and see everyone I can, and tell them if I'm gone and if they need help, they should contact you, or that you will be available to meet them at certain times and places."[16] Then he asked if she had any money. She told him that, for-tuitously, the bank's "money mailman" had actually delivered her cash, a large sum in various currencies, that very morning.

She gave Joe some money, and he left the apartment, accompanied by Stephen's old lover, Tony Hyndman, who had been living at Muriel's ever since she had recruited him to run errands for the resistance.[17] At one o'clock in the morning, they returned with Joe's friends Capro and Hilda Bohmer, Socialists whom Joe wanted to meet Muriel since she would be their connection. Then Joe and Tony went out again, looking for more comrades to introduce to Muriel. An hour later, they returned with another socialist, Karl Holoubek, and his wife, and they too worked out a code. But the Holoubeks had a problem: Karl would not abandon his spouse, and she would not leave her relatives in Vienna. He decided to remain, but in hiding, and Muriel promised to get him a Czech pass-port so that he could make a getaway if and when he decided to. Yet again Joe crept outside, returning finally, at three in the morning, when he couldn't find anyone else. People were either hiding or not answering their doors, but he'd left coded messages for as many as he dared.

Muriel kept pushing him to leave and, finally, Joe agreed. He would go on the 7 A.M. Orient-Express to Paris. Determined to try one more time to gather acquaintances before he took the train, he left the apartment, first looking for his close friend, Josef Boehmer, known as "Peperl." Peperl, an inactive Socialist, was one of the very few people on the left who had a car, and such transporta-tion would prove useful to Muriel in the days and weeks ahead.

At some point during the night, Muriel too, along with some of her English friends, went out to deliver money to people who had to depart immediately. Some had legal passports, but others did not and would have to cross moun-tain passes into Switzerland. A larger group, those who needed false passports, would be Muriel's focus in the days ahead. Seeking out the most exposed peo-ple, smuggling their photographs to Czechoslovakia, then transporting faked passports back into Austria, would be her main job, along with hiding some people and escorting others to safety across the border.

Muriel would also aid some fortunate individuals to acquire American visas by providing them with affidavits of support. These documents, in which an American citizen guaranteed that the individual named was financially solvent and would never need to be supported by the government, allowed a number of Austrians to gain admittance to the United States. In addition, Muriel would enlist her brother Nelson as well as many friends in America to write these affidavits. She would, in the end, secure hundreds of affidavits and save hun-dreds of lives. Some of those she rescued were Jewish analysts—among them her friend Dr. Bornstein—and others were Jews who had some affiliation with the psychoanalytic community.[18]

Just before dawn on Saturday, March 12, Muriel and Joe were reunited in the apartment with only a short time before the Orient-Express was scheduled to leave. Tony offered to accompany Connie and Fini on the train while Joe continued to waver. Although he had agreed to go, he was afraid for Muriel. She would lose her anonymity as "Mary" because now, without her cover, she would be directly in contact with the RS members and others needing help. Also, he knew what was in store for his country and those who remained there once the Nazis were actually in control.

Nevertheless, Joe eventually capitulated, giving Muriel instructions all the while he packed. "Manfred Ackermann. He is the most important. If he gets in touch with you, try to get him a passport immediately."[19] Ackermann, a respected intellectual and labor leader, head of the central committee of Revolutionary Socialists, an active anti-Nazi, and a Jew, was to be aided first: Joe had already sent word to Ackermann that if he found himself in trouble, he should go to Muriel's apartment.

Now it was time for Muriel to awaken Connie. She was sending her and Fini to Arosa, a tiny hamlet in the eastern Swiss Alps, with Tony traveling with them long enough to ensure that they were settled and that Joe was safely on his way to Paris. Then Tony, determined to find more ways to be useful, would return to Muriel in Vienna. She walked into her daughter's room and kissed her to wake her. When Connie opened her eyes, Muriel asked, "Would you like to go to Arosa to ski?"

"Yes," she answered. "When?"

"Now," said Muriel. "Get up, get dressed, wear your ski suit."[20]

Connie dressed in her ski clothes, and Muriel took her and their little black dachshund, Klex, out to buy rolls and milk for breakfast. The bright child knew immediately what had occurred when she saw the huge swastika on the hospital across the street. But the little girl who always asked questions, made only one remark that morning: "I guess the Nazis got ahead of the referendum."[21]

Muriel tried hard to transmit resolve and confidence rather than anxiety to her daughter during their last moments together—she knew that their separation came with an uncertain future. For her part, Connie was delighted to go on a skiing trip and, and in spite of the ominous swastika, had no idea that she wouldn't see her mother for a long time.

Back in the apartment, Muriel told Joe, "I don't know whether you'd better tell her anything about your part in it all." He decided to warn Connie that

Austrian and German Nazis might recognize him at the border or on the train. But she was too smart for his awkward efforts. "Wouldn't it be better if I just pretend I don't understand German?"

"Much better," he said with a smile.[22]

Moments later, wearing ski outfits and carrying ski equipment, Joe, Connie, Tony, and Fini left. Muriel did not go to the station with them. She said goodbye at the door of her apartment and then watched out the window as they walked away. As she would later hear from Tony, their train crossed into Switzerland without incident, although German stormtroopers controlled every large station.[23]

For the first time in years, Muriel was on her own. She felt both anxious and brave. As an American, her position was not as precarious as that of the local citizens. On the other hand, her work in the resistance could make her a target for detention, or worse. She was determined to finish her examinations, to help Joe's Socialist comrades, and to save as many Jews as she could.[24]

Later that morning, Muriel, learned, along with the rest of the world, that overnight Austria had "ceased to exist." Hitler issued a proclamation to the Austrians that promised a true plebiscite in April and then set off for a triumphant march into the country of his birth.[25]

Muriel, alone in her apartment, began her work. She would first seek out those with whose well-being Joe had entrusted to her, the endangered Jews and Socialists. She had so much to do, and quickly, that she could not take many precautions. The people who would now contact her would get in touch directly. Some were not careful by nature, while others had not been politically active and didn't know how to be cautious. Many would just show up on her doorstep. She would feel uneasy at times, that she was being followed and that it was only luck that she was not detained during these first weeks. And she would be correct. As she later learned, the Nazis were watching her.[26]

On Saturday afternoon, she contacted Socialists Hans Pav, Emil Sladky, and Little Otto Bauer, all of whom she already knew, as well as Manfred Ackermann and Lisl Zerner. She also called on her physics tutor, Franz Urbach, to convince him to take his family and go. She had known the physicist since 1933 and, since he was Jewish and also working on quantum theory, she felt certain he would be apprehended almost immediately. "You must go to America at once," she told him. "I am going to write you an affidavit of support."[27] He fled a short time later, with his wife Anni and their young son, using Muriel's affidavits to obtain visas to the United States.

Upon her return to her apartment, Muriel was heartened to find a young English friend, Shiela Grant Duff, waiting for her. They had been together in

Russia in 1932 on a whirlwind tour of Soviet facilities at a time when many left-leaning radicals were interested in the Soviets. Now a journalist based in Prague, Shiela had come to Vienna to report on the *Anschluss*. Muriel found comfort in talking to this well-informed woman to whom she could tell her story and pour out her worries without fear of endangering either of them. Shiela kept her company through another interminable night as she waited to hear about Joe. Hoping for a call from Tony by eight, Muriel found herself despairing when by midnight he still had not contacted her.

On Sunday morning, March 13, having no idea if Joe was safe, she nevertheless went out to see as many endangered Viennese as she could, including active Socialists Hans Kunke, Ferdinand Tschürtch, Karl Czernetz, and others. None had legal documents or, at that point, any getaway plans. Later that day, analyst Anya Maenchen and her husband Otto, a Socialist and a historian, came to see Muriel about getting out. That afternoon, one of Muriel's closest friends, Ania Herzog, visited to discuss her indecision about what to do. Ania mentioned that her friend Hermann Broch would call Muriel for advice as to how to get over the border. Unused to the secret ways of the resistance group, Broch began calling Muriel too often, asking "coded but nevertheless indiscreet questions, usually relating to a lost umbrella, which I could not quite figure out, and which caused me great uneasiness." Nonetheless, both Broch and Herzog eventually got away.[28]

On the street, what she witnessed so horrified and shocked her that she was almost immobilized, a rare feeling for her. All the while under siege from the noise of the shouting hordes, the rumbling tanks in the streets, and the screaming planes overhead, Muriel saw with her own eyes that Austrian anti-Semitism was more virulent than she ever could have imagined—indeed, it was said to be worse in Austria than in Germany, as one Viennese woman would write.[29] Muriel couldn't understand how anyone could stand by and watch what was happening in Vienna without doing anything. She didn't seem to grasp that other people did not possess her endless generosity, as well as her courage. Within hours, it seemed, Vienna had become a different city. Jewish schoolchildren were forced to sit in the back of classrooms as the school day began with a shouted "*Heil Hitler!*"[30] Almost at once, Nazis put up signs banning dogs and Jews, as journalist Gedye wrote:

> It is not so much all the brutalities of the Austrian Nazis which I have witnessed...It is the heartless, grinning, soberly dressed crowds...fighting one another to get closer to the elevating spectacle of an ashen-faced Jewish surgeon on hands and knees before half-a-dozen young hooligans with Swastika armlets and dog-whips...[31]

The Gestapo dragnet would eventually sweep one third of Austria's Jews into Hitler's grasp. Austrian writers who made it to freedom left a complete record of the early days of the *Anschluss*, describing roundups, purges, torture, and deportation. "I came from hell," said one woman who got away.[32]

Muriel was horrified by the new landscape: Jews scrubbing cobblestoned streets with their bare hands. Men, women, and children, beaten and broken, left lying in gutters.

Viennese Jews were in shock:

> What was completely new to me was the feeling of being a second-class human being, totally exposed to the brutal impulses of any passerby, without any recourse to the law.[33]

Whenever she contacted Socialists and other Austrians who were Jewish, Muriel tried to convince them to leave immediately, but many people refused. Some had relatives they would not abandon. Others were in denial. Finally, there was their loyalty to their beloved Vienna, with its beauty and charm, its long musical history, its lush Vienna Woods. The Viennese had a difficult time giving up on their city, even as it became an abyss.

> Vienna is a very, very powerful place, when you live there and you've been immersed in the culture of it... And Jewish people like us were part of a very large extended family and everybody was still there. I had ten aunts in Vienna, sisters of my mother. I had an uncle and an aunt who were siblings of my father. I had my grandmother there.[34]

For those who managed to escape during those first days, the journey consisted of body searches by eagle-eyed Nazis in train stations that suddenly resembled refugee camps.[35] Some exiles would never recover, and suicide became commonplace.

The *Anschluss* meant that the Socialists were once again, as they had been in 1934, in total disarray. Some got away, but others were captured and sent to Dachau. The invasion also meant the end of the Austrian Jewish community. In 1938, about 200,000 Jews lived in Vienna. After March 1938, two-thirds of Austria's Jews would go into exile while the remaining 65,000, unable to elude the Nazis, would be deported. As the result of "persecution, expulsion and extermination," a half century later in 1983, only 10,000 Jews remained in the city.[36]

Meanwhile, Hitler received a roaring welcome in every town he entered, surrounded by hordes of troops in brown and black uniforms. By the time he arrived in Vienna on March 14, the *Anschluss* law, which began "Austria is a

province of the German Reich,"[37] had been signed. Now, not only Jews but all
RS activists who had managed to avoid being seized over the weekend were on
the run.[38] Those militants who were caught were imprisoned. Practically the
only Socialist left in Vienna at this time who was able to go out on the street to
accomplish something without being arrested was Muriel. With Joe's departure, the organization's full weight fell on her shoulders.

In light of her vulnerability, Muriel's abandonment by Joe is hard to understand. He knew she faced real peril. Given a choice between saving the many
or the one he loved above all else, however, he was, with great reluctance, true
to their joint cause. Clearly, he had confidence that Muriel would survive and
somehow manage to exploit her relative freedom "to help others with her two
apartments, her financial resources, her connections with other foreigners, and
finally with her own passport."[39] And he was right. Muriel, along with other
equally brave unsung heroes, would manage to help many people escape the
Nazis in the months ahead.

CHAPTER 13

THE THIRD WOMAN

M uriel lived by a self-imposed mandate during the *Anschluss* and its aftermath, believing that she and others of like mind had a great responsibility, as Stephen Spender would write in his memoir, to resist Nazism and try to
prevent a world war.[1] Her lifelong passion for democratic principles, beginning
with her youthful attraction to the women's suffrage movement, and continuing through her college-era adoption of radicalism and Socialism, all made
her appreciate her own freedoms and privileges. And she never forgot that the
killing of innocent creatures was the source of her family's wealth and had
thus enabled her comfortable lifestyle. These experiences and circumstances
informed who Muriel was, and once she decided to risk her own life to save others, she rarely looked back.

Now, in March 1938, with Joe out of the country, Muriel's real work began.
Her life had become increasingly dangerous: she would face arrest and deportation to a concentration camp if the Gestapo found out that she was helping to
liberate Jews, Socialists, and, the most vulnerable, Jewish Socialists.

As the first German units arrived in Vienna, people moved from hiding
place to hiding place, or simply stayed home, waiting in terror for the knock
on the door. During their initial roundup, the Gestapo took 20,000 people into
custody, holding a few temporarily but some permanently.[2]

A handful of those on the run succeeded in escaping from Vienna while
others tried and failed. Robert Danneberg, the respected comrade who had
insisted that Joe and Otto Bauer reconcile their differences some time earlier,
boarded a train along with Karl Hans Sailer. But when the train was turned
back at the border and halted briefly, Sailer leaped off and ran into the woods,
while the exhausted and disheartened Danneberg remained in his seat. Sailer
hid and later escaped to America. Danneberg, however, was arrested and on

April 4 was among those on the first transport to Dachau. Despite desperate attempts to save him on the part of many in the United States and other countries, including Muriel's repeated efforts, he was killed in the Dachau gas chamber in 1942.[3]

As Muriel's days grew busier, they often came to be occupied by enormous and complicated maneuvers to save individual lives. Manfred Ackermann, the Jewish Socialist whom Joe had asked Muriel to help if possible, heard that the police had come for him on Saturday morning. He immediately shaved his head, removed his glasses, and had a passport photo taken of the new man he had created. After spending Saturday night at a friend's house,[4] he sought Muriel's help on Sunday evening, March 13.

Muriel was still at home awaiting news of Joe when the bell rang. Through the peephole, she saw a man, a woman, and a little boy, all appearing to be in great distress. As they entered, the man addressed her as Mary and told her in a low voice that he was Ackermann. After a brief discussion, she agreed to take his new photograph to Brno on Monday morning and to smuggle a fake Czech passport back for him. He was afraid for his life, so she offered to put him up at the Lammgasse apartment, where she had successfully hidden Joe for years.

He agreed reluctantly to Muriel's plan though he was nearly immobilized by fear; Ackermann's wife and child would accompany them to the apartment because a group would look less suspicious than a single man. Then the family would double back and return home since they were not in immediate danger. It was Ackermann, an active Socialist, the Nazis wanted, not—at this time at least—his family. Ackermann would stay in the apartment for a day or two until Muriel could return with his passport.

Later that evening, the family arrived at the apartment and Muriel gave Ackermann an extra set of keys and showed him where everything was. But he was barely listening as he pulled down the shades, nervously reminding her not to forget about him, to come back for him soon. The rest of the family returned to their home, and Muriel went back to the Rummelhardtgasse apartment, hoping to hear that Joe had arrived in Paris.

She was still waiting for news the following morning, Monday, as Hitler marched triumphantly into Vienna as if he owned it, with nearly 2 million citizens cheering him on, as one eyewitness would write in his remembrance:

> I witnessed the hysterical city...I walked through the streets, and saw the armoured Nazi cars cheered by the crowds. The Viennese, reputed for their Gemüetlichkeit [coziness], revealed faces distorted by hate mixed with ecstasy, as they shouted hysterically "Heil Hitler, Sieg Heil, ein Volk, ein Fuehrer." It was a deplorable and frightening sight![5]

Later that day, as 50,000 enlisted men and officers in the Austrian army swore their allegiance to Germany,[6] Muriel, traveling on her British passport, arrived at Otto Bauer's home in Brno. Handing Bauer several photographs of Austrians, including Ackermann, she said she hoped he would have the passports soon. Bauer told her that Ackermann's would be ready on Tuesday morning but she would have to come back later in the week for the others. She stayed in Brno overnight and the next morning rushed back to Vienna, the ticket to Ackermann's freedom in her hand.

To make sure she wasn't followed, Muriel took a series of trams and taxis from the railroad station, finally getting out at a corner near the Lammgasse. When she walked into her apartment, it felt empty. She called out Ackermann's name, but she could tell that he was gone.[7] Frightened, she assumed that he had been arrested and that the police were now waiting for her as well, either outside or at her other apartment.

Muriel's immediate dilemma was that she was carrying an illegal passport. She didn't want to be found with it on her, but neither did she want to destroy it. Finally, she decided to call the Rummelhardtgasse apartment, hoping that her loyal maid, Frau Käthe, would let her know if anything was amiss. She found herself suddenly unsure of her ability to keep things on track and so was thrilled to hear Tony's voice when he answered the phone[8]: He would be able to tell her whether it was safe to come home, and he would surely have news of Joe. Using prearranged codes, she asked him to look in the kitchen to see if they needed anything. He told her to call back in ten minutes so he could check the cupboards. Then he went outside and found the street empty. When she called again, he was able to say that she should just come home—they had everything they needed.

Arriving at her apartment, she hid Ackermann's passport in a pile of papers and asked Tony about Joe. While he could assure her that Connie and Fini were securely ensconced in Arosa, he had no idea whether Joe had made it to Paris, although he had been fine when they parted in Switzerland days earlier.

Upset by this news, and forcing herself to shake off her deepening concern, she told Tony that Ackermann had disappeared. Suddenly the phone rang and when she answered, the caller used a code name to identify himself as a comrade. When he said he was in her neighborhood and asked if he could stop by for a few minutes, Muriel invited him up for a cup of coffee.

Moments later, a tall, blond man arrived, introducing himself as Robert, a friend of Ackermann's. Robert, an Austrian and inactive Socialist, provided the information that solved the mystery of Ackermann's whereabouts. Alone in Muriel's Lammgasse apartment, he had become so terrified that he couldn't bear it and had called Robert to rescue him. Robert picked him up and hid him.

When Muriel said she had Ackermann's passport, Robert offered to take it to his beleaguered friend.[9]

His suggestion unnerved her. Everyone was under suspicion during this time, and although Robert had the right code words, he was still a complete stranger. She later recalled that when she hesitated, he said, "Hubert got to France safely."[10] With this phrase, Muriel suddenly, for a brief moment, felt the pure joy of unmitigated relief. Hubert was Joe's most recent code name, and this meant not only that was Joe safe, but that the man standing in her apartment was not a spy.

Robert and Muriel set about figuring out how the terrified Ackermann could depart from his homeland without giving himself away. Trains were being watched. Despite its neutrality, Switzerland already had guards at its border, and its citizens seemed inhospitable to sheltering men and women targeted by the Nazis. By March 28, two weeks after the *Anschluss*, the Swiss would require all people with Austrian passports to have special entry visas, a position the politically neutral nation would maintain for the next seven years.[11]

Security at the border of Fascist Italy was more lax, so Muriel and Robert decided that Ackermann should be taken to a place as close to the Italian border as possible. She contacted Joe's friend Peperl, who had a car,[12] and he agreed to drive Ackermann, with Robert accompanying his frightened friend, to Wiener Neustadt, a town 45 kilometers south of Vienna. From there, after Robert purchased the train tickets, Ackermann would take the train into Italy.

At 9 P.M. on Tuesday, Peperl arrived at the designated corner in his large Buick, which was decorated with a Nazi flag. At the last minute, he suggested that Muriel go along as additional cover, and the four of them took off for Wiener Neustadt. As they drove out of Vienna, the German army was on the road, heading toward the city. Soldiers in marching columns and officers on horseback greeted them, and they waved back. Arriving at their destination, Muriel gave Ackermann a small amount of money—all she could spare, for she would need the rest of her cash for the days ahead. She decided that she would contact her brother Nelson in the south of France as soon as she returned to Vienna; he would be able to wire Ackermann more money. Many years later, a grateful Ackermann would recall how Muriel saved his life, and "wish[ed] that god would bless her."[13]

An exhausted Muriel drove back that night with Robert and Peperl, knowing that the next day would be just as tiring. During those first few weeks, no one was immune: Even Austria's greatest banker, Baron Louis Rothschild, a Jew, was arrested and imprisoned. He would spend a year on the top floor of

Vienna's Hotel Metropole until his family ransomed him for a sum reputed to be as high as $10 million.[14]

Although many active Socialists were finding their way to more secure locations during this first week after the *Anschluss*, the Socialist leader Otto Leichter chose to stay at home. When two men in leather coats showed up on Tuesday, he walked outside to meet them, telling his youngest son, Franz, that if the men were Gestapo there to arrest him, he might just as well go out. Instead, the men turned out to be Czech government officials who had brought false passports for a number of prominent Socialists such as Leichter and his wife, Käthe. Passport in hand, Leichter immediately set off for Yugoslavia, only to be turned back at the border for a reason that was never made clear to his family or his comrades.[15]

Leichter would have to try again to escape but now, having failed to get away, he decided to avoid his own apartment and immediately headed to Muriel's. The maid let him in after he said he was a friend of Joe's, and he soon made himself comfortable, even eating the supper of sandwiches and milk that the maid had prepared for her employer. When Muriel arrived home late from her hair-raising adventure with Ackermann, and before she could scream at finding a strange man in her living room, Leichter jumped up, addressed her as Mary, and reminded her that they had met. After Muriel acknowledged that she did recognize him, the friendly Leichter asked to stay overnight since the Gestapo were probably looking for him. But, he said, he would leave for Czechoslovakia early the next morning: he had a passport and hoped that this time he would be able to make it across the border.

Muriel agreed, and was astonished at how relaxed Leichter was compared to Ackermann. Whereas Ackermann had been too nervous to eat or sleep, Leichter had polished off the supper intended for her and asked for an alarm clock so he could rise at 5 A.M. The contrast between the two men fascinated her. After all, she had spent more than a little time studying psychology, during her own lengthy analysis and in her medical studies, and she found the vast differences in human behavior especially interesting. The next morning at 6 A.M., Muriel rose to find that her guest, true to his word, had already gone.[16]

A day or so later, she returned to Brno to pick up the remaining passports that Bauer had promised to have ready for her. But when she arrived at the Brno depot, she found waiting for her not only Otto Bauer, but Otto Leichter as well, both, in her opinion, quite conspicuous. She was frightened at the men's risky behavior. The Nazis had spies in Brno. As the two men approached her, she told them quietly but firmly to pretend they didn't know her, to act as if they were waiting for someone else, adding that she would meet them later. She left the station and went into the town, spending time at a café, then sitting for a while in a church—all to ensure that she hadn't been followed. Then she took another tram and finally a taxi, angry that these two men should be so thoughtless, especially Leichter, who had so recently eluded capture by the Gestapo.[17]

Arriving finally at Otto Bauer's, she picked up the five passports he had for her and left for her hotel. But in her room, as she opened the package, her nerve suddenly left her, and she panicked at the thought of smuggling the passports into Nazi-controlled Austria. Her terror mounted as she thought over what had just occurred in Austria; the invasion had instantly transformed the nation into a totalitarian state. Within the first 24 hours, the Gestapo—aided by police and various Nazi paramilitary organizations—had arrested thousands and were busily collecting the records of the Austrian police, particularly the Austrofascist *Staatspolizei* (state police), with its lists of known Socialists, Communists, Jews, and other groups. Daily life also had changed as people were not only hauled off to prisons and camps, but were committing suicide in large numbers. In the last two weeks of March alone, immediately after the *Anschluss*, 79 Jewish people chose to kill themselves rather than face the German occupation.[18]

Arguably, the violence was at its most vicious during these early days. Many years later, Muriel would hear that an American friend had visited Austria to see for himself if it was as bad as he had heard. As he wrote in a letter,

I went directly to Innsbruck and then to Hochsolden... The eerie thing was that things were so much as they had been portrayed that I could hardly get over the sensation that I was in a movie theater. Uniforms everywhere..."*Juden verboten*" [Jews forbidden] everywhere. Huge scarlet banners, window displays of evil looking knives inscribed "*Blut und Ehre*" [blood and honor]... My hotel had been taken over by the village Nazis and so had the ski school.[19]

In her hotel room that night in Brno, Muriel, who couldn't get images from recent events out of her mind, didn't sleep at all. The next morning, with feelings of dread, she resumed her mission and boarded a train for Vienna. After a short time, as the train approached the Austrian border, instead of the usual guards entering cars to inspect bags, an officer ordered everyone off the train with their luggage.[20]

Still on the Czech side of the border, Muriel, shaking, disembarked carrying a small suitcase, the passports secreted on her body in her corset. She followed the other travelers through a temporary fenced-in passageway, the demarcation between Czechoslovakia and Austria. Her mind was racing. She later remembered thinking: "I don't know what's coming... maybe I should not try to go into Austria at all this moment and should return to Brno." But it was too late: she was already in no-man's land. The Czech guards barely glanced at her passport, but as soon as she arrived on the Austrian side, Nazi officials shouted that women and children should go to one line, men to another.[21] Apparently they planned to search the passengers, down to their undergarments.

Somehow she kept from panicking as the line of women and children inched forward. As she watched people being escorted into tiny cubicles, Muriel knew her worst nightmare was about to come true: she would be stripped and the passports found. She could not bear to think about what might happen next.

Forcing herself to think about options rather than about being arrested, she decided that when it was her turn, she would create a disturbance, yelling that she was an American and that she refused to allow such an indignity. Feeling slightly relieved that at least she had a plan, she was further encouraged when, arriving at the head of the line, she saw that only every third woman was being taken into the cubicle. And she was not the third woman. Told to move on, she was not examined. For now, she was safe.

Back on the train, trembling from the near miss, she spent the remainder of the ride repeating to herself what Otto Bauer had told her only the night before: she would not have to continue running passports over the border. His comrade, Czech senator Heinrich Müller, a Prague Social Democrat, had a friend at the Czech consulate in Vienna, from whom he would be able to obtain new, clean and legal passports for those most at risk. Muriel had given Bauer about a dozen passport photos on this trip and now she could simply wait in Vienna for Müller to deliver the new passports to her without having to make the dangerous border crossing herself.[22]

Using Bauer as a conduit, Muriel arranged with the Czech senator to meet at a crowded and anonymous spot: the heart clinic in the hospital across the street from her apartment. She would carry a book, *The Microbe Hunters*, so that Müller could find her; he would make himself known with a coded greeting. Muriel waited anxiously. She would only learn which day the meeting would take place when a postcard arrived from "Maria" stating the date of her "planned vacation." Finally, the card came and at the agreed hour, Muriel went to the heart clinic, wearing a simple hat and a loden cloak, and carrying her book and the day's newspaper in a string bag.

When a man in short leather pants and a Tyrolean hat, toting a knapsack, walked up to her and said the right thing, she knew it was Senator Müller. She took him to her nearby Lammgasse apartment; she had not been inside the place since the night she had discovered Ackermann missing. They sat and talked and Muriel, knowing she didn't have to go anywhere or do anything at that moment, enjoyed Müller's company and began to relax during this brief respite. She even allowed herself to get sentimental, weeping with joy when her

Czech visitor took out his cache of new passports, meant to save twelve more lives. The sympathetic senator waited until she had stopped crying and then paid her a compliment that she would later recall:

> I've known many beautiful, courageous and interesting women in my life, but the most interesting one today.[23]

They left the apartment together, a perfectly composed Müller returning to Czechoslovakia and a somewhat shaky Muriel going back to the Rummhardtgasse apartment to figure out how to deliver the passports. She knew that a few would go to Little Otto Bauer and his family. As head of the Alliance of the Christian Social Democrats, a subset of the Revolutionary Socialists whose members were religious Catholics, Little Otto had already had his house searched and his printing materials confiscated by the Gestapo. Imprisoned for two weeks, he had been released with strict instructions not to leave the city.[24] He knew what that meant, and so did Muriel—seizure of Little Otto by the Gestapo was imminent.

Muriel had reserved passports for the parents and two of the Bauer children. Little Otto had told her earlier that his two oldest daughters, ages 14 and 16, could get away on their own. The girls had planned to stay with friends near the Swiss border, then take a day tour bus to Switzerland—and freedom—where papers would not be checked. But this plan fell through, so now two additional passports were needed for the girls.

Little Otto asked Muriel if she would travel to Prague to call on a professor friend who had daughters the same age. Perhaps he would give their passports to Muriel for his daughters to use. She agreed to go, and on Saturday took the overnight train to the beautiful Czech capital. Unfortunately, when she met with him, she discovered that Little Otto's professor had no passports to give her; he didn't even have any for his own family. Shocked—to Muriel, it seemed obvious that Czechoslovakia was next in line for invasion by the Germans—she could not understand why this man was so unprepared for his own family's exodus that he had not obtained the papers they would need. Apparently, she thought, fantasy still reigned among the middle classes. She left the professor, discouraged and depressed.

After listlessly spending the day in cafés and restaurants, Muriel finally boarded the evening train back to Vienna, relieved to be on her way. Haunted by the daunting problems she faced, she remained sleepless and therefore was wide awake when the train crossed the Austrian border in the darkest hours of the night and a Nazi guard entered the car to check her documents.

He questioned her in stern tones about arriving in and leaving Prague the same day. The Nazi clearly thought that a trip from Vienna to Prague and back within 24 hours was suspicious. Muriel kept talking about her planned return to England, emphasizing that she was an American. Trying not to babble and to keep her wits about her, Muriel mentioned her travels and the habit she had of making quick trips to favorite places of the past. She had no more than one day to revisit her beloved Prague, she said, since she had been there many times and had a busy schedule right now. Finally, though still somewhat disbelieving, the official handed her passport back and left.[25]

Thoroughly unstrung, Muriel finally arrived home. Her quiet apartment seemed an island of calm in the midst of a city in turmoil. The Nazis were settling in Vienna, with evident results, perhaps the most offensive being that the headquarters of the Austrian Adolf Eichmann, an *SS-Untersturmführer* (the rank of major) had become the central Vienna location for the hegira of Jews from Austria—an "office" supervising thousands of Viennese Jews' purchase of freedom as they were forced to relinquish their money, real estate, and possessions to the Nazis.

They were the lucky ones. Within a short time, Eichmann's operation would change from an operation of emigration to one of extermination, overseeing the murder of more than 4 million throughout Europe, most of them Jews. Like Eichmann, many Austrian Nazis would be transferred to administrative jobs, assigned to ensure the smooth operation of Hitler's plan to annihilate the Jews.[26]

On April 10, barely a month after the *Anschluss*, when Hitler held his promised referendum, more than 99.75 percent of Austrians voted yes to uniting with Germany. While people like Muriel had recognized that *Anschluss* meant the end of Austria, others believed the Nazi narrative: that they could heal Austria, revive it, but only in union with the German Reich.[27] The truth was revealed after the referendum's results were released and Hitler swiftly banned the name "Österreich," and moved to suppress the Austrian identity by forcing the Nazi-imposed name of "Östmark" on the nation.

As Muriel continued trying to get people to safety—including the Bauers, which was especially difficult because the family was so large—conditions worsened. By mid-April, all Jewish children were expelled from Vienna's schools and moved to separate facilities. Soon, Germany's Nuremberg Laws, with their heavy prohibitions against Jews, governed Austria. Some Austrian towns forbade entry to any Jews. Park benches and other public spaces in Vienna were off limits. Jews could no longer hold civil service jobs or practice medicine or law.[28]

Though Muriel still intended to graduate, the University of Vienna medical school had shut down after the *Anschluss,* and the two Jewish professors who had been scheduled to examine her were now gone: one had killed himself, the other had vanished.[29] She was not the only student left in limbo. With only a few weeks left until the end of the school year, the foreign students, all Jewish, were anxiously awaiting news of their fate: Would they be allowed to graduate?

In the midst of this uncertainty, one day in April, near her apartment, Muriel ran into the Wolf-Man (Sergius Pankejeff), her former Russian teacher. As usual, he was overwrought, so she invited him home but grew fearful once they were inside that his loud, excited voice might attract the concierge: Muriel's safety depended on avoiding anyone's attention, so she sought anonymity and tried to be unobtrusive and always quiet.

In her apartment, the Wolf-Man told of his recent tragic personal problems and his frustrating stab at emigrating: he could not get his travel documents in order because he had no tax receipts, and anyone trying to leave Austria had to prove he or she didn't owe back taxes to the government. More important, he had no passport because he had been stateless since World War I when he relinquished his Russian citizenship. Now, not officially a citizen of any nation, he could not get out of Austria.

Clearly about to have a breakdown, the Russian begged Muriel to help him. To calm him, she said she would try, suggesting that if he succeeded in getting away, he should travel to London to see Dr. Brunswick for some analytic sessions. Now, on top of the Bauer family of six, and the scores of others she was trying to assist, she took on the seemingly impossible job of helping this highly neurotic and nervous man slip out of the country. Muriel couldn't help feeling sympathetic toward the Wolf-Man, who, although in no danger from the Gestapo, was so seriously emotionally ill that he appeared to be a menace to himself.

In a moment of compassion, she wrote to Freud's great friend, Princess Marie Bonaparte—the great-granddaughter of Napoleon's younger brother, a psychoanalyst and Freud's patient and protégé—and several others, seeking the guarantees required by the consulates before they would grant the Wolf-Man a visitor's visa. Soon he received a Nansen passport, an international identity card issued by the League of Nations to refugees who were stateless.[30] Muriel gathered the guarantees she had collected for him and his Nansen passport and they went together to the British consulate.

Meeting at 6 A.M. one day in late April, they found the consulate surrounded by a two-block long queue of people who had been waiting overnight, camped out with blankets. Despite the angst and pain evident on the faces of those on line, "the greatest tragedies were those of the persons who never got inside the gates at all," Muriel would later write. Once in the consulate, Muriel heard a British official making anti-Semitic remarks. By now aware that she should not even think about complaining, she just stood and fumed silently that a representative of the British government would express such hatred of Jews. Nevertheless, the trip was successful for the Wolf-Man. He finally obtained a visitor's visa to England, and Muriel saw him off.[31]

She returned to the Bauers, but before she could deal with them, at the end of April she was forced to make a quick trip to Paris and Arosa. Old friends from America had dropped off their young son, nicknamed Pups, at her apartment. Planning a six-month archaeological expedition in Turkey, they had earlier arranged for their child to stay with Muriel and Connie. Muriel had not been able to get in touch with them for, just as the *Anschluss* occurred, they were on board a ship crossing the Atlantic. When they arrived in Paris, Muriel was there to meet them. After explaining what had just happened in Austria, she said that the ten-year-old boy could stay if they agreed that he would be safest with Connie and Fini in Switzerland.

They assented, so Muriel took Pups and boarded a train back to Vienna that would first make a quick stop in Switzerland. At the train station near Arosa, she only had time to embrace Connie and promise to visit her soon, say goodbye, and then re-board. Leaving Connie, she was of two minds: it was easier this time because she hoped to leave Vienna in a matter of weeks. But, what if something were to happen to her? Who would take care of her child?[32]

Pushing such ruminations aside, she returned home to learn that in addition to the Bauer family, Nuna Sailer and her six-month-old baby needed her assistance. Nuna was the wife of Karl Hans Sailer, the energetic Socialist who had escaped after jumping off the train he was riding alongside the doomed Robert Danneberg. An active Socialist, Nuna had no passport and doubted that she could run through the woods carrying a baby.

Muriel invited Nuna to her apartment. The two women were similar in appearance, with dark hair and eyes, so since Muriel had both American and British passports, she offered to give the British document to Nuna if the other woman was willing to take the risk. She also suggested that the young mother disguise herself as a British tourist and carry skis as well as a suitcase embossed with Muriel's initials.

Since Muriel's British passport was issued before she had Connie and so did not include a child, Nuna would have to leave the baby with Frieda, another comrade, and Muriel would then try to get the baby out. Nuna agreed, reluctantly of course, as leaving her child was difficult. But with Muriel's passport, skis, and suitcase, she escaped successfully and the baby was eventually rescued, taken to Switzerland by another trusted friend. Relieved that Nuna and her child were safe, Muriel turned her attention again to the Bauers. Almost at once, she was granted a tiny opening. Frieda had a friend at the Czech consulate in Vienna. Muriel asked if this contact would add two more children to the bulky family passport for four that Muriel had obtained earlier from Senator Müller.[33]

Frieda agreed to try and Muriel warned her to be extra careful at the consulate—though loyal, Frieda had difficulty being totally discreet. Nevertheless, Muriel pursued this option because she saw no other way. To her great relief, Frieda had learned from her past experiences and carried out her assignment carefully—no one got arrested and the daughters were successfully added to the Bauer passport. Muriel still needed a tax receipt for them but felt she could no longer wait to get the family out. With each passing day, the likelihood increased that the Gestapo would come back for Little Otto.

Muriel had crossed the border many times without being asked for proof that she had paid her taxes, but such an advantage was due to her being American. The Bauers were a different story. One slip-up and all six would be shipped to Dachau. Muriel decided they should try for Italy. She would accompany them, traveling in a different car on the train so she could watch them but not be part of their group.

She had a plan, too, for the dreaded tax receipt: if she were asked for hers, she would make a scene, yelling that Americans should not be bothered with such things. Then, if the Nazis tried the same thing with the Bauers, she would yell some more, shouting that they'd never get any more tourists, especially from England or America, if they treated passengers like this.[34]

Finally, at ten o'clock on a night at the very end of April, Muriel and the six Bauers boarded adjacent compartments on the train for Italy. All of them quite wide awake with nerves, they rode the train through the night. To their amazement, they passed through the dawn border check with no incident, and continued on into Italy. Muriel was almost giddy with the cessation of tension, as she later wrote:

> We were so happy to get over. I stood outside their compartment door and smiled. I would have liked to go in, but Otto just looked at me and gave me a little sign by shaking his head. Then I realized, Italy is a fascist country too and we'd better be careful.[35]

From the railroad station in Venice they took a vaporetto to the Piazzo San Marco, where they could finally relax. Little Otto's son never forgot the day, as he would later recall:

> We went to a very fancy restaurant…It was the best meal I'd ever
> had…You only had to eat half of it and they came with a new plate.
> And dessert was ice cream in the shape of an animal. Then she put us
> on the train to Switzerland.[36]

Muriel wished for the day to be over, almost in disbelief that the stress of
this work would cause her to want to leave her beloved Venice, a city she adored
from past visits. That night, they all went on to Zurich, where the Bauers would
be met by Swiss friends and Muriel would see Joe, albeit briefly. The lovers,
separated by distance and war, had only moments to embrace, to say how much
they loved each other. It was a train-station meeting, fraught with longing and
passion. They clung to each other for a few minutes, trying hard to find privacy
in the busy terminal. Then it was over.

The group went on to Paris, all except Muriel, who was sad and lonely for
Joe. She returned to Vienna where, over the next few weeks, she helped a number
of people make last-minute escapes. One was the sociologist Alfred Weissman.
Muriel arranged for a companion—very likely Tony Hyndman—to accompany
him to Switzerland. Her former tutor, the physicist Franz Urbach and his wife,
Annie, were more difficult, for even after she obtained passports for the couple,
Franz refused to use his, afraid that traveling with a fake document would cause
him to be arrested. In the end, according to Annie Urbach's recollection, Muriel
bribed a low-level official in the Gestapo who allowed her to pick up a real passport that had been sent to the Swedish embassy for the Urbachs. Once the couple
arrived in Sweden, Muriel supported them financially for some time.[37]

Muriel, still in touch with Stephen Spender through all these dark days,
used his British connections to obtain contracts for at least half a dozen young
Jewish women to work as domestics in the United Kingdom: these contracts
allowed them to emigrate to England. A medical school colleague of Muriel's,
Stefanie, was trying, along with her fiancée, Karl, to obtain affidavits of support so they could flee to America: they were both Jewish. Muriel could not
submit the affidavits for them since, as she later wrote, "the American consul
in Vienna would not accept any more from me, claiming that I had already
given too many." After many efforts, Muriel finally located another official
who would accept her affidavits. The couple went through countless frustrating
experiences, including bureaucratic rigmarole of an exasperating nature, but
finally managed, with courage and luck, to get safely to the United States.[38]

There were so many individuals asking for her help that Muriel did not
always come through to her own satisfaction. She ended up feeling "more than

guilt, an immeasurable sadness," as she would recall, that she did not save one particular man who had requested an affidavit. She should not have had so many principles about asking too much of others, she later realized. "Are these scruples valid, face-to-face with death?" she would later write.[39]

By May 1938, it had become increasingly difficult to make a getaway and the exodus out of Vienna slowed down. Even individuals for whom she had managed to get passports decided to stay. Some people knew that a few of those passports made in Brno had not turned out well and were useless, and so refused to use them: one comrade, Lisl Zerner, had burned hers rather than be caught with it on her. In another case, after Swiss police discovered that his passport was a forgery, Karl Czernetz had been arrested at the border.[40] Muriel argued with those who chose to stay behind, telling them that they would surely end up in the custody of the Gestapo if they remained.

She also felt that within a short time, passports would no longer matter, as entry into neighboring nations would come to a stop. Just as frightening was the realization that, even if people managed to get out of Austria, most of them had no place to go: Even democratic nations outside of Europe were reluctant to accept those fleeing from Hitler. By late spring, every country with an embassy in Vienna, with the exception of Mexico and the Soviet Union, had shut down and sent their staff home.[41]

After a short trip to see Connie—a joyful but bittersweet reunion since Muriel knew she had to leave again almost immediately—and relocating her, Pups, and Fini to the Hotel Kastanienbaum at Vierwaldstaetter Lake, a few kilometers south of Lucerne, Muriel returned to Vienna for what she believed would be the last time. The medical school had reopened, without its Jewish professors. Gone too were most of the Jewish students from other countries. Despairing at the fate of her professors and the others who had been apprehended by the Gestapo, Muriel now wanted nothing more than to graduate and run away herself, fearful that by now the Gestapo had become aware of her.[42]

Nevertheless, she continued to work with those who still had a chance of getting out. She tried with Steffi and Hans Kunke, young Socialists who agreed to use passports Muriel had obtained for them but were unwilling to leave without their close friend Ferdinand Tschürtch, who was so disabled that Muriel could not find a passport to fit his appearance. But it was too late: the couple and their friend were arrested a short time later and all three died in concentration camps.[43]

Another Viennese Socialist, Käthe Leichter, whose husband Otto had spent the night at Muriel's apartment weeks earlier, was a reluctant émigré, even though she had been given a false Czech passport only days after the *Anschluss*. She and Otto had decided that she would stay in Vienna to make arrangements for the escape of their two sons, even though as a feminist with a doctoral degree, a member of the training committee of the Revolutionary Socialists, and the editor of *The Information and Intelligence of the RS*, she had a long and distinguished history of activism, making her a target of the Gestapo.

Although she knew she was in danger, Käthe nevertheless hesitated: she had household matters to settle, including storage of furniture. More important, she had an elderly mother whom she was loath to abandon. Leichter continually wrote to his wife, imploring her to follow him to safety in Paris. Muriel also took several messages to Käthe from her husband, under his code name "Uncle Stefan."[44] But Käthe continued to delay, almost defiant in her belief that good would win out. As her son Henry would write:

> She had strong nerves and an unquenchable optimism which simply did not permit her to be scared, and, rather, led her not to recognize the danger she was in.[45]

"I won't let these bums scare me," she would tell Henry as she calmly went about her business. But by the end of May, after some Nazi hoodlums painted *Jude* on the house and she noticed Gestapo agents following her, Käthe finally agreed to leave. She would travel with Henry on the Czech passport given to her by Muriel and would find someone to take Franz, her youngest son, out of the country.

One night, as young Henry was busy memorizing the details on his new passport, Käthe met with fellow Socialist and trusted old friend Hans Pav, who, as sports editor of the *Arbeiter-Zeitung*, had worked closely with her husband, Otto. Käthe confided her plans to her fellow party member, who was all ears.

Pav was finally someone Käthe could talk to, or so she thought. Unknown to her, Pav had been arrested by the Gestapo and then released, after Nazi agents developed him into "their most effective instrument for infiltrating and then betraying a number of underground cells," according to historian Radomir Luža.[46] Pav would inform on countless people, mainly women, during the very late spring of 1938. Knowing nothing of this perfidy, however, Käthe and other Socialists had no reason to be suspicious of their comrade.

On May 30, Käthe went out to buy a hat to wear as a disguise. Arriving home, she called the house in Mauer where the Leichter family had lived previously to find out if anything had happened there. The landlord told her that the Gestapo had appeared that morning in order to arrest her. She hung up and immediately called her mother. A man answered: unless she went immediately to her mother's place to turn herself in, he would take the elderly woman into custody. Käthe quickly sent Henry to stay with friends, reassuring him that although she might be arrested, her imprisonment would be brief. He believed her.[47]

The moment Käthe set foot in her childhood home, the Gestapo arrested and detained her until they could ship her to Dachau a short time later. Käthe was eventually taken to Ravensbrück, the women's concentration camp. She would be murdered with poison gas at Bernburg, a euthanasia institution, in March 1942.[48] Her mother later committed suicide.

By June 1938, three months after the *Anschluss*, the Jews of Austria "felt like hunted animals."[49] Early that month, on June 4, Sigmund Freud finally left his beloved Vienna, his ransom to the Nazis paid by Princess Marie Bonaparte. The princess handed over enough money so that Freud could take with him his library and sculpture collection, as well as his famous couch. At the age of 82, Freud took his family and moved into London's 20 Maresfield Gardens, where he would spend the last year of his life.[50]

Muriel's own Jewish background, on her father's side, finally came to the fore at this time. At the university, where she was taking the last of her final exams, Muriel noted that the other American students, all Jewish, would not be allowed to graduate with the larger group; they would have their own small ceremony later on. Muriel, on the other hand, would be allowed to attend the main graduation ceremony.[51]

She cared nothing about the ceremony itself since the school had already become what she called "a Hitler university," but she wanted to receive her diploma. Muriel had first registered at the university in 1932 as *konfessionslos* or without religion, in keeping with a lifetime of no religious affiliation. In order to obtain that piece of paper, however, Muriel was required to fill out a long form that included many questions about her background. One day in June, having finished her examinations and just about to graduate, faced with the Nazi questionnaire asking her religion, Muriel wrote "Jewish." She later tried to explain:

> I suddenly felt solidarity with them, not because they were Jews but because they were oppressed...for that reason I did something which I've never been able fully to understand since then, because it made no sense at all... [Saying] I was Jewish did nobody any good. It was a completely irrational act, but I guess one gets irrational sometimes.[52]

She had made a mistake and had imperiled not only her graduation, but possibly her freedom. Should the university authorities put their heads together with the Gestapo, she could well have become another Nazi prisoner.

University officials, inquiring why she had not previously registered as Jewish, interviewed her repeatedly. Finally they told her, as she remembered, "You know we can't allow Jews to graduate at present." But she argued with them, insisting that they review the details of her childhood—the lack of religious upbringing, the fact that her mother was Protestant. After extensive debate back and forth, the university officials changed their minds, possibly after consulting Article 5 of the Reich Citizenship Law of 1935,[53] which defined the meaning of a Jew. Muriel later recalled their words:

> Since it was your mother who was a Protestant and your father who was Jewish, and it is the mother that counts, and since your husband was definitely a Protestant, you are a mixture of the first degree, but under these conditions, we will allow you to graduate.[54]

In the end, her mother and her former husband Julian, the son of a Church of England clergyman, had saved her. After a few more minor bureaucratic hurdles, Muriel was set to graduate with the larger group along with one other foreign student, the son of an Indian rajah. On June 18, she stood on the podium, one of a hundred graduates. In the audience, among the guests were two that she had invited, John Emlyn Williams, Central European correspondent for the *Christian Science Monitor*, and an elderly woman, a friend of her mother's, who lived in Vienna. After the initial "*Heil Hitler!*," the rector made a speech, and then diplomas were handed out. Muriel accepted hers with a sense of accomplishment—it had been an arduous six years. At the end of the ceremony, the audience rose as if in one body and shouted "*Heil Hitler!*" again. Then it was over, and Muriel rushed home to begin packing, relieved that no one had noticed her small act of defiance—that she had neither raised her arm nor shouted during the ritualistic salutes.

After the past few nightmarish months, Muriel could not leave Austria fast enough. She had received permission to take her belongings and furniture out of the country as long as she allowed two Nazi officials—men whom she had to pay by the hour—to watch as she packed. The process of packing and loading the "approved" vans bound for Paris, her destination, took an excruciating five days while every single item was scrutinized.[55]

She next had to obtain a French visa in order to enter France legally. Her experience at the French consulate, coupled with her time at the British embassy aiding the Wolf-Man, upset her greatly as she discovered that even the so-called democratic countries had prejudices, especially against Jews, and did not seem all that welcoming to the desperate Austrians who needed safe haven. As she had feared, it was impossible to obtain a French visa, so she decided to let it go for now; she would try again in the little Swiss town of Zug, which had a French consulate and was a stop on the way to Arosa where she would head first, to see Connie.

Muriel had by this time spent 12 years in Vienna. She had watched the systematic looting of the Viennese Jews as the Nazis liquidated Jewish assets, dispossessed Jewish tenants, and plundered Jews' bank accounts. The Aryanization of Jewish economic assets was so successful that a year after the *Anschluss*, almost no Jewish businesses remained. While most Austrians heartily welcomed the Nazis, the excessive enthusiasm of some led to their perpetrating outrages on their Jewish neighbors. Everyone who survived the German invasion had a story: the cook who snatched the radio and the jewelry, or the neighbors who, given the key and asked to watch over the now-vacant apartment and its furnishings, looted it instead.[56] But worse, much worse than that, Muriel had seen friends and comrades displaced or shipped to concentration camps. (By the end of the war, Austria would be practically empty of Jews, all of them having emigrated or been murdered.)

Joe's old friend Karl Holoubek was one Muriel had tried but failed to help. Hating the idea of a life in exile and with a wife who refused to leave her Viennese family, Holoubek had nevertheless held on to the passport Muriel had given him at the end of March. But he had not used it. Finally, days before her own departure to meet Joe in Paris, Muriel made one last try. This time Holoubek agreed to go and said he would meet Muriel and Joe in Paris within the week. But as it turned out, Holoubek's fate was already sealed: his closest friend was Hans Pav, the traitor. Before the week was out, the Gestapo came for Holoubek. He never made it to Paris.

On June 25, 1938, Muriel boarded a train from Vienna for the last time, leaving the city she had grown to love, and now—after the *Anschluss*—to fear. She would make a stop in Lake Lucerne to see Connie, but her final destination was Paris and the security of Joe's embrace.

Muriel's maternal grandfather, Gustavus Swift, founder of the meatpacking empire Swift and Company. Courtesy of Andrea Selch, Archivist, The Morris Family Archives

Muriel's mother, Helen Swift. Courtesy of Andrea Selch, Archivist, The Morris Family Archives

Muriel's father, Edward Morris. Courtesy of Andrea Selch, Archivist, The Morris Family Archives

The Morris family mansion at 4800 Drexel Boulevard in the Kenwood section of Chicago. Courtesy of Andrea Selch, Archivist, The Morris Family Archives

The two youngest Morris children, Muriel, on the left, and her sister Ruth, wearing a bow. Courtesy of E. M. Bakwin

Another bow: Muriel, in one of the many formal portraits taken of the Morris children. Courtesy of E. M. Bakwin

From the 1922 Wellesley yearbook, the year she graduated. Courtesy of The Wellesley College Archives

Muriel in Vienna, in her early thirties. Courtesy of Dokumentationsarchiv des österreichischen Widerstandes (DöW)

1938, after the *Anschluss*: Nazis block Jews from entering the University of Vienna. From the Holocaust Encyclopedia. Courtesy of The United States Holocaust Memorial Museum

Muriel in 1945, with friend and fellow Social Democrat Friedrich Adler, son of Viktor Adler, founder of the Austrian Social Democrats. Courtesy of Dokumentationsarchiv des österreichischen Widerstandes (DöW)

Brookdale Farm in Pennington, New Jersey, Muriel's home for the last four decades of her life. Courtesy of The Stony Brook Millstone Watershed Association

Muriel and Joe at Brookdale Farm. Courtesy of Dokumentationsarchiv des österreichischen Widerstandes (DöW)

Muriel at age 50, in Frankenmarkt, Austria, with a protégé, Guntram Weissenberger, and his mother, Juliane. Courtesy of Guntram Weissenberger

Joe was the love of Muriel's life. Courtesy of The Wellesley College Archives

Muriel posed for a formal portrait by noted German-born photographer Josef Breitenbach. Courtesy of Josef and Yaye Breitenbach Charitable Foundation

Muriel Gardiner was given flowers when her husband, Joseph Buttinger (on the right), was presented with the International Rescue Committee's Freedom Award in a ceremony at the Austrian Consulate in New York on June 6, 1978. Courtesy of The International Rescue Committee

Muriel at 83. Courtesy of The Wellesley College Archives

CHAPTER 14

AMERICA:
HOME FROM THE WARS

When Muriel boarded the Orient-Express in Vienna on that early summer day in 1938, she knew she would not see this storied city again for a very long time. With war on the horizon and the German takeover of Austria a fresh and painful memory, she felt much older than her 36 years. Yet as soon as she sank into the plush cushions, the ornate and sumptuous car with its lacquered inlaid floral design, art deco lighting, and exotic flourishes helped remove her from what she had left behind and prepared her to think of what lay ahead in Paris. Having in the past rejected luxury, this time Muriel savored the grace and comfort of her compartment, her tension melting with each click-clack of the train's wheels. An indomitable realist, however, she recognized the gravity of the European situation.[1] She would have little time to relax before she became immersed in new resistance efforts, which she would conduct from Paris this time. The war loomed as reports of Nazi aggression in Czechoslovakia suggested that a conflict that had once seemed to be confined to a small part of Europe appeared to be spiraling into a full-blown war.

As crucial as the political front was, Muriel also found her thoughts constantly shifting to Joe and Connie. Joe wanted to marry Muriel but, with two marriages and divorces behind her, she preferred a relationship without legal ties, as she would later explain: "I loved him and thought I'd probably live the rest of my life with him, but I just didn't particularly want a marriage ceremony." She had learned a lot about herself over the past years. Even though she found Joe to be intellectually stimulating, as well as easygoing and sexually satisfying, she did not believe that she was marriage material. She would write, "Perhaps I knew I would in time be 'unfaithful.' "[2]

And then there was Connie. Muriel had brought her up in an insecure world and had been engaged in politics and resistance work almost from the beginning of her daughter's life. Indoctrinated, whether she realized it or not, in the same school of child-rearing as her own mother, Muriel had hired nurses and governesses to feed, clothe, bathe, and dress her daughter—all well trained, competent, and kindly, but still substitutes. As her train ride continued, Muriel, who would be stopping overnight to see Connie at Lake Lucerne on her way to Paris, found herself dreading telling the girl that she would be leaving again immediately, even though the plan was that she would find them a flat quickly and then send for her daughter.

It turned out that Muriel needn't have felt such remorse. In spite of her statement about having had an "awful childhood," Connie would also remark that she had adjusted to her mother's frequent comings and goings:

I just trusted her to come when she could, and she did...The world was in such turmoil...It was just not a time when childish things were important and I was old enough to know that there were more impor-tant things than me in a world...that was turning upside down.[3]

Pulling herself together on the train, Muriel was determined not to rumi-nate any longer and to focus instead on her more immediate problem: she had no French visa, and France would be an important part of her future. At this point, it had become the country of refuge for Europeans fleeing Hitler from every nation. Its historic enmity with Germany, as well as its tradition of "liberty, equality, and fraternity," made France the safest haven for the refugees.[4] For now, the Socialists who Muriel had helped to evade the Gestapo were largely gathered in Paris, still hoping to survive and perhaps even prevent a sweeping Nazi vic-tory by forming coalitions with Communists and other left-wing groups.

Muriel disembarked on her way to Lake Lucerne to try again for a French visa in Zug, the capital of the small German-speaking canton of that name in Switzerland. Disappointed when the official at the tiny French consulate told her he would give her only a transient visa, she had no choice but to accept it. She would, he said, be able to change it for a permanent one when she arrived in France. Hurrying out of the consulate, Muriel calmed herself with that final assurance.

Finally arriving in Lake Lucerne, she spent the day with Connie walking in the meadows of alpine flowers around the hotel where she and Fini lived, and then continued on to Paris, where she and Joe, meeting in his rented room, had a passionate reunion. By the next day, Muriel had found a flat, an unpre-tentious place on the rue Mouton-Duvernet in the 14th arrondissement, with a courtyard where Connie could ride her bicycle; it was near the Luxembourg Gardens, the Parc Montsouris, and even a large public swimming pool, all places the child would love.[5] Then she sent for Connie, Fini, and their young guest, Pups.

Within a short time, the family was settled into the flat. Joe was busy with his Austrian émigré comrades, most of whom lived clustered near each other for support and camaraderie in the northeastern part of the city. Before Muriel's arrival Joe and the others had opened a headquarters at 20 rue Trudaine in the 9th arrondissement; the light-filled space on the first floor on a quiet street quickly became noisy with the group's vocal disagreements. In July 1938, they held a moment of silence for Otto Bauer, the great theoretician and leader of the Austrian Social Democratic Party, who had died of a heart attack, alone in a hotel room at age 56. Later, the Socialists would unite under the umbrella of the Auslandsvertretung der österreichischen Sozialisten (AVOES), the exile organization of the Austrian Socialists, led by Joe and the Socialist leader Friedrich Adler, a physicist, and the son of Victor Adler, founder of the Austrian Social Democrats.[6]

Muriel knew that before she could be of any help to Joe and his comrades, she needed to get that elusive French visa. As it turned out, the consul in Zug had misinformed her: she would not be able to transition from the visa she had to a permanent one. Not only was this worrisome, but because she had only the transient document, she had been labeled a "suspicious person" and was required to check in every month with the French Prefecture of police.[7] This was merely a trivial nuisance, however, compared to her new mission. She had been asked to become a courier for the Socialists in exile by returning to Austria. It was an incredibly risky assignment. She agreed instantly.

Between the early summer of 1938 and the outbreak of the war a year later, Muriel would be the only contact between the exiles in Paris and the small circle of comrades still in Austria who defiantly tried to maintain some activity even under the Nazi regime.[8] Despite communiqués from Lore (Leopoldine Moll), the former resistance contact in Vienna (she has been released after her arrest), and Muriel's lawyer, a Dr. Kaltenegger, telling her that she should not go back—the Gestapo believed her to be a foreign agent and "were after her"— Muriel intended to return to Austria. Her only concession would be to avoid Vienna, where she was more likely to be known.

That summer, she enrolled Pups in camp because she felt he needed more companionship with children his own age, and then took Connie and Fini off for a seaside holiday in the south of France.

In August, Henry, the oldest son of the Socialist Otto Leichter, was allowed to visit his mother, Käthe, in a Gestapo jail in Vienna's Hotel Metropole on the

Ringstrasse. There he learned the name of her betrayer, Hans Pav. Henry later described the moment:

> Although a Gestapo man was present at all times...he did not bother us...She would not have been Käthe Leichter if she had not conveyed to us political news, most important of which was the name of the man who had betrayed her...it never occurred to me that this would be the final good-bye and that I would never see her again.[9]

A short time later, Henry Leichter escaped from Vienna, and his younger brother Franz was taken to Friedrich and Kathia Adler's home in Belgium. Finally, the brothers reunited with their father in Paris. Muriel would later become their benefactor, paying their passage to America, then supporting the family once they arrived. Meanwhile, Hans Pav continued handing Socialists over to the Gestapo, including several women who had led the Socialist Workers' Assistance (SAH) that provided funds to families of imprisoned comrades. The SAH had operated successfully for four months after the *Anschluss* until the Gestapo shut it down, taking its entire staff into custody. Muriel had been part of this secret circle, leaving money behind for them when she left Vienna.[10]

Muriel still didn't know about Hans Pav's treachery and upon her return from her brief vacation, she met with him in Switzerland. It isn't clear why they got together—or why he didn't betray her too. In any event, her luck held and she soon returned to Paris.

Nervous about traveling back to Austria, Muriel decided to make her trip a bit safer by obtaining a new British passport under her maiden name, Helen Muriel Morris. To do this, she had to go to England. Taking Connie and Fini with her to London, she followed the bureaucratic rules for securing a new passport. She obtained character references through friends and relatives and then published her passport application for two consecutive weeks in a public notice in the *Times*.[11] While waiting for the document to come through, she forced herself to put aside her worries and determinedly toured the city with Connie, seeing old friends, visiting the zoo and the parks. Her last day in London would prove memorable: she and her friend Auge, the Viennese architect who had built her little house in the Vienna Woods, sat together, sipping tea in a verdant park:

> I had an already nostalgic feeling that this was to be the last time I would look on such a sunny, peaceful scene...this hour of sunshine lingers in my memory as a farewell to a precious tranquility about to disappear forever.[12]

Days later, shiny new passport in hand, Muriel returned to Paris where she soon moved her family into a new flat, this one in the 16th arrondissement, and visited with her brother Nelson who was in Paris with his wife, Blanche, a former actress. Pups left them when his parents arrived from their expedition in Turkey and took him home to America. Connie started second grade in the American School, leaving Muriel free to take a two-month course in gynecology and obstetrics at a Paris hospital.

War loomed that autumn of 1938, and the comrades in Paris were profoundly gloomy about recent developments. At the September 29 Munich conference, the leading European powers had agreed to permit Germany to annex the Sudetenland in western Czechoslovakia, where half the residents were of German origin. British Prime Minister Neville Chamberlain capitulated to Hitler's will to such an extent that afterward, as historian Saul Friedländer wrote, "no one would lift a finger in defense of the hapless Jews."[13] Within two weeks after the signing of the Munich Pact, Hitler occupied the Sudetenland, and the government of Czechoslovakia resigned.

In the midst of all this bad news, Muriel pressed on with her hospital courses, taking time out only for a second meeting with Hans Pav at Saint Moritz in Switzerland, passing on to him a message from Paris: no former Social Democrat was to engage in any political activity at this time. It was simply too dangerous. She urged him not to return to Austria, still having no idea that he was under the protection of the Gestapo. Years later, when she learned of his double life as a Gestapo spy, rather than condemning him, which was not her way, she wrote, "I think he thought he had to do it to save his life. They threatened him somehow . . . It would be of enormous interest to me to psychoanalyze such a person."[14]

After her meeting with Pav, Muriel returned to Paris, where she spent as much time as she could escorting refugees to various consulates and beseeching American friends for more affidavits.[15] Joe took her to see his close friend the Socialist Josef Podlipnig, who schooled Muriel for her return to Austria. Podlipnig told her whom to see, where they lived, and how to talk to them once she located them. Exhilarated to be back in the game, Muriel felt ready to travel clandestinely again, the way she had for so many months before the *Anschluss*, crossing borders under the noses of the Gestapo in order to help save lives.

Occasionally, however, she would wonder if it would be foolhardy to undertake this mission. It was much riskier now. After all, she had been told that the Gestapo in Vienna were looking for her. She cast her doubts aside, however, and remained committed to doing dangerous work—conspiracy had become second nature to her. Now, despite what she had grown to recognize as inevitable feelings of fear and separation anxiety because she would be leaving Connie and Joe and journeying back into danger, she continued her preparations for the Austria trip.

In addition to the Gestapo, there were other dangers associated with this journey. First, she would be traveling without a permanent French visa. But much more serious was the bad timing of her visit, shortly after *Kristallnacht*, the night of November 9 to 10 when Nazi party officials, the SA *Sturmabteilungen* or Storm Troopers, and the Hitler Youth rampaged and destroyed Jewish shops, homes, and synagogues in every city, town, and village in Germany, Austria and Nazi-occupied Sudetenland, focusing on Berlin and Vienna with their large Jewish populations. This orchestrated pogrom resulted in 91 deaths, the destruction of 267 synagogues, the looting of 7,500 businesses, and the arrests of more than 30,000 Jewish men, who were sent to concentration camps. Rapes and suicides were also reported.

Kristallnacht was "a turning point," the culmination of which would be the Holocaust.[16]

But Muriel didn't waver.[17] Her mission was urgent. The Socialists in Paris believed that their comrades who remained in Austria could remain alive only if they were completely neutral and engaged in no political activity. It was imperative that they communicate this message, which Muriel was to deliver. Her instructions were to convince those with whom she talked that conspiracy and political resistance would be futile now and would only result in more people being transported to camps to be murdered.

Her trip to the Austrian provinces was planned carefully to include major population centers: Klagenfurt in Carinthia, Salzburg, and Linz. Comrade Podlipnig told her that Socialists trying to survive under the Nazis would only trust her if she recited to them their own last conversation with him before he left Austria. She spent days memorizing what he had said to each person on her list.

Though she had been to Salzburg before, Muriel had not visited the other cities. Although her papers listed her profession as student, she knew that with her age, 37, that looked suspicious. Nevertheless, the new passport with a new name—Helen Muriel Morris—that she had obtained during her autumn visit to London as well as the detailed instructions from Podlipnig were reassuring. In mid-November, carrying only a small suitcase, a guide to Austria, and books on history and architecture, Muriel took the night train to Klagenfurt.

She arrived at dawn in the historic capital of Carinthia, the southernmost region in Austria, where Joe had spent his childhood. Checking her bag at the station, she set out for town, guidebook in hand. She meant to find the local barber, who was a comrade. Locating the barbershop easily, she had spoken only a few words of Podlipnig's message when the man joyfully embraced her. He then brought over some friends to meet her, and they spent hours sharing information: Socialists in Austria had little or no knowledge about their comrades in Paris or about what was happening in Germany, France, and England. Nor did the Nazi overseers allow into the country any truthful data about Hitler's aggressions and the coming war. As a result, Muriel was a living newspaper, recounting to her eager new friends the events of the day.

After spending hours in this warm, welcoming environment, Muriel stayed overnight alone in a drafty hotel, her next destination the nearby St. Veit an der Glan, the charming and picturesque little town where Joe had spent many years and where his old flame, Gisela Rauter, still lived, working in an electrical-supply shop. Joe had kept in touch and had told Muriel where to find Gisela. When Muriel saw her, to alleviate any suspicion the young woman might have had, Muriel immediately said she had come from Seppl, which was Joe's old nickname. But Gisela, who did not remember meeting Muriel four years earlier in Vienna at the Lammgasse apartment, was hesitant. After a discussion during which Muriel detailed their earlier get together, Gisela lit up happily at the memory, relaxing a little as the women began to talk. Again, Muriel repeated her message from the group in Paris, and she told Gisela what was happening outside her small town. Joe, she added, was well.

At Muriel's next stop, Salzburg, she met with comrades named Kirtel but the woman was "cold as ice and hard as nails."[18] She insisted on seeing Muriel's passport and, after handing it over, Muriel broke down in tears. Finally, getting nowhere with Frau Kirtel, she retrieved her passport and set out for the station. As she walked, Herr Kirtel pulled up alongside her on his bicycle and apologized for his wife's suspicious behavior.

Upset by this encounter, Muriel nevertheless got back on the train, heading for Linz, the capital of the state of Upper Austria, where both Hitler and Adolf Eichmann had spent their youths. The Mauthausen concentration camp, with its murmured stories of death by torture, was nearby, and its very aura seemed to hover in the air.[19] Checking into a hotel in Linz, Muriel hoped to find her contact that evening, but Podlipnig had not known the man's exact address. Making sure that no one was watching her, Muriel set off to find him, but as night fell, it grew too dark to see. She would have to return the next day.

But this night would prove her emotional undoing. She managed to fall asleep despite her feelings of apprehension. Then at 6 A.M., she heard a loud banging on her door. Bolting upright, she heard the dreaded shout: "Geheime Staatspolizei! Gestapo! Open up!" Heart pounding, she put on her robe and opened the door: a young Nazi officer stood there. He talked brusquely, asking her name and nationality, and demanding to see her passport.

Her knees began to tremble. "Well, at this moment I was scared to death, really," Muriel would recall. Should she act like an indignant tourist? Or remain cowed? Pretending to look for her passport, she desperately tried to figure out how to handle this long-feared confrontation with the enemy.[20]

Finally she remembered advice that a lawyer in Chicago had given her years earlier about what to do in a civil court case when questioned by an attorney:

> Answer all questions, politely but briefly; never offer more information than asked for; never ask a question unless there is something you have not understood.[21]

For several long minutes, the officer scrutinized her passport, then peppered her with queries: Why was she in Linz? What was her profession? What was her purpose in visiting the city? What was she studying? Had she ever been in Linz before? Why did she speak German so well? She tried to respond clearly and briefly. After what seemed an eternity, the Nazi left, but Muriel remained standing by the door, passport in hand, still shaking.

When she was finally able to pull herself together and dress, she went down to the hotel lobby where the desk clerk alleviated much of her fear by offhandedly remarking that the Gestapo made routine early morning spot checks on guests. His unintended reassurance meant that no one knew her identity and that the encounter had been routine.

Relieved, Muriel ate a huge breakfast, having learned during her earlier resistance work that eating relieved her anxiety.[22] Then she went to scout out the neighborhood from the night before. She still could not find the correct house so she returned, frustrated, to town and waited for nightfall, thinking that her aimless wandering would be less noticeable under cover of darkness, That day, she pretended to be a tourist, pausing for anything that qualified as a "sight." In the evening, after much walking around, she finally found the location. The comrade and his wife and children greeted her warmly after she recited Podlipnig's last conversation with the man, and they sat and talked all evening, with Muriel feeling less isolated in the company of fellow Socialists.

Muriel couldn't wait to get out of Austria—she was leaving Linz the next day and eager to return to France.[23] Arriving back in Paris, she quickly resumed her everyday work of arranging for false passports, obtaining affidavits of support, and giving funds to those on the run from the Nazis. But she would also maintain her pattern, a holdover from the Vienna resistance days, of seeking respite whenever she felt strained by her conspiracy work. In late December 1938, she gathered up Joe, Connie, and Fini for skiing at St. Moritz (Joe had managed to acquire a safe-conduct pass, allowing him to travel out of France legally).

After a few days, Muriel sent Connie back to Paris with Fini, and she and Joe continued on to Davos to rendezvous with some old Socialist friends from Vienna. The group, staying at the same hotel, had to pretend at first that they didn't know each other, then that they had just met and liked each other. After this merry interlude, Muriel and Joe returned to Paris, where their mood soon plummeted upon hearing that as of January 1, 1939, Germany would require Jewish women to add "Sara" and Jewish men to add "Israel" to their names on official documents. By the end of the month, there was even more grim news in the form of a speech by Hitler in which he threatened "the annihilation of the Jewish race in Europe."[24]

Muriel continued working with the large refugee population in Paris even after Germany invaded Czechoslovakia on March 15, the assault capping months of anti-Semitic persecution in that country. The six-month-old Munich Pact, in which England, France, Italy, and Germany had agreed that Czechoslovakia would cede the Sudetenland to Germany in order to prevent an all-out war, had proved worthless.[25]

Czechoslovakia now joined Austria—the two nations had fallen without an official shot being fired. In the wake of the German occupation of Czechoslovakia, Britain and France announced that they would protect Poland, Hitler's likely next victim, with armed resistance.

Muriel's reaction was to leave at once for America, where she could achieve two crucial goals. If she wanted to save Joe's life, she had to marry him so that he could emigrate to the United States on a preferential visa as the husband of an American citizen. Otherwise, he would wait years for his number to come to the top of the U.S. quota list. Reconciled to the necessity of marriage, Muriel abandoned her reluctance to engage in a legal union. It now seemed critical to Joe's safety that the couple wed. But he was currently stateless, having renounced his Austrian citizenship when the Germans included Austria in the Third Reich. And he could not marry without papers. Muriel believed that she could obtain the documents he needed through her connections in America.

In addition, she had to take exams in the United States in order to practice there and wanted to do this before she forgot all the medicine she had learned. On March 23, 1939, Muriel left for New York with an entourage: Connie, Fini, even their little dachshund Klex, who she had managed to ship back from Vienna.[26]

Muriel had not been home for years, and in spite of the horror she had just left, her excitement grew as the ship neared the dock: "I had had no idea what a welcome I would receive," she would later write. "Although it was late in the evening, a group of close friends...were waiting for us on the pier. I was overwhelmed with joy and gratitude."[27] The women waiting for her were friends from

Wellesley, from childhood, from her summers in Greenwich Village. Reuniting with these much-loved, comparatively carefree young people who knew nothing of political chaos, resistance, conspiracy, and Nazism—how magical to be with them and in New York!

It was a glorious homecoming. The welcoming committee immediately carried Muriel and her family off to a hotel and helped settle them in. Happily, the hotel was in the Village, and Muriel felt immediately at home. She quickly contacted her lawyers and set about finding a way to marry Joe. And she found tutors at Beth Israel Hospital in downtown Manhattan who would help her prepare for her medical exams. She then started a rigorous study regimen to learn the English names for the medical terms she knew only in German. Unsure of herself, she fully expected to fail her exams.[28] The lapse of time since she had taken classes, the language barrier, and her work with the resistance that had taken up the majority of her attention, all convinced her that she couldn't possibly pass this first attempt.

To her surprise and satisfaction, she pulled it off, succeeding on every examination. But her other, more important agenda was obtaining Joe's documents, and there she had failed. She had no experience in bribing officials, and neither she nor her lawyers knew anyone with real authority in such matters. But just when she felt at her lowest because of this, Joe—waiting patiently for her in their Paris flat—cabled her with astonishing news: the former French Prime Minister, the Socialist Leon Blum, had obtained papers for him. He was now legal, he wrote, and if Muriel rushed back to Paris, they could marry.

She did.

But not before she took Connie on a quick visit to her mother, Helen, at the family compound in Green Lake, Wisconsin. Then she and Connie, accompanied by Muriel's closest friend, Gladys Lack, sailed for France on the fast and luxurious *Normandie*.

Muriel and Joe married on August 1, in *la mairie*, the town hall, of the 16th arrondissement, with Connie and Fini, Gladys as her witness, and Socialist friends Kathia and Friedrich Adler as guests, as well as Pups's father, Bob Casey, who was visiting. A garden party followed the ceremony. With bunches of apricot and yellow rambling roses, limitless icy champagne, and delicate hors d'oeuvres, everyone could forget, for at least an hour or so, what was going on in the rest of the world—though war, not celebration, would surely commandeer their attention in the near future. Later, Joe would proudly pen, "Muriel Gardiner was now legally Muriel Buttinger, which illegally she had already been for over four years." Despite Muriel's surplus of names, he wrote that she would nevertheless always be "Mary" to the many Austrians whose lives she had saved.[29]

After the ceremony, Muriel, Joe, and Connie took a brief family honeymoon at Juan Les Pins, then returned to Paris where Muriel sent Connie, for safety, to a sleep-away camp at Etretat, near Le Havre in Normandy. The camp, run by the American School, was on a windy beach that Connie loved and, as Muriel assured her, she would be joining her mother and stepfather very soon to go home.

Because he was married to an American citizen, Joe quickly obtained an American visa, and Muriel booked passage for the three of them to New York on the *Queen Elizabeth*, sailing on September 6. At about the same time, Tony Hyndman—with whom Muriel had kept in contact—offered to marry Fini so she could obtain a British passport, as, he told Muriel, Stephen's friend W. H. Auden had done in 1935 for Erika Mann, Thomas Mann's daughter. Muriel gave Tony a large sum in order to "settle" Fini in London, and the pair left for England, where Fini soon secured a housekeeping position with Anna Freud, while Tony—whose relationship with Stephen Spender had long been over—spent the money on himself.[30]

Pleased that Fini was safely out of Europe, Muriel started allowing herself to daydream about going home when the brutality of life in a war zone once again showed its face: on August 23, Hitler and Stalin signed the Nazi-Soviet Non-Aggression Pact in which Stalin assured Hitler that he would not have to fight a two-front war.

Muriel, a lifelong supporter of the 1917 Russian Revolution, a Socialist with Marxist leanings for many years, took this news of an alliance hard. She thought she had long ago gotten over her illusions about Russia, but she still believed that a vast difference existed between the Nazis and the Communists. This pact, she would later claim, "was one of the worst political shocks" of her life. She felt the trauma so acutely that, although she was an inveterate realist, she thought that maybe Britain's Chamberlain would not dare to oppose both Hitler and Stalin. Thus, she was one of the few who believed that the danger of war had lessened a little, as she later said. "I didn't think that France and England would declare war, and there of course I was quite mistaken."[31]

But within days of the Hitler-Stalin pact, Britain mobilized its fleet and began civilian evacuations of London. Helpless, all Muriel could do was hope for the best for her many friends then in London—now including her dear Fini—and anticipate her own September 6 voyage to the safe haven of the United States.

She began gathering French exit visas, required by the government of France before one could leave the country but almost impossible for refugees to obtain. Although securing the document was easy for her because she had been born in America, it was a different story for Joe and Connie, both of whom had been born in Austria. "Oh, this business of being born in other countries!" Muriel would say years later, the frustrations still clear in her memory.[32] She ended up seeking help from the American Legion post in Paris, whose members gladly aided this sister of a World War I veteran—her brother Nelson. To Muriel's elation, within days she had obtained French exit visas for her family.

But, not long after she had safely tucked the precious permits away, the gravest news of all came. On September 1, Germany invaded Poland. Struggling to maintain her equilibrium, Muriel occupied herself by scrubbing the kitchen floor after Joe had called her from the rue Trudaine office to tell her of the invasion, knowing that performing simple manual tasks would relieve her despair over particularly critical news.[33]

Two days later, on Sunday morning, September 3, Muriel was again at home alone when the telephone rang. It was Joe, who told her in French—the only language the government of France now allowed for speaking on the phone—that Britain, France, Australia, and New Zealand had declared war on Germany.

A day later, the British Royal Air Force attacked the German navy. Thankful that Connie was safely in Normandy, Muriel despaired at the next phone call from Joe: the government of France had declared German refugees, including Austrians, to be enemy aliens, and ordered them to report to a giant stadium, Stade Olympique de Colombes, on September 6—the day Muriel, Joe and Connie were scheduled to sail. Now, with Joe's new status as an enemy of France, he might never get out.

On September 5, the United States declared its neutrality. The next day "Joe became an instant German," as Connie would recall,[34] when the French placed Nazis and anti-Nazis together in the stadium so that the physical hardships the Socialists would suffer were compounded by the discomfort of being in close quarters with the Fascists they had resisted for so long. Joe and 2,000 others had gathered as ordered, bringing with them knapsacks filled with toiletries and food for three days.

When German- and Austrian-born women were ordered to report to another site, Muriel took in the two daughters of Little Otto Bauer, then 15 and 16, whom she had earlier helped to escape from Austria; their father had been interned along with Joe and the other comrades, and their mother was still in Switzerland with the two younger children. Muriel correctly believed that the girls would avoid the internment if she hid them in her flat.[35]

For a week, Joe and the others at Colombes ate bread and liver paste after the food they had brought with them ran out. They were then transferred to Meslay-du-Maine, several hours from Paris. The small tents erected by the French on the large grassy field couldn't protect the 2,000 internees from the wind and cold. Without blankets or adequate food and water, with no lights other than flashlights, they slept outside, wet and chilled, unable to even wash themselves. The field was soon an ocean of mud.

Muriel wasn't about to sit still while anyone suffered, let alone someone she loved. She planned to go to Meslay to see the camp commander, and, after displaying Joe's papers and their marriage license, to plead with him to release her new husband. But before she could travel, Muriel herself needed an additional document, a safe conduct, obtainable only from the French government. After a considerable effort, the hallowed document (with a one-week limit) was finally in hand and she strode off to the camp.

In spite of her energetic petitions, the commandant would not release Joe. For once, Muriel felt she might lose her fight. Reminding herself of the stakes, she raved on, wearing the officer down until he finally permitted her to talk briefly to Joe through the fence. She left, deep in thought about how best to help not only her husband but the other Socialist prisoners as well. She was accompanied on the train back by a sobbing young Frenchwoman who had brought to the camp an elaborately decorated birthday cake that she had not even been allowed to show to her internee-husband.

Because her safe conduct had not been examined, Muriel felt she could use it again and determined to return to the camp with dozens of blankets. In the Socialists' office, she told her plan to those few comrades who remained free: they were a small and, to her, unlikable lot, including Hans Rott, Oskar Pollak, Karl Hans Sailer, and former *Schutzbund* head Julius Deutsch, whom she detested.[36] Deutsch, puffing up and talking as if to a grand audience, said he had already ordered quantities of blankets, as well as crates of lemons to prevent scurvy, and so it was unnecessary for her to duplicate his efforts. But Deutsch's blankets and lemons never arrived, and his ineffective bluster made Muriel dislike him even more.

Rosi and Poldi Bauer, Little Otto's daughters, had sewn sleeping bags out of warm, waterproof material that Muriel had purchased, and she sent them to Joe and the others, who had now been interned for about three weeks. In late September, with war preparations all around, including blackouts and air raids, Muriel made another difficult decision: she would send Connie back to America as soon as possible. Europe was becoming more dangerous. The Red Army had crossed the Polish border to the east on September 17, and after days of bombing, Warsaw surrendered on September 27. Two days later, the Germans and the Soviets began to carve up the once independent nation, and Muriel foresaw that it was inevitable that Paris would come under siege. While she was concerned about ship travel in wartime, she thought it would be safer for Connie to risk crossing the ocean than to remain in Paris.

In order to tell Connie of her decision, Muriel went to see her at camp at Etretat. She would stay with her Aunt Ruth, her mother explained, until Muriel could get home. Although Connie didn't protest, Muriel knew the girl was unhappy at the prospect of leaving her mother and traveling alone during wartime. Muriel asked a friend at a local travel agency to secure passage for her daughter on the first ship out, as there were only a few sailing, and space was scarce. She also asked him to find a kindly woman who would be aboard at the same time who would "just sort of keep an eye on" Connie, as she would recall.[37]

Her reliable friend took care of everything, booking Connie on the next ocean liner out of Le Verdun-sur-Mer, in Bordeaux, and arranging for her to share a cabin with an American woman, her mother, and a third woman. The now eight-year-old child would also have Klex with her for company. Early on the morning of October 7, 1939, Muriel escorted Connie to the train to Bordeaux. Air raid warnings could be heard in the distance as Muriel left the apartment carrying Connie's suitcase with her daughter keeping a tight hold on her dachshund's leash. At the train, Muriel greeted a young American man, a teacher who had promised Muriel's travel agency friend that he would watch over Connie, both on the train and in Bordeaux until the ship sailed.

It is almost unimaginable today to think of sending a young child alone on such a voyage. But Muriel felt certain that this was best for her daughter. In addition, she knew her child. She had been on ships before and was brave. Still, Connie would later recall her fear and loneliness on the 3,000-mile voyage.[38]

Once her daughter was safely in New York at her Aunt Ruth's, the relieved mother would receive a letter whose very complaints reassured her:

> You told me Miss Moscatello would not be seasick. She was the most seasick person on the ship. You told me Miss Moscatello would be nice. She was the most awful person on the ship and she made me wash my ears every day.[39]

Any lessening of tension at news of her daughter's safe arrival was soon absorbed into Muriel's worry about the continuing political storm in Paris: the French and British governments had decided that the Austrian émigrés then in France should form an Austrian government in exile, but Joe and his comrades in the internment camp refused. Some of the Austrians were Austrofascists—supporters of Chancellor Kurt von Schuschnigg's regime just prior to the *Anschluss*—while others were monarchists who hoped to reestablish Otto von Habsburg as emperor.[40]

Even among loyal Socialists, there was factionalism about the government in exile, with more than the usual dissent. When French officials contacted Joe, he announced that the issue could only be explored if he and the other Socialist leaders were released from the camp. A short time later, on October 12, 1939, he was among a small group that was freed.

This group then wrote a resolution to keep Austrian émigrés from participating in an Austrian government in exile.[41] The resolution prohibited them from committing the Socialist Party to the restoration of Austrian independence in any way. Joe and his Socialist friends spent two days arguing about this. It finally passed unanimously.

Joe and his clique viewed as reactionaries not only members of the old Schuschnigg supporters, monarchists, and semi-fascists, but also non-political émigrés who wanted an independent Austria. To Joe and his comrades, a return to a former state of affairs—an Austria before the *Anschluss*, a semi-fascist state without a parliament, free elections, or political parties—would be conservative and anti-liberal. Only Julius Deutsch continued negotiations with the Socialist French government.[42]

Soon Deutsch and his coterie were out of power: the group around Joe now took the lead, refusing to form a government in exile or to participate in any efforts to restore their homeland's independence. But Joe's thinking at times verged on the naïve, as historian Franz Goldner would write:

> His total lack of understanding of the power relationships prevailing in Europe after the Anschluss is evident. Buttinger adhered to the views he had formed within the framework of his political activities in Austria from 1934 to 1938. He kept those views…clinging to the principle of passivity…offer[ing] bitter resistance to all efforts to restore Austrian independence.[43]

Muriel and Joe exemplified the times in which they lived. Although she had perhaps even keener perception than her husband, and in spite of the couple's explicit support of equal rights for everyone, Muriel understood that men made policy and women followed their lead. Thus whatever Joe believed politically, Muriel also believed. From the earliest days of her resistance work, she had had little or no influence on organization or planning.[44] But she was a superb conspirator—quick-witted and courageous in the field. The endless political maneuverings of the Socialists, who rarely agreed about anything, were not for her.

But at least the group felt that anyone who could get away should go. Joe, with his American wife and American visa, was one of the lucky ones, and his colleagues urged him and Muriel to sail as soon as they could.

Muriel gave away furniture and household items to friends who had to remain behind, storing some personal items—letters, photographs, and art works, including several by Konenkov—in the Paris warehouse of the British firm Wheatley and Company. She also left money with her friend from the travel agency to pay any bills related to the storage. Such efforts to be responsible showed a deep part of Muriel's psyche, her ingrained sense of doing right by others—and her ability to deny the dark when she needed to be positive: she would in fact lose everything after the Nazis occupied France. Wheatley's was plundered whether the stored objects belonged to Jews or not, and Muriel's art and memorabilia all disappeared, never to be seen again.

At the end of the month, impatient to be in America with her daughter, Muriel was finally able to book passage for herself and Joe. They were to sail on November 7 on the S.S. *Manhattan*. Muriel had the exit visas she had worked so hard to get, and of course the couple had their passports and ship tickets, but, as usual in wartime, nothing went as planned. Even though it was early November, Muriel and Joe arrived in Bordeaux in broiling sunshine, then finally went on to Le Verdon-sur-Mer, where it seemed equally unseasonably warm. More than a thousand people stood on the huge dock trying to get on the ship. Muriel, in front of Joe on line, was handed a boarding card after the officials examined her papers. But Joe was stopped. When it was his turn, after he had gone through the first checkpoints and arrived at the last desk, an elderly French general in full war regalia appeared about to end everything.

"You were born in Austria. You used to be an Austrian. You can't leave France," the general said to Joe, as Muriel would recall.

"Well, I gave up my citizenship immediately and I am married to an American and I have my exit visa," argued Joe.

"Can't leave France."

"The authorities gave me an exit visa," Joe disagreed.

"This is up to the military," said the general.[45] This long exchange led to impatient shouts from the crowd behind them so the general suggested they leave and return after everyone had boarded. Muriel immediately came up with a plan: she would give Joe her boarding pass. She later recalled their final day in Europe:

We were not absolutely in despair...I was pretty sure that in the worst case, Joe could board with my pass, and lose himself in the crowd inside. With my American passport, I could probably bluff my way on, or insist on a new boarding pass on the grounds of having lost mine. Still it was hard waiting the many hours until the crowd had thinned. Finally the last people were in line. Night had fallen.[46]

By 10 P.M., the remaining stragglers were on board, the ship's lights were dimmed for the blackout, and Muriel stood in the shadows while Joe went up to the officials to get a boarding pass. Asked his profession, he answered passionately, as Muriel would recall: "Journalist. And I want to write for the cause of France against the Nazis when we get to America." The military men at the gate were tired, in a hurry to be done, and said to the stubborn general, "Look, we have to let him go. He's going to do a lot for France when he gets to America."[47] Joe soon had his own boarding pass, returned Muriel's to her and, tired but relieved, the couple walked up the gangplank onto the *Manhattan*, which would be the last American ocean liner to cross the Atlantic until the end of World War II.

The next morning, at sea, Joe shaved off the mustache he had worn as a disguise since he first went underground in 1935. Muriel too was reflecting on her identity: fleeing from the turmoil of a Europe at war, she realized with a start how far it all was from her pampered childhood. She had transformed herself from a daughter of privilege to a woman of purpose. Now almost 38, faced with the prospect of returning permanently to the country she had left nearly two decades earlier, Muriel felt her emotions vacillate from anticipation to uneasiness, her excitement tamped down with trepidation. What would the next few years be like? More troubling than such predictable ambivalence was what Muriel knew to be her deepest concern: Would her life ever be as meaningful again?

CHAPTER 15

A HEALING TIME

Muriel and Joe arrived in New York shortly before Thanksgiving 1939, and Connie's smiling face was the first thing Muriel saw as she stepped off the gangplank. Accompanied by Margarita Konenkov, Connie wanted to be there to welcome her mother, whom she had not seen for more than a month, back to America. Thrilled to be home but still reeling from those last weeks in Paris and in shock over the war in Europe, Muriel barely had time to adjust to being in the United States again before she resumed the work with refugees that had been so important to her for the past five years.[1]

Muriel set about finding her family a place to live as Joe scrambled furiously to deal with cables and letters already arriving from imperiled people in Europe. Those early days in New York were a rush of decision making, readjustment, and, of course, Muriel and Joe's continued involvement in Europe. The war had only just begun, but they knew it was only a matter of time before more nations fell to Hitler. This time, however, Muriel could be involved only indirectly, trying to help refugees escape from the Nazis by using the only means now available to her: letters of intervention, affidavits of support that stated that the émigrés would not be a financial burden,[2] and, of course, money.

Muriel also had to deal with issues on her own home front. Connie's behavior at Ruth's appeared somewhat problematic. The child had addressed Muriel's sister as "Hey Aunt listen Ruth,"[3] a way of getting attention and making herself heard among her talkative cousins. Ruth had enrolled her niece along with her own offspring at the exclusive Dalton School in Manhattan, but it was Margarita Konenkov who had been Connie's closest companion, taking Muriel's place for the last month.

Muriel's mother, also in New York that autumn, finally met her daughter's third husband. Although Helen had initially opposed Muriel's marrying a man

four-and-a-half years younger than she, once she met Joe, she agreed that he
seemed mature for his years and she accepted him: Joe and Helen got along well
during this brief encounter. The short, muscular Austrian who had never before
been out of Europe seemed exotic to Muriel's relatives. They also thought that
Connie, a rarity in her precocity and outspokenness, was like no other little girl
they had ever met.[4]

The family rallied around Muriel and Joe, welcoming them warmly, with one
exception: Ruth's husband Harry Bakwin, a pediatrician, was politically conservative, the polar opposite of Muriel and Joe. While Muriel demurred whenever
politics arose as a topic of conversation, Harry baited and provoked, seeming to
enjoy the argument that ensued. As a result, uncomfortable with confrontation
as she'd always been, Muriel withdrew. The resulting distance between the sisters prevented them from overcoming their old childhood differences.[5]

Taking Connie from Ruth's to the new apartment—Muriel had rented
a small place on the Upper East Side—she and her family settled in quickly.
Despite Harry Bakwin's prickliness, Muriel agreed to spend Thanksgiving at
their house, though, as she explained to her relatives, she had to leave soon after
to spend Christmas in Chicago with her mother. The real reason for this journey was political, however. Joe had learned that Helen knew the president of the
University of Chicago, Robert Maynard Hutchins, a man with a personal connection to President Roosevelt. In Chicago, after arriving at her mother's, Muriel
and Joe soon found their way to the university and President Hutchins's office.
Easily convincing him that the United States should pressure France to release
the Austrians still interned in the French camp in which Joe had been imprisoned, Muriel even persuaded Hutchins to contact Roosevelt about the matter.
He was not, however, able to convince the president to act: "The president felt he
could not get involved in France's internal political issues," Joe recalled.[6] This
was, of course, a reflection of American isolationist foreign policy at the time.

Muriel continued her practice of keeping her political life separate from her
relatives; they knew nothing of the missions she had undertaken in Europe during
the 1930s. Nelson, the exception to this, did know about her resistance involvement and had actually helped on several occasions. Her brother Edward, on the
other hand, with whom she had not gotten along well as a child, had believed
since her Wellesley days that her political beliefs "were absolutely crazy." Ruth
learned of her younger sister's dangerous resistance work only decades later. Her
politics fell somewhere in the middle of those of the two brothers on the spec-
trum, but the separation between the sisters grew when Ruth offered her poor
opinion of psychoanalysis—a result of her brief, unhappy treatment with Anna
Freud. Though Ruth would soon aid refugees in New York, providing many of
them with free medical care, the two sisters would never be close friends.[7]

After the holidays, before returning to New York, Muriel, Joe, and Connie skied at Stowe, Vermont, along with Edward's youngest son, who was four years older than Connie, and two Austrian friends who had already arrived in America. Soon Muriel and Joe were back in New York. Joe continued to answer letters and cables from Europe, sending money when possible, and, at the least, always providing advice and information to people in crisis. Muriel studied for her February 1 New York State medical boards, and it was no surprise to anyone but Muriel herself when she passed them with ease.[8]

At the end of March 1940, the urgency of refugee aid became even more of a priority, and Muriel rented a new, larger apartment on Central Park West, knowing she would probably need extra space to house émigrés from Europe. As Muriel continued to pursue the courses and certificates she would need in order to become an accredited physician in the United States, she also shifted her focus. She no longer aided people in fleeing Europe, except to provide them with an American haven if she could. Instead, she sent money with the help of her longtime lawyers and through various refugee organizations.

For his part, Joe contributed by sending information—names of people who needed assistance. Often, the efforts of Muriel and Joe were helpful, but overall they had many failures, for the odds were against them. The democratic nations, particularly the United States and Great Britain, had a complicated set of immigration regulations that more often than not made it difficult, if not impossible, for refugees to gain entry into these countries.

Still, between 1933 and 1945, half a million Germans and Austrians left their homelands, and approximately 132,000 finally made it to the United States. Scores of these who reached the United States owed their lives to Muriel's generosity. But the United States' official anti-immigrant legislation and anti-Semitic attitudes managed to keep out most of the refugees—75 percent of whom were Jewish. Two-thirds of Americans surveyed by *Fortune* magazine in 1938 said they did not want refugees allowed into the United States, no matter what they were facing in Europe. The majority of Americans approved of the outdated Immigration Act of 1924, which set quotas at 2 percent of each "Caucasian nationality" based on an 1890 census. This restrictive policy reflected American attitudes prevalent at the end of the Great Depression: anti-Semitism, "America for Americans," isolationism, and fear of refugees.[9]

Later, when the war broadened to include all of Europe, Nazi persecution turned to Social Democrats and others who opposed Nazism who were not Jewish. But everywhere, it was always much worse for those who were Jewish. And there often was no place for these people to go. A bill introduced in the U.S. Congress to admit 20,000 Jewish children above the regular refugee quotas was amended by its opponents to admit the children only if the regular quotas were reduced by 20,000. The then useless bill died after its original sponsor withdrew, thwarted by the response of his fellow legislators.[10]

Muriel never let up on her efforts. Once refugees managed to get to America, she provided temporary support and places for them to stay. She found people jobs, paid to educate their children, bought them food and other necessities, and, through Ruth, made certain that they received much-needed medical care. Later on, she even gave interest-free loans to individuals who wanted to buy their own homes.[11]

During the war years, by Joe's count, the couple received more than 1,300 letters requesting help. Historian, Hitler biographer, and émigré Konrad Heiden, who lived for a time in Muriel's Manhattan apartment, wrote:

> The Buttingers freed many people and saved many lives, or at least helped to rescue them…They procured visas and entry papers, provided resources for the long journeys and when necessary also intervened with the government.[12]

While Joe spoke of his political duty to help comrades left behind in Europe, Muriel's motivation was different. She had long believed that the best use to which she could put her fortune was in the aid of all people in need.[13]

In early 1940, it became clear that even an affidavit of support would not in itself do much. Since the United States worked on quotas, allowing admittance to a certain number of émigrés from each country of origin, if a person's quota number had not yet come up, American consulates in Europe ignored an individual's affidavit of support. Joe advised everyone writing to him for help to seek visas to countries such as Mexico that did not have quotas. Muriel paid for some of these Mexican visas, which were then sent to a number of refugees.[14]

Most troubling were the requests that came from relatives of individuals already in concentration camps, such as Gertrude Danneberg's heart-wrenching letters from London to Muriel and Joe on behalf of her husband, Robert, Joe's Socialist comrade who had been in Buchenwald since 1938. Gertrude, financially solvent with proof of a $3,000 account in a New York bank, had in her possession affidavits, "good" quota numbers, and even tickets and visas for Haiti. Nevertheless, she was unable to free her husband, as she would write:

> You can't imagine how it affects us to know how our most beloved person is suffering. I have news from him, and that is a help to not lose courage He urges us to have courage and patience. We naturally have

to take an example from his wonderful attitude, and hold our heads up, even when is seems so difficult.[15]

During this period, Muriel's failure to help Gertrude Danneberg saddened her as did another more personal sorrow. Thirty-eight when she arrived in New York, Muriel tried to have more children and became pregnant fairly easily, but none of the pregnancies came to term. She suffered four miscarriages. These losses took a toll on both her body and her psyche, as she very much wanted to have a child with Joe and knew how much Connie longed for a sister or brother. But she bore her pain stoically and kept her emotions to herself, as she had always done.[16]

The news from Europe continued to horrify Muriel, as country after country fell to the Germans: Norway, Denmark, Belgium, the Netherlands, Luxembourg, and, finally, France. When word came on June 22, 1940 of the fall of France, and the subsequent German occupation of most of that nation, it seemed like a far-off bell mournfully tolling death and the loss of freedom.[17] Rescue work now took on a new urgency for Muriel and Joe as the Europeans who had earlier sought shelter in Paris were again on the run. These most hunted of people, some of whom had been refugees since 1933, now had to flee again.

As they retreated from Paris, Joe's Austrian comrades continued to write to him and Muriel. From the south of France, a group of them settled mainly in Marseille and Montauban, then tried to reach America via Spain and Portugal. But the major difficulty all the refugees faced was the "surrender on demand" clause in the Franco-German treaty, mandating that the government of France turn over any individuals requested by the Nazis. Joe's comrades and the others were hounded creatures once more, especially with entry barred to both Fascist Italy and Fascist Spain.[18]

"The situation was desperate: this time we were really caught," Henry Leichter remembered, until salvation came—for him—from New York, as Muriel's connections and Joe's perseverance worked hand in hand to acquire American visas for their Austrian cohort.[19]

In the summer of 1940, Muriel, Joe, and other progressive Americans organized what would later become the Emergency Rescue Committee (ERC). Joseph Lash, a former antiwar Socialist who was now Eleanor Roosevelt's friend and protégé, arranged a meeting with the First Lady for Joe and the German anti-Fascist Karl Frank. At that meeting, the two men informed Mrs. Roosevelt that, although the Presidential Advisory Committee on Refugees had approved 576 names, only a handful of visas had been issued. The men asked that the United States issue immediate emergency visas under special order of the president.

Angered at her government's intransigence, Mrs. Roosevelt had for some time been barraging her husband with memos and phone calls on the matter—Joseph Lash called it "the running argument"—but to no avail. Finally, after her talk with Joe and Karl Frank, she engaged in a 25-minute telephone conversation with FDR, in the presence of the two émigrés, ending with this threat:

> If Washington refuses to immediately supply the necessary visas, the German and Austrian refugee leaders, with the financial support of many Americans, will rent a ship, load it with as many as possible of the endangered refugees in France, cross the Atlantic and sail up and down the eastern coast of the United States, until the American people, furious and ashamed, compel the government through demonstrations to allow these victims of political persecution to enter the United States.[20]

Muriel, Joe, and the others in the ERC knew that individuals could only escape now if they could get to Lisbon, the port of last hope since American ships could no longer embark from now-German-occupied Bordeaux in France. From Lisbon, fleeing refugees could find safe haven in Cuba, Santo Domingo, Venezuela, Mexico, or other nations with relatively open immigration policies. If they tried to continue on to the United States, immigration restrictions would prevent all but a very few from gaining admittance.

But Joe and Karl Frank's fight for emergency visitors' visas had apparently worked, for a few days after Eleanor Roosevelt's conversation with her husband, the United States issued a number of these documents for refugees. The ERC would soon form a coalition with the American Friends of German Freedom and other small groups, meeting on occasion at Muriel and Joe's Central Park West apartment. In a short time, this private refugee organization would send an American volunteer, an editor and journalist named Varian Fry, to Marseille. Over the next year, he and the ERC would save some 1,500 men and women, using emergency visitors' visas, getting people over the foothills of the Pyrenees into Spain, then into Portugal where they could, with luck and the necessary documents, book passage and sail to a safer place.[21]

By the late summer of 1940, more than 20 Austrian comrades had notified Joe and Muriel that they were safely in Lisbon. Then, on September 3, a large contingent of them sailed to New York aboard a Greek passenger ship, the *Nea Hellas*: Manfred Ackermann, Little Otto Bauer with his family, Otto Leichter and his two sons Henry and Franz, Friedrich and Kathia Adler, Karl Hans Sailer, Walter and Rosa Sonnenfeld and their son Kurt, and others.[22]

Kurt Sonnenfeld recalled that his family's precious American visas had arrived for them in Montauban after Muriel had sent an affidavit vouching for his family to the American consulate in Paris. Although Kurt and his parents survived, he would recall that two of his aunts and uncles who had been with them in Montauban, as well as several friends from his Socialist youth group in Vienna, did not. Apprehended by the Nazis, Kurt's friends and relatives, as he later learned, were transported first to the French transit camp Drancy, on the outskirts of Paris, then to Auschwitz.[23]

As the *Nea Hellas* steamed toward New York, Muriel rented nearly two dozen apartments for the Austrian comrades, who would soon arrive homeless, jobless, and stateless. After the ship docked, Muriel opened her large apartment to those for whom she could not find quarters: Little Otto Bauer and his family lived there for two months. Friedrich and Kathia Adler stayed for four weeks. She also paid school tuition for the Leichter boys and sent medical and living expenses to Joe's brother Loisl and his pregnant wife Friedl, who were still in Europe.[24]

Angered at the Spanish government's arbitrary border policy—Spain would close or open its borders for no apparent reason—Muriel tried to convince some U.S. officials to intervene. When that didn't work, Muriel and Joe hoped that prominent Catholics in Spain might affect the border policy. But, as Joe wrote, the Catholics refused to get involved:

> The scandalous manner in which the local Catholics, but also the immigrant German and Austrian Catholics, especially the Austrians, behave with regard to this question can hardly be exaggeratedly represented.[25]

Muriel continued to send money. Between May 1940 and October 1942, according to documented records, she spent dollars, francs, pounds sterling, and escudo on behalf of countless men and women, paying for ship passages, documents when they could be bought, living expenses, and bank accounts— the equivalent in today's money of more than $1 million.[26] At the same time, she was pursuing her goal of becoming a psychoanalyst. Required to undertake an internship and a residency, then further and more specialized study, once again her superhuman ability to keep her life compartmentalized—indeed, maybe her compulsion to do so—was helping her to accomplish so much at one time during an incredibly tense period.

Muriel had raised her daughter with no gender-related limits, as if being a girl carried no special strictures, and had allowed Connie almost total freedom. The nature-loving girl, miserable living in the city—and probably playing subtly on Muriel's guilt over her long absences—convinced her mother that the family should move to the country. In June 1940, within days of learning that half of her longtime friend and lawyer Wolf Schwabacher's rambling two-family farm-house in Pennington, New Jersey, was available, Muriel decided to purchase the half-share for $23,000. Since the home came already furnished, she, Joe, and Connie moved in immediately.[27]

Pennington was only 60 miles from New York, and they retained their apartment there both for visits to the city and as a place to house refugees. Muriel would come to love Brookdale Farm, as the house in New Jersey was called, and to appreciate its barn and outbuildings and 200 wooded acres. The three-story farmhouse would be her home for the rest of her life.

Connie soon turned her country bedroom into an animal sanctuary, with a partially sand-covered floor and nests and other habitats for creatures she found in the woods, as well as for domestic pets.[28] Muriel and Joe continued to go back and forth to their apartment in New York City—although there were times when they would arrive on Central Park West and find the place so packed with refugees that they had to stay in a hotel—while Connie spent all her time at Pennington, cared for by servants and attending a public school in nearby Princeton.

In 1941, having grown even closer to Wolf Schwabacher and his family now that they lived together, Muriel established a trust fund for Wolf's daughter, Brenda, of $50,000 (more than $700,000 in today's currency). Life at Pennington meant comfort and stability to Muriel during the war years, since even her medical studies had become somewhat erratic because of the many different institutions in which she studied.[29]

In New York, too many people made too many demands on her, but here in the bucolic New Jersey countryside, where she would spend almost all her time from now on, there was a tranquil regularity to the day. Each morning, she ritu-alistically ate the same breakfast: bacon, toast with apricot jam, and coffee. Then she read the paper before beginning her day's work. Evenings were similarly comforting: martinis around the pool in good weather, or by the fire in bad.

But the war and refugee needs were never far away. In early 1941, Muriel called on Albert Einstein to help out when Joe's brother Loisl was thrown into a Canadian jail. A neighbor of Muriel's who had become a friend, Einstein had been ensconced near Pennington since 1935 at Princeton's Institute for Advanced Studies. Loisl, his wife Friedl, and their baby had spent weeks cross-ing the Atlantic on a Greek freighter, their passages paid by Muriel. After the freighter was attacked several times by German U-boats, it limped into a Canadian port, where Loisl's incomplete papers landed him in jail. Allowed one call, he contacted Joe, and Muriel sprang into action. Within days, or so the story goes, the influential Einstein had sent an affidavit, and Loisl was released. The family lived first at Brookdale Farm, then in an apartment Muriel rented for them in New York as Loisl, now Louis, took a position as a teacher in a private school.[30]

As the war in Europe wore on, in September 1941 news reached Americans of a German proclamation that all Jews under the Greater German Reich were required to wear a yellow star, "a perversion of the Jewish Star of David." The Nazis began widespread and systematic deportations of Jews and other so-called enemies of the Reich. The Jews of Eastern Europe now lost any hope they may have held onto. At best, they would be imprisoned. And, according to the most terrifying rumors, they all would be murdered.[31]

Muriel continued to find refuge in the Pennington farmhouse, and this time, no matter how bad the news from the war, she never allowed it to deter her from her path of becoming a physician. She was hired as a psychiatric consultant at the Sunnyside Progressive School in Long Island City and the Walden School in New York, under the supervision of her old friend from Vienna, Dr. Berta Bornstein. Then she began a one-year medical internship at the New Jersey State Hospital at Trenton.

Trenton's program head had been Dr. R. G. Stone, a follower of Dr. Henry A. Cotton, both of whom believed that mental illness was always the result of a physical infection. Both men performed "surgical bacteriology" to rid people of emotional disorders. Stone, who admitted to Muriel that he did not like women doctors, never deviated from his bizarre theory: Muriel saw countless patients who had had their teeth, ovaries, tonsils, and other organs removed because they were diagnosed as schizophrenic. If the Trenton facility had an uncircumcised male patient, he was promptly circumcised; women would be just as quickly divested of their reproductive organs.[32]

Muriel's experiences at Trenton changed forever the way she viewed medicine and, even, life itself. In a series of essays that she wrote about the institutionalized racism at Trenton, and the overt racist cruelty of its doctors and nurses, Muriel was able to work through the pain she experienced while interning at this hospital. In "Hospital Bed" wrote about how a nurse dismissed the fears of a young patient about to give birth as "just nigger superstition." She witnessed an auxiliary policeman who had beaten a man, then dragged him off in handcuffs, shouting, "Come on, you drunken nigger." Fellow physicians were no better, routinely using the racist term. In one incident, Muriel was assisting the unsteady hand of a surgeon as he removed not only an ovary with cysts, but the normal second ovary after he learned the patient was "colored."[33]

In an especially moving essay, "I Didn't Ask to Have It," Muriel wrestles with her own demons, as well as with the callous and brutal racism she witnessed at Trenton. Again the patient is "a young colored girl." She is 16, pregnant and terrified about giving birth. Encouraging the patient not to give up despite her unwanted pregnancy, Muriel gives her money to get home, lends her an umbrella, and promises to take good care of her when she returns for her next checkup. At that checkup, the young woman goes into premature labor at only six months into her pregnancy. The baby is born with a "hare-lip and cleft palate...so malformed that the poor little nose had only one nostril."

It was unlikely that the infant would survive.

> In a surge of horror and pity for the poor creature, making such efforts to start its miserable life, I covered its face again with the towel and held my hand over the gaping space that should have been a mouth. The movement was instinctive and unthinking—I felt only the cruelty, the impossibility of letting it live.

But as the baby shuddered, she remembered that he was still alive with at least a miniscule chance of survival. Desperately, she tried to help the baby now, tying the umbilical cord, wrapping the tiny creature in a blanket. Then she asked the nurse to put the infant in a heated crib; she would return in a few minutes to check on it, she said, adding a warning that the young mother was not to be told anything.

Up on the hospital roof, Muriel argued with herself. Was it fair to keep this child alive, a child that would live with horrible deformities and health problems?

> It's my problem. I have to know what I think. The baby will die anyhow, but I have to know what is right to do...I can give it oxygen and coramine and still know it will die. I can satisfy my conscience and still not have it on my mind that I've kept this miserable thing alive.

She wrestled with the moral question until she decided, finally, to give the baby oxygen, though she knew that it would not survive. She went back to the nursery and asked a nurse, an elderly woman, "What does the chief usually do for a premature baby with malformations? Does he do anything special to keep it alive?" The nurse's answer shocked her...but only for a few seconds—she had come to expect this kind of response: "Sometimes he does. But if you're talking about that little nigger baby, I don't believe he'd lift a finger. There are too many niggers in the world already." Muriel suddenly grew furious: "That baby's going to have every damn thing the hospital's got, to keep it alive," she snapped. She ordered the emergency procedures and medications and walked into the nursery. The baby was already dead.[34]

Until Trenton, she had thought she'd faced down the worst in human nature while in Austria. But Trenton was a different kind of awakening, right in her own country and only miles from where she lived.

The bombing of Pearl Harbor by the Japanese on December 7, 1941, took her attention and emotions away from the nightmare of Trenton. One day later, the United States entered the war. Joe was immediately proclaimed an enemy alien, along with all Germans, even though he was an Austrian. This situation fortunately changed after the newly formed Austrian Labor Committee immediately petitioned the State Department asking for Austria's "right of self-determination." Within a month, to Muriel's satisfaction, Joe and other Austrians would be reclassified as non-enemy aliens. By this time, convinced that there was no place in America for the old Social Democratic factionalism, Joe dropped out of politics completely, giving up all connections to his former party, and leaving the foreign office of the party to his friend Friedrich Adler.[35]

Despite the hell that was Trenton hospital, and even though the war would put so many at risk, Muriel continued to find tranquility in her farmhouse and her family, as Stephen Spender would later write after visiting her in Pennington:

> Now that [Muriel] had returned to America she seemed more fulfilled
> and happy than I had ever seen her. She was absorbed in her work
> among the insane and brought to it the great gift of never allowing
> insanity to obscure her recognition of the individual personality under
> the psychotic mask. Devoted to her home, her friends and her work
> for humanity, [Muriel's] life was beautiful, and this was a fact which
> all who knew her felt as though it were a part of her physical presence.
> Her unselfish achievement was not based on a dramatic renunciation.
> It came more out of a fullness of living than from self-denial.[36]

But though Pennington provided an oasis, Muriel's thoughts were never far from those who suffered—from the patients she had seen for the past year to the victims of the war, especially the Jews of Europe whose destiny was forever changed by a handful of German Nazi officials at the infamous Wannsee Conference on January 20, 1942. Fifteen men met at a villa in a Berlin suburb to put their seal of approval on what they called the "Final Solution"—"the systematic, deliberate annihilation of the European Jews."[37]

During 1942, Muriel importuned several officials about individuals in camps who were waiting for deportation or others who had obtained their visas but were still unable, for various reasons, to flee; this group had a particularly high rate of suicide attempts. She and Joe contacted officials in several organizations, including the American Friends Service Committee and the Jewish Joint Distribution Committee, and sent them the names of men and women in Europe for whom she pledged to undertake all financial responsibility.[38] Despite her assurance that she would support these people, that they would never become a burden on the U.S. government, almost all of these pleas went unanswered.

In March 1942, a group of Socialists imprisoned at the French internment camp at Gurs contacted Muriel and Joe. The hardships they faced at the camp were nothing compared to their fear that, since they were only 20 kilometers from the demarcation line between Free France and the German-occupied region, they too would be delivered to the Germans, as some of their comrades had been. Illness and death, as well as deportation, they wrote, were thinning their ranks. Their fears were justified. In November 1942, when Germany occupied all of France, the French government turned over the remaining nearly 4,000 Jewish Gurs internees to the Nazis, who soon transported them to Drancy, then on to extermination camps in occupied Poland. Five of the six men who signed the letter to Joe and Muriel would eventually perish there.[39]

By the end of 1942, almost 4 million Jews would be killed. Among them were Joe's Vienna comrade Robert Danneberg, and Otto Leichter's wife, Käthe, one of the first concentration camp prisoners to be killed by gas. Her oldest son Henry would recall that news of her death was "the hardest and saddest hour of my life."[40]

Muriel, sad and frustrated that she and Joe had been unable to help these people—along with so many others—continued to send money. Soon, at the suggestion of Wolf Schwabacher, she created the New-Land Foundation. Wealthy all her life, but always uncertain how to invest her money, Muriel never wanted to discuss this matter with her family since, as she would later say, "they all thought I was a dope" concerning financial matters.[41] Thus she leapt at the lawyer's suggestion that she create a philanthropic and humanitarian foundation. At its creation, New-Land's stated aims were peace, arms control, civil rights, justice, population control, and leadership development. The foundation continues today, providing grants to individuals and groups whose ideas and ideologies match those of its founder.[42]

At the start of 1943, both Connie and Joe became U.S. citizens, and Muriel, who, according to Connie, ran things at home, decided that Joe should formally adopt her daughter. The adoption went though, despite an almost comic inspection of the Pennington house by an official who tried desperately not to faint when she viewed the unconventional menagerie in Connie's zoo-like bedroom. Despite Muriel's hopes for a tighter nuclear family, however, it would not happen, according to Connie's later memories: "Joe was good to me but he wasn't very interested in me. He had other things. He was my mother's husband and he didn't feel like my father."[43]

When Muriel's internship finally ended in 1943, she hesitated about embarking on a psychiatric residency, the next step toward becoming a psycho-analyst, because she assumed that she would shortly be called to Europe. The war would end soon, she felt, and she wanted to be free whenever that happened to do hands-on refugee work abroad. Thus, to avoid complicating her training, instead of a residency, she took a position as assistant medical director of the New Jersey Department of Health, as a field worker in the Bureau of Venereal Disease Control.

The war went on and letters continued to arrive at the Pennington address or the West End Avenue apartment, asking for money and help. Soon, Muriel learned that the IRC, or International Rescue Committee, formerly the Emer-gency Rescue Committee, would be organizing aid for those Germans, Austri-ans, Italians, and Spaniards who would need assistance before they could return to their homelands. She felt certain she would be asked to become involved. She was correct. The IRC chose her to lead its Paris office, where she was man-dated to provide food and lodging as well as counseling to refugees needing repatriation.

Within days of President Roosevelt's shocking death on April 12, 1945, Muriel left her adored farmhouse, once again said farewell to those she loved, and flew to Paris on a U.S. Army plane.

She arrived in Paris at midnight on April 19, snatched a few hours sleep at a friend's flat, then set out for the IRC office at the Place de la République. Less than two weeks later, on April 30, Hitler committed suicide. On May 8, V-E Day, the Allies formally accepted the German surrender. German-born Ernst Langendorf, who wrote that at the end of the war he was the first American soldier to set foot on Marienplatz—the square in front of the Munich *rathaus*, or town hall—had been helped to freedom five years earlier by the ERC's Varian Fry. About V-E Day, Langendorf would write:

> War over, Hitler kaput, Mussolini executed, mon dieu, great words, one really can't grasp the entire meaning of all these events which hap-pened in such short intervals. These days I did quite a lot of discussing with my fellows. And we agreed that humanity has a new chance for a start. But will it be used? We are rather pessimistic, all of us.[44]

Caught up in the contagion of V-E Day in Paris, Muriel laughed, talked to strangers, was kissed by five different people, drank too much, and held a little girl on her shoulders so the child could see over the crush of tens of thousands in the Place de la Concorde.[45] The great worldwide effort to aid the millions of war victims soon began in earnest, with Muriel doing her part as head of the IRC's Paris office. The Allies had a fund of $25 million, administered by the International Refugee Organization (IRO), and the IRC was mandated to distribute nearly a million dollars to aid more than a thousand political victims. Many of them, separated for years from their homes and families, were isolated and confused and required considerable counseling before they could be resettled. The refugees also needed legal intervention because their homelands were now under the control of the Allies.

Muriel wrote home to Pennington of the unshod and unclothed Europeans, who were in desperate in need of underwear, sleeping garments, slippers, shoes—the most basic clothing could not be found in Paris other than on the black market, which only a very few could afford. The food was paltry, too, with no coffee or fresh fruits and vegetables: she herself existed on bread, potatoes, and a "hot brown liquid" that tried but failed to pass for coffee. Her letters to Joe and her friends are filled, in the beginning, with pleas for clothing and other items for the refugees, and sweaters and boots for herself. Paris was cold. The city was filling up with needy people, she would write:

> Thousands are returning from prison camps in Germany now, weekly, perhaps daily. One sees men on the streets in striped prisoners' coats with "Buchenwald" or some other camp name on their sleeves. Everyone in France is, naturally, terrifically indignant about the treatment of the men in the camps.[46]

The IRC office would soon become, to Muriel's great dissatisfaction, rife with factions: she quickly saw that certain refugees, after the war, made all of life into a political event, much as they had done before the war. While her responsibility was to decide who and how to help, she soon found different groups struggling to receive the IRC's attention and funds. Within a very short time, Muriel realized that the Committee's work would be nearly impossible. There were too many cases, too many disabled and wounded Spanish veterans, too many hungry children for her to manage all at once. In addition, although she attempted to run the office in her usual efficient style, she was often thwarted by internecine battles among the Committee's staff members.

She soon began to feel sorry for herself, an emotion completely unfamiliar to her. In May she wrote Joe that the Committee was run sloppily and that her associates were touchy and emotional. The office moved to a new space on May 3, but when Muriel first walked into the empty rooms, she found lice and other vermin, no electric power, and no phone service. Despairing, she wrote long complaining letters to her husband, and then apologized for "blowing off steam."[47]

She occasionally saw her brother Nelson, who was in Paris, and some of his friends. But when they insisted she attend a party, she wrote Joe that the guests were "tiresome, boring, irritating, and of no earthly use or pleasure to anyone,"[48] and vowed never again to be roped into such an outing. Any time off from the Committee, she decided, she would spend quietly and alone.

Often homesick for Joe, Connie, and Brookdale Farm, Muriel quickly grew discouraged by the endless needs of the refugees and the in-fighting among the Committee's staff. But at the end of May, having been in Paris only six weeks, she felt a little more alive and herself again as she now had more of a social life, drinking in cafés with soldier acquaintances and enjoying herself a bit. She had an occasional date with a "Scotch soldier," as she wrote, finding Scots relaxing to be with—most likely because they were different from the Austrian, German, and French Europeans with whom she was familiar.[49]

In June, she began suggesting to Joe that he and Connie get visas so they would be able to visit her. Occasionally going out with soldiers did little, it would turn out, to relieve her deep loneliness. Muriel was also stymied and overwhelmed with Committee work. The political factions, the power struggles, the squabbling among the Committee members and those they were supposed to aid—the chaos threatened to destroy her sense of order, commitment, and duty. Her talents were organizational and methodical and this chaos at the IRC made her feel truly lost for the first time in her life.

"I spend all my money on airmail letters, cables and cognac,"[50] she wrote in June. Worse, as more and more people returned from the concentration camps, as increasing numbers of prisoners of war were released, it became clearer than ever just what the toll of this war had been. It was an enormous wave of devastation, and the IRC, one small effort in Paris, could barely make a dent. Other groups and organizations were on the scene, too, all struggling to aid those whom war had turned into human wreckage. Heartbreakingly, the few surviving Jews were worse off than anyone. They not only had no homes to go back to, but usually, no relatives either. Muriel wanted nothing more than to return to her home, to the peace of Pennington.

Learning in late June that her mother had died, she asked only where Helen, who was 76, had been buried and whether Joe and Connie had attended the funeral.[51] Her letters convey no sadness. Over the past years, Helen and Muriel had gradually, even unconsciously, become little more than polite strangers to each other.

Muriel now began to plan for either Joe and Connie's arrival in Paris or her own leave-taking. By July, she was so lonely that she found herself fantasizing about going into Connie's bedroom at Pennington to play with the girl's pet hamsters, who she viewed as unspoiled, simple creatures when compared to people. And she missed being with children, who she now saw as the "only

normal human beings"—"anyone over 12 or 14 is already condemned to this
tired, lifeless life of war-torn Europe," she would write.[52] Muriel wanted someone to take over the Committee, and she suggested to the chairperson in New
York that the organization send a man. Perhaps he would have less difficulty
controlling the uncompromising factionalism.

Muriel also became angry with a group of Austrian refugees who called
themselves the Richter group, after one of Joe's old code names. She resented
their use of the former name because she thought it psychologically harmful
and regressive for anyone who had been in the Austrian resistance to cling to
pre-1938 ways and beliefs. She believed that this postwar period was a wonderful chance to sweep away the cobwebbed ideologies of the past.[53]

Seeking someone with whom she could really relax, Muriel at last found
a friend in Clara Thalmann, a revolutionary and former Communist who had
been in the French resistance. Muriel and Clara went together to operas and bal-
lets and strolled the Paris streets. Muriel also continued to go out at night with
her Scottish soldiers, sitting in cafés and sipping cognac until the wee hours.[54]

But soon, a new issue in the office erupted, as Muriel wrote to Joe—the
Committee was now plagued with the issue of secret agents and their importance in rescue work:

> That's the problem of all the agents of the deuxieme bureaux of the
> various countries, past, present, and suspected...a very large number
> of people 1) definitely are [or] 2) are suspected of being agents—often
> for more than one government...Now with the American intelligence
> service well entrenched in France and European countries...we are
> often enough asked to assist some well-known agent...[55]

On one of her outings with Clara Thalmann, she visited Otto Bauer's grave
at the Père Lachaise cemetery. The place aroused in her not awe at its intricately
carved monuments, but distaste for the way humans disposed of their dead:

> Pere Lachaise is a horrible and depressing place. I don't know why the
> human race hasn't found something better to do with its dead than
> stick them in the earth and build ugly monuments, cluttering up a
> good piece of land.[56]

This same dislike of burials, expressed by her some weeks earlier upon
hearing from Joe about her mother's funeral, would remain a life-long conviction. She felt that people should find a simpler way of doing away with the body
once a person had died.

Being in Paris immediately after the war had altered Muriel, in some ways as much as the Trenton hospital had: along with her new dislike of certain human behaviors, her awareness of simple beauties and joys was heightened as she recalled her life at home. She wrote Joe:

> I realize more than I ever did before how nice the house and the garden
> and the pool are, and the kids running around and annoying us, and
> the animals getting dirty and smelly and annoying us, and all the other
> things that didn't always seem so perfect take on a rosy glow from the
> distance of war-torn Europe.[57]

This acute sense of pleasure in the moment would remain with her for the rest of her life.

In August, she spent three weeks at the IRC office in Zurich and so was in Switzerland when the United States dropped atomic bombs on Hiroshima and Nagasaki. She knew it meant both the end of World War II and the escalation of man's inhumanity to man, as she would write:

> We have to find a new word for barbarism or something like that, to
> express ourselves for dropping a thing like this bomb on human beings.
> We'll find it, like so many expressions this war brought us. But for the
> time being this kind of killing or being killed is over.[58]

Despite her urgent need and wish to return home, she didn't want to give up completely on providing aid to the European refugees, concentration camp survivors, and returning prisoners of war. Perhaps, she mused, she could work in Europe as a physician or a social worker at some point in the future. But, for now, she just wanted to leave Paris, and though she forced herself to stay the course, by the end of August, she wrote to Joe: "I can't take it anymore…I am walking on hot coals…Not all the sense of duty I have will make me stay in the Paris office much longer."[59]

Although she had been urging Joe and Connie to join her in Europe, she now cabled Joe not to come, to stay at Pennington so that she could immediately go home. Expecting some resistance from him at her sudden change of plans, Muriel was surprised at his quick agreement. His cable said that all was well and he would be at home, waiting for her. "You never let me down," she wrote. "I ought to know that by now."[60]

Finally, in early September 1945, she boarded a U.S. troop ship, the *Santa Rosa* and, jammed among 4,000 others headed for America, Muriel sailed home to the people—and the place—she loved.

CHAPTER 16

A FULLNESS OF LIVING

It was the fall of 1945, and only a few weeks after Muriel's much-desired return to Brookdale Farm from Paris, when it was Joe's turn to leave. The IRC appointed him director of its postwar European operations, and he left immediately. Muriel missed him more than usual, almost as if she was finally allowing herself the luxury of spousal love, though her life was as busy as it had always been. She resumed her medical career even as she began an ambitious program of sending packages and money to people in war-ravaged Europe.[1]

Joe was headquartered in Geneva, Switzerland, and as one of his first acts, he founded a short-term refuge for 38 Austrian, Spanish, and French children whose parents had been murdered by the Nazis. They would stay in Samoëns, a village in the French Alps. When Joe wrote Muriel that IRC funds for the refuge had dried up, she provided money for the children for the duration of the program, two months.[2]

Toward the end of the year, when it first became possible to send food from America to Europe, Muriel's packages of food, clothing, and medicine went to friends of Joe's from the old anti-Fascist resistance. By February 1946, she was sending hundreds of packages to Germany and France, to a large list of friends and acquaintances whose names Joe had collected.[3]

Eventually Muriel connected with the Cooperative for American Remittances to Europe (CARE), a coalition of 22 organizations formed in 1945, and used them to put together and ship the packages, but paid for them herself. In one year, 1947, she sent 2,820 CARE packages, containing mostly food.[4] She also sent separate boxes of clothing and shoes, remembering what it had been like in Paris in 1945. Eventually, thousands of thank you letters would pour in. Some Austrians, including Joe's mother, would describe Muriel as a "good fairy" for all that she had sent to Joe's village, Schneegattern. The Unterwegers, friends of Joe's who had been left almost completely without food or essential supplies, were able to survive only because of Muriel's assistance. Their son, then just a child, would later recall, as if yesterday, the wondrous gifts of oranges and American T-shirts from "mythical figures Aunt Muriel and Uncle Joe." After the end of the war, Muriel's largesse and generosity would be praised as much as her earlier involvement in the resistance.[5]

Joe, who, in order to take the post with the IRC, had delayed completion of the book he had been writing on the history of Austrian Socialism, benefited from the letters going back and forth between postwar Europeans and Brookdale Farm. Without even trying, he was the recipient of a wealth of information about the effects of the war on people. It was through these communications that he learned much about social and political relations between Austria and Germany after the war. This information would be passed on to the CIA, which was, reportedly, closely aligned with the IRC during these tense early days of the Cold War. Joe's position in the IRC put him at the center of a vortex of intrigue and propaganda, as the Soviet Union and the countries of the Eastern Bloc began an era of mutual suspicion with the West following the end of World War II, spawning scores of secret organizations on both sides.[6]

While Joe quickly became enmeshed in the new secrets and plots swirling around the IRC—he was back in the political milieu in which he had once thrived—Muriel, who had abandoned her post in Paris partly because of political squabbling, remained happily out of the scene. Although she had been away from psychiatry for some time, in 1946 she undertook a residency at the New Jersey State Hospital at Marlboro, happy to be able to avoid the Trenton hospital where she had had such a miserable internship.

After two years at Marlboro, she was already working as a director and psychiatrist at four different clinics in New Jersey, and she felt confident with her patients for the first time. Her lengthy analysis with Dr. Brunswick in Vienna and her extensive theoretical training had given her such first-rate experience and prestigious clinical background that other residents would ask her for guidance.

Even the sudden death of her analyst on January 24, 1946, failed to interfere with Muriel's contentment. Dr. Brunswick, only 48, had died after a fall, either from an illness or perhaps a result of the effects of opiates to which she had become addicted while in Vienna—a dependence that Muriel had long known about but had hoped her analyst would be able to conquer.[7]

Muriel managed to maintain her equanimity despite external events or the actions of others although her peaceful state of mind would be challenged more than once by Joe's sexual infidelities, which she had first experienced back in 1935. Intellectually committed to the concept of sexual freedom, she nevertheless found her spouse's betrayals (and she couldn't help thinking of them in this way, though she fought such a reaction) deeply wounding and painful. Although she would work hard to accept Joe's predilections, she often found it difficult.

After Joe had been in Europe for more than a year, seeing Muriel only briefly when she could get away to visit him, he returned to Pennington. Following a short reunion, he left with Connie in August 1947 to tour England and France. Muriel's work prevented her from joining them until October, when she had a red convertible shipped to Italy where, she at last reunited exuberantly with Joe and Connie. They toured Tuscany on its nearly empty roads, taking advantage of the scarcity of cars in Europe at that time. But the trip ended abruptly after Muriel learned that Joe had once again been seeing his Swiss mistress. "It all blew up," as Connie would recall.[8] Muriel decided she couldn't take his indiscretions anymore, and she gave him an ultimatum: he had to choose between her or his mistress. She would no longer tolerate what she would come to define as his deceitfulness, as she had years before in Vienna when he had refused to give up Gisela. As Connie remembered, her mother was very much in love with Joe:

> After all these other relationships, he was "the one" and she really built him up and tried to give him every advantage. She was a Pygmalion to him. He was a dandy, and she got him the best-looking clothes, and made him very presentable.[9]

Before he left for Europe, Muriel had turned the entire third floor of Brookdale Farm over to Joe for a study and library where he could work on his English and write his book on Austrian political history, one of several books he would publish. Muriel tried to help Joe "find his place in the world" whereas she, of course, had always had a place.[10]

After their breakdown in Italy, Muriel and Joe dropped 16-year-old Connie in Grenoble, a university town in the French Alps, to live on her own before she returned to Pennington just before college. Connie had already spent half a year away from home staying with friends in New Hampshire. As a teenager, Connie had been shy and stuttered so much that she could barely get her words out.[11] Living on her own in both New Hampshire and France was Connie's first effort to create her own life away from her dominant mother. Although Muriel allowed Connie freedom and independence, she was the controlling force at home, owing in part to her confident, assured manner.

After Grenoble, Muriel and Joe spent a few days in Paris and London before returning to Pennington. Always keeping her emotions hidden from others,

Muriel would gloss over the business with Joe's mistress, writing to her friend Margarita Konenkov that her trip had been a success.[12]

But Joe's affairs would continue to hurt Muriel, according to both Connie and Stephen Spender, two of the people closest to her (Muriel and Stephen had reconnected after the war, in 1947, and remained close friends for life). Yet Muriel believed so deeply in personal freedom that she would struggle for years and eventually accept Joe for what he was—a charmer who loved women, a highly sexual man who would be unfaithful to her even though he cared for her deeply. And he did continue to stray. He later had an affair with one of Muriel's patients. He would urge women to walk up a spiral staircase in his and Muriel's New York home and then reach up under their skirts. He even made sexual advances to Stephen Spender's daughter-in-law.[13]

That both Muriel and Joe were glamorous is evident—Joe in his ascot, and Muriel, stunning with her worldliness and great wealth. But whereas Joe was careless about revealing his private life, Muriel was discreet. "Muriel was something out of a movie, her demeanor just different than anyone's," a friend would recall. But "if Muriel was out of one kind of movie, Joe was out of another. He was out of a French film. He was dashing and compelling. He was a sexy guy."[14]

The couple impressed everyone they met. A psychiatrist who first knew Muriel when he was a child would say,

> Life around Muriel always felt luxurious and seemed very special from what we ate to the people we were with. She had a style of being, a wide-eyed open curiosity where you could question anyone about anything. Joe was completely intriguing and charming. They had a magnificent open marriage and loved each other intensely, as colleagues.[15]

Muriel herself believed in the goodness and affirming qualities of sexuality—she even volunteered to be interviewed by Alfred Kinsey for his study of human sexual behavior—and realized she had to regain her sense of self or risk being dependent on Joe's choices about fidelity. At some point, Muriel had resolved to overlook Joe's affairs and her acceptance, once she had made her decision, had no limits: in her will, she left a trust fund for Joe's long-term mistress, Jeanette Roderick, whom he had known for decades.[16]

During Muriel's middle years, she considered all that she had learned after years of analysis and also revisited her old ideas about monogamy: She was once heard having sex in her bedroom with someone other than Joe. Yet, despite the open-marriage part of their relationship, "Joe was the love of her life," Connie would say.[17] And for his part, Joe loved and also admired Muriel, if not as passionately as she adored him.

> I think you are the most loved person by the many people I came into contact with in Austria. Everyone asks about you, everyone wants to meet you, and nobody can understand how such a person as you can exist in such an ugly world. Some [say] you have saved their lives.[18]

During the war years and just after, love, or at least sex, was in the air at Brookdale Farm. Muriel entertained some interesting guests, including Albert Einstein and her old friend Margarita, the beautiful wife of the Russian sculptor Sergei Konenkov. Einstein had met Margarita in the mid-thirties, while Muriel was still in Europe, when the Institute for Advanced Studies commissioned Konenkov to create a bronze bust of Einstein that stands on the Institute's grounds today.

Some years after Einstein's second wife died in 1936, a romance began between the attractive Russian woman and the world-renowned physicist. By 1945, the Konenkovs had returned to the Soviet Union. Decades later, nine love letters from Einstein to Margarita were discovered, and at that time, allegations also surfaced that Margarita had been a Soviet spy, commissioned to somehow influence Einstein, as well as Robert Oppenheimer, to align with the Russians. When asked years later if she thought that Einstein had had an affair with Margarita, Muriel would exclaim, "I certainly hope so! They were two lonely people!"[19]

The late 1940s had as much intrigue, with the start of the Cold War, as Eastern European factionalism had had before the war. During this time, events that would have seemed extraordinary to most Americans happened regularly to Muriel. Offhand references to meeting Robert Oppenheimer or befriending Anna Freud and Albert Einstein occur throughout her notebooks, though occupying no more than a line or two.[20]

By 1950, after a decade of living at Brookdale Farm with the Schwabachers—with Wolf's client Lillian Hellman hearing tales of the glamorous former member of the Austrian resistance with whom he shared a house—there was some discomfort between Muriel and Wolf's wife, Ethel, an eminent painter.[21] By that time, Muriel had become a full-fledged psychoanalyst and had opened a private practice in nearby Trenton.

Thinking that she would prefer her office to be in her house, and also feeling more and more uneasy with the dual-family situation, Muriel came to a difficult decision: she suggested to Wolf that she buy him out. He agreed and sold his half of the property to Muriel by 1951. Muriel soon expanded the pool and resurfaced the old tennis courts. She and Joe would live at Brookdale Farm for the next three decades—a period that was as peaceful as Muriel's life could ever be.

As a nod to her Socialist and progressive beliefs, Muriel became involved as a financial backer in a new political magazine, *Dissent*, founded by Irving Howe and other Social Democrats in 1954, "its underlying ethos…humanist, inclusive and 'equality-friendly,'" as an editor of the magazine wrote.[22] For years, Muriel helped fund the publication, especially pleased to do so since Joe contributed the occasional article.

Her discipline allowed her to dedicate herself to her work through her fifties, not losing focus despite losses of friends and family. Muriel hadn't blinked when she had heard that Albert Einstein had died in April 1955. She would, however, pay close attention to stipulations he left about what would *not* occur after his death—an elaborate funeral and memorial service—as Einstein's wishes would influence her own decisions later on. The scientist had expressed no wishes over what was to be done with his body and was cremated without ceremony.[23] Even through highly emotional episodes, such as the loss of her dear brother Nelson on October 6, 1955, she held steady. Nelson died of a heart attack as he and his wife Blanche were disembarking from an ocean liner. He was 63.[24]

On the other hand, a note from Connie that said, "I'm running off with Harold," got Muriel's attention.[25] At 24, Connie eloped with Muriel's old friend from medical school, Harold Harvey, 46, a man Connie had first met when she was a toddler in Vienna. This happened while he was still legally married, although not living with his wife. Muriel never objected to this marriage, because it was already decided. Connie would recall:

> He said, "I'm going to marry you." And I thought, now what do I do? Do I punch him in the nose or do I say okay? So I said okay. We were having a rather torrid affair at that point…Two days later…we got in the car and went, and I didn't have anything except a toothbrush, but what the heck.[26]

A short time later, the couple returned for a temporary stay at Brookdale Farm. Then they traveled to Italy, returning on the ill-fated SS *Andrea Doria* when Connie was eight months pregnant. On July 25, 1956, she and Harold were among the 1,660 passengers who survived the ship's collision with the MS *Stockholm*. Not wanting to wait for a lifeboat, the pair shimmied down a rope they had seen hanging from the deck, jumped into the water and swam to a nearby lifeboat from the *Stockholm*.[27] Without a doubt, Muriel's own self-confidence and determination, even in the face of frightening events, carried through to the next generation. Over the next eight years, Connie and Harold would have six children.

Not long after the young couple were safely home and Muriel's first grandchild, Joe, had been born, escalating Cold War tensions led to an uprising in Hungary. What began as a student demonstration in Budapest on October 23, 1956, soon spread across the country as a rebellion against the Soviet-sponsored government. The Soviets responded by placing armored tanks in key spots around the city. A general strike was called, and pitched battles erupted. After only a short time, the Soviets put down the revolution, quickly arresting thousands of Hungarians, deporting hundreds to the Soviet Union, and executing hundreds more. By November 10, with Budapest under Soviet control, 200,000 Hungarians had fled, and Joe and the IRC stepped in to help Hungarian refugees in Austria.

Joe remained in Vienna for months to oversee the IRC's operation there. Muriel, who had briefly became involved in political activism again, was by his side for part of the time. The couple was credited with convincing the government of Austria to allow about 100,000 refugees into the country, most of them young men who had escaped to avoid deportation. They also worked with the many displaced children who arrived from Hungary without their parents, wearing signs around their necks that simply said, "To whom it may concern."[28]

Back in the United States, Muriel made arrangements for Hungarians arriving in New York. By now she was an expert in this kind of thing. A leading Social Democratic member of the Hungarian Parliament lived in Muriel and Joe's apartment for two months with her friends and family. Their exit was followed by the arrival of the democratic ex-mayor of Budapest and his family, who stayed even longer. Muriel assisted Hungarian refugees and supported others, with the first meetings of the Hungarian Freedom Fighters Federation USA held in her and Joe's apartment.

At this point, with no idea what the future held in terms of refugees and their needs, Muriel decided that the apartment was simply too small for sheltering people and was also inadequate for housing Joe's rapidly growing library. She turned to her old Vienna friend, Felix Augenfeld, commissioning him to design a structure large enough for all the family's needs. Auge designed and supervised the construction of a four-story townhouse for Muriel and Joe on a vacant lot on Manhattan's Upper East Side. The house, at 10 East 87th Street between Madison and Fifth Avenue, would be constructed around a tree that Muriel loved and didn't want cut down. Later, they added a patio and fountain, the fountain "made by my very good Welsh friend whom I had known when he was an art student in Vienna,"[29] as Muriel would describe Richard, the

Welshman with whom she had been in love in the summer of 1928 and with whom she had maintained a friendship.

A two-story library inside the townhouse included carrels so that people could do research in Joe's enormous library of Austrian and German books and later his Vietnam collection. Muriel and Joe hired Little Otto Bauer to be the permanent librarian, and he lived in the house with his wife and daughter for many years. Later, when Little Otto's wife became ill, Muriel purchased a house for the family in Tenafly, New Jersey.[30] Over time, many others would take up residence in Muriel and Joe's townhouse on a temporary basis.

Joe's Vietnam library had its origins in his new interest in that country. Although he would take time out, briefly, for the Hungarian Revolution, Joe would spend the 1950s and 1960s obsessed with Vietnam, as embroiled in its politics as he had been years earlier in Austria's. Vietnam was for him a return to the machinations and political maneuvering he so enjoyed, for the excitement as well as ways to help people. On his first trip there, in 1954, the IRC had given him a mandate to organize a committee in South Vietnam to aid refugees from the north. He would travel often to the small nation and soon became a confidante of Ngo Dinh Diem, then president of South Vietnam.

Through an organization that he helped found, the American Friends of Vietnam (AFVN), Joe would attempt to convince the American public of Diem's positive qualities. The AFVN supported Diem's regime—because of its commitment to social reform and economic justice, which, as Joe and AFVN believed, would form the basis of a true democracy—and also American intervention in Vietnam.[31]

For years, Joe organized AFVN conferences. He traveled at Diem's side during the president's trip to the United States in 1957. During a second visit to Vietnam in August 1958, Joe renewed his faith in the Diem regime, and defended it in his *Dissent* review of *The Ugly American*. He also tried to affect the editorial policies of several influential American magazines and newspapers to favor Diem's policies.[32]

Eventually, however, he began to realize that Diem had become repressive and also unpopular. During the next several years, Joe would wrestle with this dilemma as he collected a library and began to write his own books on Vietnam. He also interacted during these years with some important figures in international politics, including such diverse individuals as the ultraconservative Francis Cardinal Spellman, as well as the perennial presidential candidate and Socialist Norman Thomas, who had spoken at Wellesley at Muriel's invitation more than 40 years earlier. Muriel, staying out of Joe's involvement in Vietnam as she worked to heal people through psychoanalysis and psychiatry, had nevertheless argued with him about it, disagreeing with his support of South Vietnam and U.S. intervention. By the end of the 1950s, Joe would have serious misgivings about Diem, growing even more ambivalent as Diem revealed increasingly unjust and authoritarian elements in his governance.[33] Muriel was more than pleased when, in 1961, Joe abruptly reversed his position and broke with Diem. After that, although he remained with the AFVN, he resisted the organization's efforts to support Diem and applauded a 1963 military coup that overthrew his former friend. From this point on, Joe would be a strong advocate for the other side, becoming an early opponent of the Vietnam War.[34]

In October 1963, a group of old-line Social Democrats associated with *Dissent* magazine met in the living room of Muriel and Joe's elegant East Side townhouse with youthful representatives of the New Left: Todd Gitlin, Tom Hayden, and others from SDS, Students for a Democratic Society. The meeting did not go well as the two groups were too far apart, both generationally and historically, to understand each other. As Gitlin would write, "They *had* politics; we *were* politics." Despite the awkward meeting, Gitlin and SDS applied for a grant from Muriel's New-Land Foundation, which they received.[35]

While Joe was working internationally during these years, Muriel remained largely withdrawn from politics, her focus during the 1960s on helping people live more contented lives. She had begun a long relationship with the Philadelphia Association for Psychoanalysis in 1948, including years under the supervision of her friend Dr. Berta Bornstein.[36]

In addition, she wrote for and edited the Association's bulletin, and because she still loved education and the young, she taught psychiatry and social work at Rutgers University. Deciding that she wanted more contact with other analysts who lived nearby, she soon realized that, despite the proximity of Princeton, she was the only analyst between Newark and Philadelphia, a "rather lonely situation," she would recall.[37] Because of this professional isolation, she convinced a friend, the psychoanalyst Samuel Guttman, to move to her area.

Not long after Guttman and his wife moved to a house a mile from Brookdale Farm, Muriel and he resolved to create an organization for psychoanalysts, modeled on Freud's Vienna Circle. It would be a small group, no more than 15 or 20 analysts who would meet a few times a year to discuss clinical and theoretical subjects.[38]

In 1960, the first meeting took place in Muriel's Pennington living room. Within a short time, a group of 15 had been formalized as the Center for Advanced Psychoanalytic Studies (CAPS) at Princeton. Within two years, CAPS had been incorporated, officers elected, and a board of advisors established.[39]

Muriel's private psychoanalytic practice lasted for only a handful of years, however, before she discontinued it. She found it too limiting to see patients one at a time and often for years on end. The practice also had other problems—the fact that her office was in her home created an atmosphere that was too relaxed and familiar. Muriel became friends with a number of her analysands and, in one awkward instance, a patient, an attractive woman, grew close to Muriel and then, uncomfortably and unfortunately, much too close to Joe.[40]

In 1957, Muriel decided, all these decades later, to return to her first interest: children. Now, she would work with their psyches, rather than their intellects. Muriel was hired as a psychiatrist in the public schools, her first job in Bucks County, Pennsylvania; she resigned in 1962 after ongoing differences with the county superintendent. She moved on to the special education division of the New Jersey school system, describing her "preventive psychiatry" with teenagers as "the best work" she had done during her lifetime.[41]

Despite not being in private practice, Muriel's involvement in CAPS continued, giving her an opportunity to share theoretical as well as clinical issues with other analysts and helping her to clarify her methodology with her own adolescent patients. The group was soon joined by Psychoanalytic Studies at Aspen, a similar organization, also founded by Muriel and Samuel Guttman.[42]

Muriel had long had an interest in the village of Aspen, beginning with a skiing trip there with Connie and Joe in 1939 just after they had all returned to the United States from Europe. Two decades later, after another family vacation, Connie and Harold fell in love with a piece of land, purchased it, and settled down. In 1962, Muriel and Joe bought their own condominium in the Colorado ski town, returning often to visit Connie and her family.

During these years, Muriel's practice of financially aiding friends and others continued. Clara Thalmann, a friend from the postwar years in Paris, was told that the loan Muriel had given her was now a gift and that Clara did not need to repay it. In accordance with her belief that nothing was more important than supporting young people who were seeking an education, Muriel sent countless people to college. A young Austrian émigré, Guntram Weissenberger, whom she first met on the ski slopes of New Hampshire, went to Harvard Business School. Peter Unterweger, the son of Joe's old friend Albin, received his degree from Rutgers University, and Jessica Lohnes, whose mother, Inga Pineo, worked for Muriel and Joe for decades, attended a private day school in Princeton and studied architecture in college. A young American named Anne Nowak graduated from medical school in Israel—all of these at Muriel's expense. There were many, many more.[43]

Muriel indulged herself also with one of the few luxuries she loved: travel. During her middle years, she crisscrossed Europe often and visited the Middle East and Moscow, among other destinations. She traveled to Moscow with

Stephen Spender in 1959, the two old friends closer now than ever. Stephen would dedicate his *Journals, 1939 to 1983,* to Muriel. A decade later, Muriel would return to Moscow, this time to visit Sergei Konenkov, now 95 and ill, but with Margarita still at his side, caring for him.[44]

In the mid-1960s, recognizing that she and Joe would not live forever and that Connie was committed to living in Aspen, Muriel decided to eventually donate Brookdale Farm and its hundreds of acres to a land conservancy, to be maintained in its natural state in perpetuity. Beginning in 1965, she gave large parcels of her land to the Stony Brook-Millstone Watershed Association. By 1984, she had given the Association a total of 585 acres—she had added to her original acreage by purchasing nearby farms—along with hundreds of thousands of dollars. Today, this watershed is the largest piece of permanently protected land in Central New Jersey.[45]

Muriel continued to see her daughter and grandchildren often, as she and Connie, although not demonstrative, shared a deep love. However, Muriel's profound feelings are on display in a poem she wrote in 1958 about Connie at 27, titled "To C":

> From crowded city streets or subway cars
> People look up, and see your face, and know
> The splendor of the mountains and the snow
> In sparkling sun or under winter stars.
> You carry scent of pine and fir-trees with you
> Carry the sky above, the snow beneath you.
> You move as though to secret music known
> Only to you, of silent-singing skiis
> Gliding through snow beneath the quiet trees
> The music of together and alone.
> Sun and untrodden snow are all about you.
> How can one know what winter is, without you?
>
> Strangers in cities chance to see your face
> And suddenly, not knowing why, remember
> The beauty of the mountains in December
> With their unhurrying time and bounteous space.
> He has heard winter's music who has found you
> With that silent symphony of snow around you.[46]

For her part, Connie would say later, "I love her a lot more than she realizes… She knows that [I love her]. I don't know if she knows, how much."[47]

In contrast to the bond between Muriel and Connie, which might not have been elucidated clearly, there was no such murkiness surrounding Muriel's feelings toward her husband. Looking back on Joe's many infidelities, but also looking forward to growing old with him—and still passionate about him— Muriel would write to her husband one morning in 1959,

> Darling—You made me very happy last night, & I go off to work happily today. I guess I had to say once without anger what I have said so often before in anger—but I don't intend to go on doing this. I don't want you (or me) to feel that I can't talk about the past without complaining, and I don't want you to be afraid I'll go on reproaching you. I don't think I'll have to. So don't be worried or sad; just love me. I love you.[48]

She signed, as she always did to Joe, "Your mouse."

CHAPTER 17

"ARE YOU JULIA?"

During Muriel's last years of formal work, late in her life, during her seventies and early eighties, she published three major books. One would affect the literary legacy of a major American author, another would add an important coda to Sigmund's Freud's own unfinished work, and a third would be an achievement in the field of mental health. For this book, she teamed up with a school psychologist to analyze children who had committed murder, or who had made serious attempts to do so. After 15 years as a member of various child-study teams, working with emotionally disturbed adolescents, Muriel began taking notes for what would eventually become *The Deadly Innocents*, an investigation of the causes of homicidal tendencies in adolescents.[1]

During these years, as Muriel continued to travel often—to Aspen to enjoy long, relaxing visits with Connie's family and to Europe either on her own or with friends or with her grandchildren—her pleasure was tempered by the losses associated with old age: illness, the deaths of close friends, and a diminution of vigor. In 1970, Muriel decided that it was time to simplify their lives, hoping to turn Brookdale Farm over to the Watershed Association. Joe, however, was strongly attached to the farmhouse and the land around it and for once, he would not give in to Muriel's wishes. He had acceded to her all their life together, which perhaps, even in small part, may have explained his infidelities. Now, stubbornly wedded to remaining in Pennington, he would not budge. Muriel, forced to find a compromise, instead arranged for them to live in a utilitarian ranch house that she had built on their land, not far from the farmhouse, so they could live more easily on one level but still enjoy the swimming pool as well as the adjacent bucolic Brookdale Farm.

She also planned to sell the East 87th Street townhouse only a decade after she'd had it built and take a smaller apartment. First, however, she and Joe had to dispose of his library of thousands of volumes. With several institutions interested in the books, Joe chose to donate his tomes on Vietnam to Harvard's Yenching Library, and then shipped his Austro-German books to a new university in Klagenfurt, in the province of Carinthia. He had spent his first years as a Social Democrat there, and he was pleased that the books would be read by scholars and students in that region.

Muriel ended up selling the Manhattan townhouse for half of its value to Phelps Stokes, an organization whose focus since its inception in 1911 has been to provide education and opportunities for Africans, African Americans, and Native Americans.[2] The couple then purchased a small apartment at 135 West 68th Street, which they would use rarely, since both preferred Pennington and their compact new house.

During these years, Muriel remained true to her lifelong values: continuing rigorous intellectual stimulation through ongoing involvement with CAPS and writing. And she never forgot to enjoy the sensual and adventurous side of life: at one annual CAPS get-together in Detroit in 1970, the 69-year-old Muriel entered the hotel lobby glowing with excitement, announcing gleefully to a group of psychoanalyst friends: "I just came in through a revolving door and a man came in with me and felt me up!"[3]

In 1971, she edited and wrote sections of The Wolf-Man by the Wolf-Man: The Double Story of Freud's Most Famous Case, meant to give readers "the human side of a struggling, passionate individual, seen both from his own point of view and from that of the founder of psychoanalysis," as she would write in the introduction. She included portions of the Wolf-Man's memoir (which she translated), some of Sigmund Freud's early analyses of his famous patient, the Wolf-Man's recollections of Freud, and an essay by Dr. Ruth Mack Brunswick, with whom the Wolf-Man had undergone further treatment. Muriel would end the book with her own analytic impressions of the Wolf-Man, whom she had known for more than 40 years. Realizing that the book would add greatly to her father's canon, Anna Freud, by now Muriel's close friend, wrote the foreword: "The Wolf-Man stands out... he is the only one able and willing to cooperate actively in the reconstruction and follow-up of his own case."[4]

Though she ended her private practice in order to work with children, Muriel's connection with psychoanalysis grew stronger over the years as she became involved with those who were in the business of preserving Sigmund Freud's legacy. Anna Freud and Dr. Kurt Eissler were the primary keepers of the Freud flame. Soon, either Muriel herself or her New-Land Foundation would be sending funds on a regular basis to several Freud-related projects; this would continue even after her death.

Throughout her seventies, Muriel was disciplined as always, and continued traveling, writing, maintaining connections—she stayed involved. When her old friend Sergei Konenkov died on October 9, 1971, Muriel set about donating an early work of his to the Soviet government in his honor. Once, at a lunch in Aspen with a young friend, Muriel saw a need to step in when she suspected the friend was a victim of domestic violence. The girl, who had a black eye, had said during that lunch that she had fallen on a ski pole. After thinking for a few minutes, Muriel said,

> You're not safe... You need to not be married to him until he has a great deal of therapy, pretty intense therapy, and until the time that he does, you're going to have it very tough with him.[5]

To this young woman, these were words of freedom: she now felt she had permission to leave her marriage.[6]

The following year, Muriel and Joe took Connie's three boys, Hal, Mark, and Joe, self-described preadolescent "ruffians" to Europe to tour Muriel's favorite cities, Vienna, Venice, London, and Paris. The boys met their grandparents' friends and overheard dinner conversations about life and death, war and peace. Their grandmother, it gradually dawned on them, was a great humanitarian and seeker of justice, "distressed as to why human beings feel this low-grade tribal instinct to kill each other,"[7] as a grandson would recall.

Returning home from this memorable trip, and planning another one for Connie's three daughters, Muriel would hear about a new book that was garnering accolades from both critics and the public: the playwright and memoirist Lillian Hellman had published *Pentimento*, a collection of autobiographical essays and stories, including a fascinating portrait of her friend "Julia" who had been a hero of the Austrian resistance during the 1930s.

Muriel paid "Julia" little heed at the time because she was fully occupied with Joe. In the early 1970s, he first became absent-minded, then forgetful, and finally lost his memory completely. Muriel's reaction to this great loss was resignation: "Here comes that sad part of life," one of her grandsons remembered her saying.[8] She was grieved by Joe's illness, but not despairing and never out of control.

As he became more ill, Joe's personality was changing, and this was the most difficult part for Muriel. He would ask her the same question repeatedly, forgetting her answer almost as soon as he heard it, and, worse, he was beginning to forget the past they shared, those years in Vienna that bound them together. But doctors offered no immediate diagnosis for Joe's condition.

Muriel knew she had to stay connected to people other than her husband. Soon she was participating in another endeavor, a program at Yale University where faculty members from the humanities and the psychoanalytic community came together to share their concerns. After Muriel's New-Land Foundation endowed the Yale program permanently in the mid-seventies, the program was renamed the Muriel Gardiner Program in Psychoanalysis and the Humanities.[9]

Over the next few years, as Muriel completed her study of children who commit murder, Joe continued his decline. By 1976, her husband, the only man she had ever loved with unalloyed passion, was diagnosed with Alzheimer's, and "the sad part of life" took over Muriel's daily existence with a vehemence and strength that would all but sap her being.

Nevertheless, she managed to find pleasure that year in the publication of her second book, *The Deadly Innocents: Portraits of Children Who Kill,* with an introduction by Stephen Spender. After all, it marked the culmination not only of Muriel's research of these troubled adolescents, but of her close relationship with many of them: "She had a boy living with her. Every time people met him, he would say, 'My name is John. I killed my mother with an axe,'" as a friend would remember. Focusing on how schools can try to prevent such terrible crimes by providing what Muriel called "preventive psychiatry," the book was based on Muriel's many visits to prisons and reformatories to interview young murderers. After this experience, she would spend several years as a volunteer psychiatrist working with inmates, "heartbreaking work since I could do so little to help these patients," she wrote.[10]

Comparable only to her efforts in the Austrian resistance, helping to save lives, Muriel found this work with troubled young people most gratifying since it was meant to avert rather than repair damage already done. Her work was clinical, as well as educational, allowing her to put to use all that she had learned during a lifetime of studying psychiatry.[11] Now she found this work, and her writing, antidotes to the growing pain of watching her husband's mind disintegrate.

Trying to keep busy, in part to avoid dwelling on Joe, Muriel offered to edit a memoir written by her old friend Auge, even as she continued her financial support of individuals and organizations. In one year, she gave $20,000 to CAPS and paid more than $10,000 for Joe's grandnephew to attend boarding school. She continued to travel, but now she crossed the Atlantic by jet rather than by ocean liner. She hated flying so much, however, that she carried with her large quantities of her signature drink, vodka and lemon juice—the mixture she imbibed every evening. Although she traveled coach, eschewing those old family values, once in the air, she asked for ice in a manner that seemed as if she were in first class, and got it.[12]

In 1978, the International Rescue Committee awarded Joe its Freedom Award, with a proud Muriel looking on. Only a year later she was forced to hire a full-time caregiver for her husband, as he could no longer take care of himself. Before Muriel hired this woman, his dependence on her had been total. He was unable to read because he could not remember what had been on the previous page, and he constantly asked Muriel questions, sometimes the same one five times in an hour. She often found that she had things to do away from home, but it was difficult to leave Joe.

Stephen Spender and his wife, Natasha, visited Pennington in August 1980, and sat with Muriel and Joe in their living room, which was filled with reminders of the past: books by and about Freud, volumes of Stephen's poetry, illustrated tomes of favorite European cities, Muriel's mouse collection—stemming from Connie's love of mice as a child, and Muriel's own intimate nickname with Joe, "Mouse"—as well as Konenkov's art in the form of busts of Muriel, Joe, and Lenin. The couple's award for aiding dissidents during the Hungarian Revolution hung on the wall.[13]

As Stephen recounted, Joe stared out the window, interrupting the conversation of the others with unconnected observations: "Look, a bird is flying across the sky...a bird is sitting on a branch...the sun is now descending in the West. It is partly hidden by a cloud, but will soon go under." Joe always retained his flirtatiousness, however, as he twinkled at Natasha: "The flowers on your dress are beautiful. But what is underneath must be still more beautiful."[14]

Despite her sadness over Joe's condition, Muriel soon became involved in both a project and a controversy that would, at the very least, take her mind off him for a while. Over the last few years, since the appearance in 1977 of the film version of Lillian Hellman's essay "Julia," Muriel had been receiving more and more calls from friends insisting that *she* was Julia. The first call came from her old comrade, Anna Frank Loeb.[15] Anna had been married to Karl Frank all those years ago during the heady resistance days, and then, in New York, had helped form the Emergency Rescue Committee with the support of Eleanor Roosevelt. Muriel now reread "Julia" closely and found herself thinking that since she had heard quite a lot about Hellman from Wolf Schwabacher, with whom she had shared Brookdale Farm from 1940 to 1951, Hellman must have heard about Muriel as well: Schwabacher had also been Hellman's lawyer.

Muriel would express surprise in talking to friends that she had never met "Julia," even though it seemed that they should have encountered each other since both were doing resistance work during the same period, in the same place.[16] And there were other similarities: both she and "Julia" came from a "very rich family," and both were intent on sharing their fortunes with others. "Julia had dark hair, a beauty unique to her," Hellman had written, a perfect description of the young Muriel. Both women attended Oxford, then went to Vienna for psychoanalysis, and finally enrolled in medical school at the University of Vienna. Julia, like Muriel, used money sent by her bank to help people fleeing the Nazis and both saved lives though their work in the resistance.[17]

The similarity was more than uncanny: it was unbelievable. It was, in its own way, plagiarism of Muriel's life.

Although it is not clear that Muriel ever knew the extent to which Hellman had used her life as a motif, the American writer had created versions of Muriel in two other works: one in *Watch on the Rhine*, and a precursor to "Julia," a woman she named "Alice" in her 1969 memoir *An Unfinished Woman*.

> Her father was a rich Jew from Detroit and she was already started on the road to Marxism that would lead her, as a student doctor, to be killed in the Vienna riots of 1934.[18]

Hellman first borrowed Muriel's life a few months after Muriel moved to Pennington in 1940 with Joe and Connie, creating the wealthy American Sara Muller, the wife of a European resistance leader, who had returned with their three children (Connie finally got her sisters and brothers) to the United States. First produced on the Broadway stage in 1941, and made into a 1943 film with Bette Davis and the Hungarian-born actor Paul Lukas, *Watch on the Rhine* took its name from the patriotic German song made famous in *Casablanca*: Nazis drinking in Rick's Café Américain loudly sang "Die Wacht am Rhein," but loyal French citizens drowned them out with the "Marseillaise."

Watch on the Rhine is another melodramatic depiction of the pitched battle between the forces of good, exemplified by Sara and Kurt Muller—Muriel and Joe—and evil, in this case, a Nazi-sympathizing double-dealing European who sold information about Sara's husband to Nazis at the German embassy in Washington, where the play is set.

Since *Watch on the Rhine* appeared on the American cultural scene not long after Muriel and Joe's return from Europe, she had missed both play and film. Now, however, more than thirty years later, Muriel, quite aware of Lillian Hellman, announced that she had "discovered quite amazing similarities between her life and Julia's."[19] Lillian Hellman recognized a good story when she heard it, and Muriel had "not only lodged in Hellman's consciousness in 1939, but…remained there for thirty-four years," as Hellman biographer William Wright would write.[20] When Hellman created a work with Muriel as her model, the results would be inspiring, bestselling, and award-winning. *Watch on the Rhine* was judged best picture by the New York Film Critics Circle, and the film's lead, Paul Lukas, won win the 1943 Academy Award for Best

Actor. Thirty-four years later, the film *Julia* won three academy awards out of eleven nominations, and was named Best Film by BAFTA, the British Academy of Film and Television Arts. Hellman failed, however, to give the person who motivated these stories credit in any way.

Muriel would later tell friends that she thought Hellman's war tale was silly: "How absurd to think that the likes of Jane Fonda could have sat unobserved, wearing that ridiculous hat, waiting for Vanessa Redgrave in the middle of a restaurant in broad daylight in Nazi Berlin!" Nothing in *Julia* seemed realistic to someone like Muriel, who was, after all, familiar with the work of the resistance. "Conspirators simply didn't act so silly. You couldn't do that and survive," Muriel said.[21] But these were all private discussions between Muriel and her friends: Muriel at first refused to say anything directly to Hellman.

Coincidentally, by the time she became truly conscious of the "Julia" situation, Muriel had already begun writing her own memoir. She had started it in 1975, inspired by Joe's earlier request to interweave both their memoirs, chapter by chapter. But Muriel found that she was unhappy revealing personal thoughts and emotions and so had dropped the project. She picked it up again two years later, resolved to simply recount her relationship with world events as they unfolded in Austria, omitting any intimate details and feelings.[22]

Her modesty was so ingrained that she wrote: "I was inhibited by feelings of privacy and by my training…in keeping confidences. I was simply unable to write openly about many important aspects of my life."[23]

But in 1976, she did finally write a letter to Hellman:

Ever since your beautiful book *Pentimento* appeared, friends and acquaintances have been asking me whether I am Julia. Unlike your Julia, I am—obviously—still alive, and I have not been wounded and my daughter lives with her family in Aspen, Colorado. But many other things in Julia's life agree with mine.

My parents were rich Americans who traveled a great deal. After my father's death, in my childhood, my mother married an Englishman. At twenty-one I went to Oxford to study English literature. I had been to Wellesley before that, and there had become a Socialist (though I did not call myself that) and had brought Norman Thomas, Roger Baldwin and others to Wellesley to talk to our Student Forum. After Oxford I went to Vienna, hoping to be analyzed by Freud, who however, referred me to a pupil of his. Wishing to become an analyst, I studied medicine at the University of Vienna, and eventually got my degree there—under Hitler in 1938! I had been inactive politically in Europe until February 1934, but from then on was very much involved in anti-Fascist and anti-Nazi work. I enclosed a little essay my husband wrote about for a psychoanalytic journal containing "tributes" to me on my seventieth birthday ["Mary," Bulletin of the Philadelphia Association for Psychoanalysis, June 1972].

Some of my loving friends even think your descriptions of Julia apply to me, and wonder whether she could be a composite of several persons. I do not at all think so, but cannot help wondering that I never—as far as I know—met Julia. Nor have I met you, though I heard of you often from our good friend, Wolf Schwabacher, with whom we shared a two-family house in Pennington for many years, and I have seen and admired many of your plays and enjoyed your books.

I hope you do not find this letter an intrusion. There is no need to answer it. I often thought of writing you before but did not want to bother you. Now, however, several more recent friends have again asked, "Are you Julia?" and one called me, having cried herself to sleep after reading your moving story.[24]

Hellman took Muriel at her word, and did not answer the letter.

In "Julia," Hellman was the hero of the story, a spin picked up by one critic who wrote that the story was "out of whack" because the author had made "the acts of bravery and devotion" hers, rather than Julia's.[25] Julia, although colorful and courageous, became secondary in Hellman's version of Muriel's life.

Shortly before Muriel's seventy-eighth birthday, the Hellman controversy heated up: on October 18, 1979, the writer Mary McCarthy said of Lillian Hellman on the Dick Cavett Show, "Every word she writes is a lie, including 'and' and 'the.'" Four months later, an outraged Hellman filed a civil lawsuit for $2.25 million against McCarthy. And McCarthy would begin a determined documentation of Hellman's lies, including "shamelessly stealing another woman's story,"[26] referring, of course, to Muriel's.

After McCarthy had been working on her defense for a time, it became obvious that Julia, Sara Muller, and Alice were all versions of Muriel. In 1980, while Hellman was furiously trying to get in touch with Muriel to ask her to state publicly that she had no claim to "Julia," Muriel was in a hospital in Rome with pneumonia and further complications. A worried Connie rushed to her mother's side and found, instead of a sick old woman, a charmer in a hospital bed, seductive and playful with her doctor.[27] All thoughts of Hellman gone from her head for now, Muriel returned to Pennington with Connie, who stayed until her mother was completely recovered. Pleased with her adored daughter's display of affectionate concern, Muriel wrote to Anna Freud:

> Connie & I love each other beyond words, but are not always able to show it, but this time we could. I also learned how much the grandchildren love me.[28]

That same year, Muriel would be honored with the Austrian Cross of Honor, First Class, presented to her at a ceremony at the Austrian Consulate in New York City.[29]

Around the same time, as she entered her ninth decade, Muriel experienced great loss: she had lost three of her oldest and dearest friends, and Joe grew worse by the day. Finally, in 1981, she saw that the only practical solution was to place him in a special facility for patients with Alzheimer's and other types of dementia since, even with help, she could no longer care for him at home. Grieving, she would write, "He remembers <u>nothing</u> of his earlier life except vaguely how he met me but even this one memory is all wrong." Missing the Joe who had been the center of her life since 1935, Muriel wrote to Anna Freud: "One has to dread each coming year more and more. Nothing can make up for this…"[30]

Meanwhile, the Hellman-McCarthy battle continued, with Muriel remaining quietly in the background, confiding privately to various friends that she was angry with Hellman for appropriating her life. She would never sue, however. She shied away from lawsuits as a form of argument, although she would soon, quite against her will, become painfully embroiled in one.

Her memoir and Joe's, written several years earlier, had been published in Vienna in 1978 as a double autobiography under the title *Damit Wir Nicht Vergessen* or "Lest We Forget." Now Muriel decided she would try to publish in English a separate version of her own time in the resistance. She would call it *The Crowded Hour: An American Woman in the Austrian Underground*, taking her title from Sir Walter Scott's borrowed line, "One crowded hour of glorious life / Is worth an age without a name." Anna Freud agreed to write the foreword and soon Muriel had a publisher, Yale University Press, and an editor, Gladys Topkis. Muriel had already spoken with Dr. Herbert Steiner, head of the Dokumentationsarchiv des österreichischen Widerstandes (DöW) or the Documentary Archives of the Austrian Resistance, in Vienna, who had confirmed that he knew of no other English or American woman in the resistance. He had also asked many resistance fighters from the old days if they knew of any Americans besides Muriel who were involved, and they had all said, "Only Mary."[31]

Muriel, at one point, considered exploiting "Julia" as Hellman had exploited her, as indicated in a letter her editor wrote to her:

> We're going to try to come up with a new title...I don't think you can use "Julia" in the title—but there's nothing to stop you from calling it "Pentimento" if you want to—titles can't be copyrighted.[32]

But since Muriel was never confrontational, although she had no problem making firm and unshakeable decisions, it was helpful to have other people state publicly what she was thinking privately. Muriel would leave the battle to Mary McCarthy. After all, it was McCarthy who had her "rapier, the verbal sword."[33]

When news of Muriel's memoir came out, shortly before its release date, Hellman tried to quash the book, calling Gladys Topkis at Yale University Press, who recalled, "I think what she wanted to do was bully us into stopping the book."[34]

In April 1983, apparently overlooking Muriel's letter to her seven years earlier, Lillian Hellman was quoted in an article:

> Miss Hellman said that she had never heard of Dr. Gardiner until this week. "She may have been the model for somebody else's Julia, but she was certainly not the model for my Julia," she said.[35]

Muriel enjoyed herself throughout 1983. Upon the publication of *Code Name "Mary"* on May 18, the Austrian Consulate in New York threw a book party. Some of the guests included people whose lives Muriel had saved—or their children. At about the same time, the spring issue of *Vogue* ran a full-page photograph of the 81-year-old in a maillot bathing suit. Muriel, the editors wrote, "remains bracing proof that the individual still makes an impact," thus acknowledging the important work she had done, and also flattering her vanity: though she never wore any makeup or jewelry, she remained vain about her body and loved showing it off, dressing in simply cut, but possibly custom made, form-fitting sheath dresses.[36]

She had another chance to show her body off when a director and producer team came to New York to make a documentary film about her, called *The Real Julia: The Muriel Gardiner Story*. They interviewed some Austrians whose lives she had saved, and they induced Stephen Spender to be in the film. Later he would say how much he disliked their probing questions about his and Muriel's long-ago affair: "Why don't they ask us to take off our clothes, and watch us make macabre love with our wrinkled old bodies?" Unlike Stephen, though,

Muriel might have enjoyed it. In Pennington for more filming, Muriel went skinny-dipping in her pool. When she emerged, naked and dripping, she called out to the filmmaker sitting poolside, "Not bad, huh?"[37]

The month *Code Name "Mary"* was published, Lillian Hellman's psychiatrist, Dr. George Gero, left a message for Muriel: Would she write a statement saying that she was not "Julia?" He called a second time and repeated Hellman's request. Muriel responded that she had never claimed to be "Julia." Finally, Hellman herself called and said she would like to meet Muriel. But Muriel was then ill in bed and so invited Hellman to Pennington. Hellman agreed, then said she would like to bring a "charming young man" with her. Muriel assumed that meant she would bring a lawyer, and so responded that she too would have a friend by her side.

When Hellman called a second time, Muriel said she had pneumonia and had to postpone their meeting. Then Hellman said she wanted to explain why she had never answered Muriel's letter—the one Muriel had written in 1976. But neither woman could hear well so both finally agreed to have Hellman's secretary tell Muriel's assistant why Hellman had not answered the letter. Hellman then said perhaps she would have her lawyer explain instead. Then, since she had to think this over, she said she'd call back. She never did.[38]

Hellman died a year later, on June 30, 1984, never having met Muriel Gardiner, her *leit-motif*, her hero.

CHAPTER 18

THE CHOICE

Muriel would follow Hellman by eight months.

She managed, during her early eighties, to take pleasure in her life but found her enjoyment considerably diminished by an ugly lawsuit against her and others regarding Sigmund Freud. Freud's legacy had required considerable attention and backing from Muriel, as well as from others, including his daughter, Anna, and the eminent psychoanalyst Dr. Kurt Eissler. Almost from its inception in the 1950s, Muriel had helped fund the Sigmund Freud Archives.[1] Established under the laws of New York State, the institution had been created to collect Freud's manuscripts and store them permanently in the Library of Congress. There, conscientious archivists carefully followed Anna Freud's and Eissler's proscriptions about when to open each document to scholars.

Muriel, who maintained a close relationship with both Anna Freud and Eissler, was convinced that Freud's legacy should be preserved. She had even purchased his last residence, 20 Maresfield Gardens in the Hampstead section of London, thus allowing Anna to live out her years there. The site would later become home to the Freud Museum. Muriel also financed a worldwide search for items missing from Freud's correspondence, paying for letters and other items that she then donated to the Library of Congress for the use of scholars.[2]

In 1982, as a result of a $30,000 donation from Muriel's New-Land Foundation to pay an annual salary to the archives' new projects director, Jeffrey Masson, Muriel found herself entangled in the kind of imbroglio she had always tried to avoid: a lawsuit. The suit arose from what one news publication had dubbed "the Watergate of psychoanalysis."[3]

In late 1981, Masson made a public statement that, in his view, Freud had incorrectly abandoned his original seduction theory—"Masson even implied that Freud had changed his mind because he could not face the prevalence of child molestation and abuse in Vienna...."[4] Though he had been hired only two years earlier, Masson was swiftly fired for airing this controversial opinion. Just as quickly, he filed a $13 million lawsuit against Muriel, New-Land, Muriel's grandson Hal Harvey, the Freud Archives, and Eissler.

This legal action devastated Muriel. She had first met the soon-to-be defrocked projects director in 1978, and recalled that: "My first impression of him was that he was slick. 'Slick' may be too strong—'facile' may be the right word." Nonetheless, Muriel and Masson had enjoyed a warm relationship and, even after he was fired, Muriel observed, with no rancor, "I consider him a good and energetic worker and a worthwhile scholar."[5]

After the lawsuit was filed in 1982, Muriel, who never spoke negatively about anyone, said only that she could no longer treat Masson with civility: "A decent person who considers himself your friend doesn't turn around and sue you."[6] The firing of Masson arose from an assumption by Eissler and the board of the Freud Archives that there was a single orthodox interpretation of Freud, and their professed belief that deviation from that convention was akin to apostasy. For this, according to the board and Eissler, Masson should lose his job. Muriel agreed with them, for the most part, unable to see that Eissler and the others were bullying their employee in the same way that hated political figures had oppressed those they disagreed with throughout her lifetime. Her loyalty to Anna Freud and Kurt Eissler simply overcame any doubts she might have had.

But this lawsuit was the very thing she was trying to avoid with Lillian Hellman, for she was convinced that people could and should find peaceful ways to resolve their disputes. Masson's legal action came not long after Muriel, her heart breaking, had placed Joe in a nursing home.

She also was facing her own complex health issues. Her grandson Hal would recall,

> The lawsuit upset her greatly. It really bothered her. It kept her from sleeping and these were the last years of her life—it was the last thing she needed. So we settled the suit...It wasn't a huge amount of money, but to blackmail somebody by torturing an old woman who is nothing but benevolent? That's low.[7]

Muriel wanted to do anything to cut short the lawsuit. She ended up paying Masson $150,000 to drop the case, giving him half in August 1982 when the settlement was signed, and the final $75,000 in May 1983. A year later, Masson filed yet another lawsuit, this time for libel against the writer Janet Malcolm, but in this case, the defendant chose to fight.[8]

In the midst of all this drama, on October 9, 1982, Muriel's dear friend Anna Freud died. Anna's house, containing Freud's library and many of his papers, needed organization, and Muriel and the New-Land Foundation stepped in, sending Hal to London. Only in his early twenties, the competent young man was nevertheless on New-Land's board of directors. He hired a caretaker to secure the house and began talking to curators and museum administrators. Eventually, over the next years, Hal and Muriel's attorneys inventoried the house, packed it up, rebuilt it, hired staff, installed security systems, and opened the Freud Museum.[9]

Muriel and Hal's approach to the Freud museum emphasized education and inquiry—they had the goal of turning it into a British institution. Today, the museum, in a large house on a leafy London street, receives continuing support of £90,000 annually from New-Land and is a British-registered charity.[10]

Despite her loss of friends like Anna Freud and Joe's illness, Muriel continued to relish the good things in life, the public attention that came from the 1983 publication of *Code Name "Mary,"* visits with Connie and her children and seeing friends. She would not, however, visit Joe because of the distress it caused him, not her. Even though he could not really recognize her, he became agitated at the sight of her, as if she represented all he had forgotten but could still sense vaguely, at least enough to grasp that he had lost something. Instead of going herself, she sent Inga Pineo, Joe's former caregiver, now Muriel's assistant, for regular visits to the man she had loved for so long. Feeling her years, early in 1984, Muriel began to plan a move to a retirement home, Meadow Lakes, in Hightstown, about 20 minutes from Brookdale Farm.

Muriel was always in contact with her six grandchildren, and through this communication, she demonstrated her lifelong belief in the importance of education and was inspired to embark on her next endeavor. In correspondence with her granddaughter Ann about nature versus nurture, Muriel strongly sided with education as being the dominant component in forming character. "I am a teacher at heart," she wrote.[11] The exchange of ideas with Ann invigorated her. Suddenly, Muriel announced her intention to write her fourth book, its subject racial prejudice during the 1940s, with the material based on her work at the Trenton hospital. She had, years before, written many essays and stories about her experience. Feeling a burst of energy, she even joked about having new business cards printed: "They would read, 'Muriel Gardiner, AKA Muriel Gardiner Buttinger. Profession—pleasure. Address—travel.'"[12]

In April 1984, Marcia Burick, a member of the Wellesley Alumnae Association, visited Muriel in Pennington, anxious to meet such a clearly generous and charming woman—the hero depicted in *Code Name "Mary."* They began with tea and switched to Muriel's favorite, vodka with lemon juice, as the day wore on, which was, by Burick's recollection, probably by eleven o'clock in the morning. The two women, one young and one old, had an intimate visit that caused them to agree that they would surely continue their new friendship. Burick would later say,

> Muriel looked like Vanessa Redgrave, tall and elegant, with irregular features. She was so in love with her husband. She just kept talking about how wonderful he was and how happy they had been.[13]

Later that month, Muriel heard that she would be a recipient of the Wellesley Alumnae Achievement Award, the college's highest honor, for the year 1985. She had first been nominated in the late 1970s, and it had taken six years for her to win the award: "They had to name her sister first,"[14] one alumna recalled. Ruth received the award in 1983. One can only imagine Muriel's emotions upon learning that she would, finally, receive the same honor as had her older sister, with whom she had been in competition for 80 years. It probably didn't escape her notice—or Ruth's—that once again, Ruth got to go first.

In the summer of 1984, Muriel was saddened by the death of her old friend Auge, Felix Augenfeld—who had designed not only her much-loved cottage in the Vienna Woods and her Manhattan townhouse, but also Freud's special chair. Soon, however, she was immersed in a new project: she was to be a panelist at a Washington, D.C., conference on September 19, 1984, "Faith in Humankind, Rescuers of the Jews during the Holocaust," sponsored by the United States Holocaust Memorial Council.[15]

Three months after the conference, in December 1984, Muriel moved into Meadow Lakes. Her apartment had been painted and furnished with some of her belongings. But only a few weeks later, on January 7, 1985, she began to feel ill and drove to see her doctor. The diagnosis was pneumonia, and Muriel was admitted to the Princeton Medical Center. A chest x-ray revealed nodules in her left lung, and a biopsy confirmed the diagnosis: inoperable lung cancer. Connie arrived at the Medical Center within days. "[My mother] knew she was dying. She accepted that. She refused any extra treatment—no chemo, no radiation," Connie would recall. Visitors began to come. Muriel made certain that her various protégés—the many young people whose education she was paying for—would be taken care of after her death. Intending the funding to continue as a "tool to promote ideas, do good work, help people, promote friendship and the environment," as one friend would say, she set about making certain that her will was in order.[16]

She left several hundred thousand dollars to maintain the Stony Brook-Millstone Watershed to ensure that those 600 acres would remain forever wild. She also donated to the Watershed to use as an education center the little ranch house that she and Joe had lived in at the end of their lives together. She ensured that the New-Land Foundation would continue to fund the causes she had cared about all her life: world peace, justice, population control, civil rights, and newly added, preservation of the environment.

It seemed at times as if her hospital room doorway were a revolving one, with people coming in and out daily, determined to see her one more time. Connie managed to get Muriel's dearest and oldest friend, Gladys Lack, to Princeton, the wheelchair-bound woman aided all the way by people Connie had hired so that her mother and Gladys could say their goodbyes. The two women spent three days together. Joe's nephew, Dennis Buttinger, came to visit. "She had sort of invited me to come just to say goodbye," he would recall. She looked tired but also in control—as she had always been in charge of her destiny.[17]

Jessica Lohnes, who Muriel had put through school, came to say goodbye to the woman she called her "fairy godmother."

> She was a very tall woman, and slender, and her arms were sort of lanky…she opened her big arms and [we] hugged…She said, "I'll always be there for you." And, you know, she is.[18]

Muriel set up her own life, even at the end. She refused to burden anyone, turning down an invitation from Connie to come and live with her in Aspen. Connie, following Muriel's directions, bequeathed her books to a variety of places. Her sister, Ruth, also came to visit, and her grandchildren visited on many occasions—on January 26 all of them came at once, causing a sensation in the hospital.[19]

Although very ill, Muriel sat up in her hospital bed, receiving friends and family, never complaining, with a beatific look on her beautiful face, as graceful in illness and death as she had been in life, her grandson Mark recalled. When he left for the last time, "she just sort of clung to my hand a little longer, and looked at me with just very loving eyes, full of expression and emotion. I had a sense that was it. I think she knew that was the last time she'd see me."[20]

Although she knew she was dying, Muriel still had plans for the future: she wanted to go to Wellesley that spring to accept her Alumnae Achievement Award, and she had intended to be at the wedding of one of her granddaughters in August. But she also was prepared to let go, as she told Connie. Always pragmatic, Muriel had often expressed her attitude toward death; she had written in 1983,

> I feel so strongly that a sudden death, without a long period of mental deterioration is better than a life stretched out longer with suffering for the patient as well as those around him.[21]

It was a subject to which Muriel had given much consideration, especially after Joe fell ill. She had discussed it with Anna Freud, who had expressed sympathy and understanding toward Muriel's "loss" of Joe, and had written:

> There is nothing worse than to see the people nearest to one lose the very qualities for which one loves them. I was spared that with my father, who was himself to the last minutes.[22]

Muriel did not want such decay for herself, did not want those who loved her to watch her humanity slowly disintegrate as she lay dying, most likely in agony. To ensure that she would not meet that kind of end, Muriel had long kept "enough Seconal tablets to kill her," Stephen Spender would write, "hoping that if she did have a fatal illness, it would not take a form which deprived her of the will power to do this."[23]

Muriel also had no use for funerals and burials and mourning, expressing throughout her life a dislike of such traditions, a loathing of cemeteries, and an admiration for people who just got on with it, as Albert Einstein had done, eschewing long drawn-out morbid rituals. For herself, Muriel would request no funeral and no flowers.

On the last day of her life, February 6, Muriel was alone in the hospital, all the visitors gone except for Connie. Stephen Spender had not visited Muriel but the last time the two old friends had been together in Pennington, Muriel had talked, really talked, to him. She remembered her beginnings as a slaughterhouse heiress, one who had learned early on, in the way young children often do, to distance herself from what she gradually came to view as her father's killing of innocent, dumb animals for his family's gain. Gradually, she came to forgive him for perpetrating such horror. Practice in compartmentalizing her emotions from an early age allowed her the strength to save from imminent death those who were hunted during the war, while it also led her to seek an outlet for her fraught, contained emotions in the analytic dissection offered by psychoanalysis. With such a science, Muriel approached the very heart of being human even as she was able to distance herself from its tragedies.

She told Stephen that in her youth, she had felt guilty about being wealthy and thought she would be happier being less privileged. Later, she had come to appreciate her money because she had been able to use it for victims of the Nazis. Now she understand that her wealth meant that her beloved Joe would always be cared for, no matter what happened to her. Money wasn't the cause of evil in the world, she declared. How people spend it is.[24]

It would be Stephen, then, who would be the first to know. When he learned she was gravely ill, he had sent a loving reminiscent telegram to his dear friend, who responded a short time later with a telephone call. As if she were leaving for Europe, or just going on another journey, Muriel said casually, "Oh yes, I'm dying,"[25] and then went on to talk of other things. Finally, before she said good-bye, she informed Stephen gently, that she would be gone within a day or two.

And she was.

ACKNOWLEDGMENTS

Many people helped me by generously providing research assistance, technical support, translations, typing and transcribing, and editorial guidance. Others graciously spent hours talking about Muriel Gardiner and her life, and answering my endless questions. I thank all of you from my heart: Henry Albarelli; Kelly Alford; Mauro Bacolo; Michael Bakwin; E. M. Bakwin; Otto Franz Bauer; Lucy Billig; Edward Bligh; Johannes Breit; Joerg Breitenbach; Marcia Burick; Michael Burlingham; Robina Pelham Burn; Dennis Buttinger; Malcolm Collins; Alice Colonna; George Czuczka; Lara Feigel; Eugen Freund; Anna Geisler; Natascha Gruber; Irene Guttman; Ruth Hite; Jeff Hoagland; Jed Horne; Dan Jacobs; Gil Jawetz; Trudy Jeremias; Gislaine Jouanneau; Tana Kamine; Al Kastner; Anton Kris; Katie Larrick; Kathy Leichter; Franz Leichter; Andrea Leitner; Nina Lieberman; Peter Loewenberg; Jessica Lohnes; Melissa Lumbroso; Leora Magier; Janet Malcolm; Elisabeth Malleiere; Iris Meder; Tracey Middlekauff; Michael Molnar; Ann Nowak; Edith Ochs; Nancy Olson; Dennis Ostermaier; Gustav Papanek; Karl Pfeiffer; Herbert Posch; Gerd Rainer-Horn; Brigitte Rath; Esther Ratner; Krista Reynen; Murray Richman; Elise Rogawski; E. Philip Rosner; Renee Schwartz; Andrea Selch; Patricia Selch; Charles H. Silberstein; Nick Sonderup; Muriel Silberstein Storfer; Lady Natasha Spender; Gladys Topkis; Peter Unterweger; Joan Unterweger; Monique King; Larkin Warren; Brenda Webster; Marcus von Nordheim; Guntram Weissenberger; Elizabeth Zitrin; Arthur Zitrin.

In the archives, my gratitude to the scholarly and patient archivists for their help: Ian Graham, associate archivist at Wellesley College; Michelle Ladew, administrator at the Center for Advanced Psychoanalytic Studies (CAPS); the staff at the Dokumentationsarchiv des österreichischen Widerstandes (DöW), in Vienna; Stephen E. Novak, head of Archives and Special Collections, Office of Education and Scholarly Resources, Augustus C. Long Health Sciences Library, Columbia University Medical Center; Michael Simonson, archivist at the Leo Baeck Institute; Dr. Raymond Lum at the Harvard-Yenching Library; Wilma Slaight, former archivist at the Wellesley College Archives; David Smith, Librarian, St. Anne's College, Oxford; Olga Umansky, librarian and archivist at the Boston Psychoanalytic Society and Institute Archives; and a very special thank you to Dr. Leonard Bruno, manuscript specialist at the Library of Congress.

I am very grateful to Marist College, where I teach, for help from so many: from students who transcribed, typed, and filed—Samantha Accurso, Alex Shippee, and Elyse Brendlen—to Elisabeth Tavarez and Donna Moran in the president's office, and Chief Public Affairs Officer Timmian Massie. A special thank you to Marist reference librarian Ruth "Pepper" Boetcker, whose research skills are matched only by her patience and good cheer. Finally, I am deeply grateful to Marist President Dennis Murray. Without his support this book could not have been written.

As always, my gratitude to typist/transcriber without peer, Sarah Beaver, who has been with me now for five books. Special appreciation to a most talented translator, Jan Kohn, to former Austrian citizen Kurt Sonnenfeld, for patiently answering all my questions about the Social Democrats in Vienna, to Muriel's family—Connie, Hal, Ann, Joan, and Mark Harvey—for hospitality and helpfulness, and to Rachel Noto and Linda Nova for photographs.

I thank my editor, Alessandra Bastagli, and her team at Palgrave Macmillan, especially Donna Cherry, and my literary agent, Will Lippincott of Lippincott Massie and McQuilkin, who goes above and beyond. My gratitude to Ellen Schonfeld for friendship and research help, and to my daughter Sunshine Flint for ideas and editorial guidance. To my dear Laura Claridge, who spent endless hours of her precious time improving this manuscript, I can never thank you enough.

Finally, my deepest gratitude to my husband, Chris Collins. He never disappoints me.

NOTES

PROLOGUE

1. Muriel Gardiner Notes: Outlines, notes, and drafts for memoirs, unpaginated and undated, in the private collection of Connie Harvey. Hereafter these documents will be referred to as MGN.
2. Stanley Cohen, quoted in Mica Nava, "The Unconscious and Others: Rescue, Inclusivity and the Eroticisation of Difference in 1930s Vienna," in *Culture and the Unconscious*, ed. Caroline Bainbridge, Susannah Radstone, Michael Rustin, and Candida Yates (New York: Palgrave Macmillan, 2007), 265.
3. Anna Freud, Foreword, in Muriel Gardiner, *Code Name "Mary": Memoirs of an American Woman in the Austrian Underground* (New Haven, CT: Yale University Press, 1983), xi.
4. MGN.
5. Wilhelm Keppler, quoted in Dieter Wagner and Gerhard Tomkowitz, *Anschluss: The Week Hitler Seized Vienna*, trans. Geoffrey Strachan (New York: St. Martin's Press, 1971), 23.
6. MGN.
7. Joseph Buttinger, *In the Twilight of Socialism: A History of the Revolutionary Socialists of Austria*, trans. E. B. Ashton (New York: F. A. Praeger, 1953), 470.
8. Wagner and Tomkowitz, *Anschluss*, 40.
9. MGN.
10. MGN.
11. MGN; "The Reminiscences of Muriel Gardiner," an oral history memoir, the result of 11 tape-recorded interview sessions with Dr. Muriel Gardiner, conducted by Dr. Bluma Swerdloff in 1977 and 1981, Psychoanalytic Movement Oral History Project, Oral History Research Office, Columbia University, 77. Hereafter referred to as REMINISCENCES.
12. MGN.
13. MGN.
14. MGN.
15. MGN.
16. REMINISCENCES, 58.
17. Stephen Spender, *World within World: The Autobiography of Stephen Spender* (New York: Modern Library, 2001), 377.
18. "Hitler Arrives in Vienna," CBS, March 14, 1938, Museum of Broadcast Communications, http://archives.museum.tv/archives.
19. MGN.
20. Civilian Agency Records, State Department and Foreign Affairs Records, "Records of the Foreign Service Posts of the Department of State," RG 84, National Archives, http://www.archives.gov/research/holocaust/finding-aid/civilian/rg-84-austria.html.
21. MGN.
22. MGN.

CHAPTER 1   CHICAGO: SWIFTS AND MORRISES

1. Helen Swift, *"My Mother and My Father,"* privately printed, 39, in private family collection.
2. Walter Roth, "Nelson Morris and the Yards," *Chicago Jewish History* 32, no. 2 (Spring 2008).
3. Horace Greeley, "Editorial," *New York Tribune*, July 13, 1865.
4. Roth, "Nelson Morris and the Yards."

5. Ralph Dainty, *Darling-Delaware Centenary: 1882–1982* (Chicago: Darling-Delaware Company, 1981), 144.

6. Helen Swift, *My Mother and My Father*, 49.

7. Dainty, *Darling-Delaware Centenary: 1882–1982*, 63–70.

8. Louis P. Cain, "Innovation, Invention, and Chicago Business," http://www.encyclopedia.chicago history.org/pages/643.html; Frederic Cople Jaher, *The Urban Establishment: Upper Strata in Boston, New York, Charleston, Chicago, and Los Angeles* (Urbana: University of Illinois Press, 1982), 460; "Union Stock Yard Gate," http:egov.cityofchicago.org/Landmarks/U/UnionStock. html.

9. Dainty, *Darling-Delaware Centenary*, 78.

10. Ibid., 57.

11. *Chicago: City of the Century*, WGBH-Boston, January 2003.

12. Ibid; http://science.jrank.org/pages/5779/Refrigerated-Trucks-Railway-Cars.html; http://www. jbsswift.com/media/releases/Swift_History_6-05.pdf.

13. *Chicago: City of the Century.*

14. Helen Swift, *My Mother and My Father*, 137.

15. "Gustavus F. Swift Dead, Well Known Chicago Packer Expires Suddenly," *Chicago Daily Tribune*, March 30, 1903.

16. MGN.

17. Ira Morris, *Heritage from My Father*, privately printed, in private collection, p. 57.

18. Louis F. Swift, in collaboration with Arthur van Vlissingen Jr., *Yankee of the Yards: The Biography of Gustavus Franklin Swift* (Chicago: A. W. Shaw), 1927, 118–120.

19. Edward M. "Pete" Bakwin, telephone interview by author, December 11, 2008; Dainty, *Darling-Delaware Centenary*, 145.

20. Morris, *Heritage from My Father*, 57-59.

21. MGN.

22. Matthew Josephson, *The Robber Barons: The Great American Capitalists*, 1861–1901 (New York: Mariner Books, 1962), 284, 286.

23. Jaher, *The Urban Establishment*, 471. From Muriel Gardiner, REMINISCENCES: "Although both my grandfathers had been born poor, and had worked as farm boys, both had succeeded in building up impressive meat packing industries, and they and their children had become rich before I was born. My father and my mother's seven brothers continued to be hardworking in these businesses as long as they lived, putting work and prosperity ahead of all else."

24. *Chicago: City of the Century.*

25. Jaher, *The Urban Establishment*, 472, 487, 488.

26. Kathleen De Grave, Introduction, in Upton Sinclair, *The Jungle: The Uncensored Original Edition* (Tucson, AZ: See Sharp Press, 2003), 45.

27. Morris, *Heritage from My Father*, 161-162.

28. MGN; E. M. "Pete" Bakwin, interview by author, December 11, 2008.

29. MGN.

30. Morris, *Heritage from My Father*, 43.

31. "Morris-Swift Nuptials—Joined in Wedlock Before Numerous Friends—Banquet and Dance," *Chicago Tribune*, October 2, 1890.

32. MGN.

33. Philip D. Armour, quoted in Charles R. Geisst, *Wheels of Fortune: The History of Speculation from Scandal to Respectability* (Hoboken, NJ: Wiley, 2002), 26.

34. Josephson, *The Robber Barons*, 284, 286.

35. Louis F. Swift, quoted in Jaher, *The Urban Establishment*, 499.

36. Helen Swift Morris, quoted in Jaher, *The Urban Establishment,* 499.

37. Muriel Gardiner, interview by Brenda Webster, APA Workshop, December 1975, digital only, in the Oral History Interview Records, The Boston Psychoanalytic Society and Institute, Boston, MA.

38. Helen Swift, *My Mother and My Father*, 135.

39. Kathleen D. McCarthy, *Noblesse Oblige: Charity and Cultural Philanthropy in Chicago, 1849–1929* (Chicago: University of Chicago Press, 1982), 100, 102.

CHAPTER 2   HAPPY, FOR THE MOST PART

1. MGN.
2. REMINISCENCES, 290.
3. MGN; REMINISCENCES, 288.
4. MGN; REMINISCENCES, 284-285; Helen Swift Morris, quoted in Jaher, *The Urban Establishment*, 499.
5. REMINISCENCES, 285; MGN.
6. MGN: "The only two spankings I ever received were when, at age three, I had hurt my sister. I remember both spankings very well. First my mother carefully explained to me that, since I had hurt my sister, I must find out what it felt like to be hurt. Then my father laid me on the couch, took my clothes down, and spanked my behind. I was hurt, humiliated and angry. With the tears streaming down my cheeks, I cried with each stroke: 'I like, I like it; do it again!' This was the first time. The second time I held back my sobs and my words. When it was over, I stood up and said solemnly to my parents: 'If you ever spank me again, I'll run away from home and I'll never, never come back.' I think it was the only time in my life that I ever threatened my parents. It must have frightened my mother; she told my father not to spank me again. After this, my punishments consisted of being shut up in the guest room with no toys, or being deprived of privileges."
7. REMINISCENCES, 365.
8. MGN.
9. MGN: "He loved to tease and to play practical jokes. I did not mind the verbal teasing too much, but he made me miserable by tickling me repeatedly and 'blowing down my neck.' As the tickling of course made me laugh, neither Edward nor anyone else took my misery seriously, and I could not defend myself. This form of torture continued into my teens. I have wondered, since then, why my mother never interfered. She must not have realized that I was really suffering. I know she would not allow us to hurt each other physically."
10. Helen Swift, *My Mother and My Father*, 146.
11. "Gustavus G. Swift Dead," *Chicago Daily Tribune*.
12. MGN: "We docked at Liverpool and went by train to London, where we were driven in a hansom cab, in rain and darkness except for the lighted gas lamps, to the Savoy Hotel. The cab driver wore a top hat and had a waterproof sheet spread over his knees, as he sat on the high seat above the cab. It was rare for me to be out after dark when the street lamps were lighted; perhaps this was even the first time. This may be why the memory of this evening comes back to me with a pleasant glow of excitement whenever I revisit London, even up to the present. The hansom cabs have long since disappeared; the street lamps are no longer gas; but the feel and smell of the city are the same, and on a rainy evening the recurring magic of that first glimpse of London can move me to tears."
13. REMINISCENCES 266, 364.
14. MGN; REMINISCENCES, 362–363.
15. Ibid.
16. Ibid. "As I have said, we were taught early to value money and to save it. But Mother must have wanted to educate us to be generous also, and one such lesson has remained a painful memory. It took place in the blue guest-room in our Chicago house. I was sometimes sent to rest there in the afternoon if I was tired or sick. I was also often confined there as a punishment. On this particular day—and I do not know why I was there—Mother came into the blue room and asked me, without prelude: 'Muriel, would you lend me five dollars?'

    "I was taken aback and did not know how to reply. No one had ever asked to borrow a large sum from me before, although Ruth or I might occasionally borrow ten cents from the other. I would have to take the five dollars out of my bank—money which I was supposed to save. Quite probably I did not want to, but more certainly I thought it might be 'wrong.' 'I don't know,' I finally answered. 'Well, then I'll ask Edward; he's always willing to help me,' Mother replied, leaving the room."
17. Ibid.
18. Ibid.
19. Ibid.
20. "About Green Lake: What Makes Green Lake Great," http://www.visitgreenlake.com/visitgl/page.asp?p=about.

21. "Heidel House Resort & Spa: Heidel House Heritage," http://www.heidelhouse.com/closerlook/heritage.asp; REMINISCENCES, 283.

22. Connie Harvey, interview by author, November 5, 2008. However, according to E. M. "Pete" Bakwin, a nephew of Muriel's, the pony cart was given to his mother, Ruth, by Sir Thomas Lipton, a close friend of Helen Swift Morris's. Email to author, July 22, 2010.

23. Helen Swift, *My Mother and My Father*, 128–129.

24. MGN.

25. Ibid.

26. Ibid.

27. Ibid. "I appeared outwardly, I think, a happy, cheerful child, active physically and mentally, full of curiosity, and generally but not persistently obedient and well-mannered. My inner problems showed themselves in an assortment of neurotic symptoms, which of course were not recognized as such at the time. The earliest manifestations—as far back as I can remember—were temper tantrums [and night terrors]. My mother tried to account for the night terrors as a result of my being overtired. The word "nervous" which I occasionally heard on the lips of others, was forbidden in our household; it was something to be ashamed of; in any case, a child could not be nervous. The temper tantrums were of course just naughtiness, and so I myself considered them, though I was aware of the fact that I could not always stop them. Mollie called them conniption fits."

28. Ibid.

29. "Death Comes to Nelson Morris," *Chicago Tribune*, August 28, 1907.

30. "Will is Broken by Morris Heirs; Agreement made out of court to divide $30,000,000 among widow and four children," *Chicago Daily Tribune*, October 15, 1907.

31. REMINISCENCES, 291–292.

32. REMINISCENCES, 364–367.

33. "Chicago to Honor Dead Fire Chief," *New York Times*, December 24, 1910.

34. Muriel Gardiner, quoted in documentary *The Real Julia: The Muriel Gardiner Story,* produced by Dan Klugherz, distributed by Altana Films, 1987.

35. MGN.

36. Ibid.

CHAPTER 3   ROOTS OF DISCOVERY

1. Edward Morris House Collection, 1913–1919, Architecture and Urban Planning: Selected Modern Manuscript and Archival Collections, Special Collections Research Center, University of Chicago Library, http://www.lib.uchicago.edu/e/spcl/arplan.html.

2. Porter E. Sargent, *A Handbook of Private Schools* (Boston: P. A. Sargent, 1916), 277.

3. MGN.

4. Ibid.

5. Ibid.

6. Ibid.

7. Ibid.

8. Ibid.

9. Ibid.

10. Kelly Alford, interview by author, November 6, 2008.

11. Muriel Gardiner, interview by Lucille Ritvo, December 1968, MP3, in the Oral History Interview Records, The Boston Psychoanalytic Society and Institute, Boston, MA.

12. MGN.

13. Ibid.

14. Ibid.

15. "Charity Bazaar a Winner When These Girls Run Booths," photo caption, *Chicago Daily Tribune*, November 10, 1912.

16. "Weeds Too Thick for Pack to Follow the Hunt," photo of Muriel Gardiner on horseback, *Chicago Tribune*, September 21, 1913; "Hats Off to the Weather Man," *Chicago Tribune*, November 23, 1916.

17. "Ed. Morris Dead: Left $40,000,000," *New York Times*, November 4, 1913; "Edward Morris, Packer, Is Dead; End Comes as Surprise to Friends, Though He had Been Ill Long Time; Estate of $40,000,000, *Chicago Tribune*, November 4, 1913.

18. "Morris Millions in Trust, Packer's Widow Controls—Will Be One of World's Wealthiest Women," *New York Times*, November 12, 1913; "Measuring Worth: Seven Ways to Compute the Relative Value of a U.S. Dollar Amount, 1774 to Present," http://www.measuringworth.com/ uscompare/. In 2008, $3,000,000 from 1913 is worth $67,282,187.50.
19. "Edward Morris, Packer, Is Dead," *Chicago Tribune*, November 4, 1913; Edward Morris House Collection, 1913–1919.
20. Gardiner, *Code Name "Mary,"* 11.
21. Muriel Gardiner, interview by Brenda Webster, December 1975.
22. REMINISCENCES; MGN.
23. MGN; Muriel Gardiner, interview by Brenda Webster, December 1975.
24. "Clothing Wet, Ardor Undampened, 5,000 Women March," *Chicago Tribune*, June 8, 1916.
25. "Vassar Girl, Aid in Strike, in Cell," *Chicago Tribune*, January 18, 1910.
26. Linda J. Lumsden, *Inez: The Life and Times of Inez Milholland* (Bloomington: Indiana University Press, 2004), 165–166; Kristen Jaconi, "Inez Milholland: A Thanatography of the Suffrage Martyr," Women's Legal History Project, submitted April 3, 2000, http://www.law.stanford.edu/ library/womenslegalhistory/papers/Milholland.PDF.
27. "U.S. Lists Stock Embargo; Show to Boom Today—Government Authorities Find Plague to be Stomatitis," *Chicago Tribune*, December 2, 1916.
28. "Mrs. Edw. Morris Marries Briton; Surprises Son. Widow of Packer Bride of Francis Neilson, Statesman," *Chicago Daily Tribune*, September 5, 1916.
29. MGN.
30. Edward J. Dodson, "In the Footsteps of Thomas Paine: Francis Neilson and the Liberal Tradition," The School of Cooperative Individualism, http://www.cooperativeindividualism.org/dodson-edward_on-francis-neilson.html; MGN.

CHAPTER 4   IN A DIFFERENT VOICE

1. Muriel Gardiner, interview by Lucille Ritvo, December 1968.
2. Connie Harvey, interview by author, November 5, 2008.
3. From college phone books of the day, according to email to author from former Wellesley archivist Wilma Slaight, March 29, 2009; MGN.
4. List of courses in email to author from Wilma Slaight, January 29, 2009; *1914–1918: The Great War and the Shaping of the 20th Century*, http://www.pbs.org/greatwar.
5. *The Real Julia: The Muriel Gardiner Story*; "Working Girl; Sister of Packing Company Head Holds Clerical Position in General Offices of Firm in Stockyards," *Chicago Tribune*, August 30, 1919.
6. Gardiner, quoted in "Working Girl."
7. MGN.
8. Robert D'Attilio, "Sacco-Vanzetti Case," http://www.english.upenn.edu/~afilreis/88/sacvan.html. For more on the FBI's General Intelligence Division, see http://www.marxists.org/glossary/ events/p/a.htm. See also http://www.fbi.gov/hq/ci/cihistory.htm.
9. Gardiner, *Code Name "Mary,"* 27; Muriel Gardiner, interview by Brenda Webster, December 1975.
10. "Voting Rights and Citizenship: Women Get the Vote," http://www1.cuny.edu/portal_ur/content/voting_cal/women_vote.html; Jaconi, "Inez Milholland."
11. Muriel Morris's dance card, Wellesley College Archives, Margaret Clapp Library, Class of 1922, 6C/1922, Wellesley College, Wellesley, MA.
12. REMINISCENCES, 9; MGN; Patricia Ann Palmieri, *In Adamless Eden: The Community of Women Faculty at Wellesley* (New Haven, CT: Yale University Press, 1995), xiv–xv.
13. Agnes Frances Perkins, *Vocations for the Trained Woman: Opportunities Other Than Teaching* (Boston: Women's Educational and Industrial Union, 1910); "Obituary: Emily Balch Dies; Won Nobel Prize," http://www.nytimes.com/learning/general/onthisday/bday/0108.html. Former Wellesley professor Emily Greene Balch won the Nobel Peace Prize in 1946.
14. Guttman, "In Memoriam," 1–7.
15. Muriel Gardiner, interview by Lucille Ritvo; Ruth Bakwin, letter to Albert Holland, November 11, 1974.

16. REMINISCENCES, 10.
17. "Women Students to Confer; Nineteen Colleges to Join in Armament Discussion at Vassar," *New York Times*, October 15, 1921; "Intercollegiate Disarmament Conference to be held at Vassar— Wellesley Delegates Chosen," *Wellesley College News* 30, no. 4 (October 20, 1921); "Intercollegiate Disarmament Conference held at Vassar," *Wellesley College News* 30, no. 6 (November 3, 1921).
18. "College Commemorates Armistice Day," *Wellesley College News* 30, no. 8 (November 17, 1921).
19. "College Votes to Discard Honor System as Impractical," *Wellesley College News* 30, no. 28 (May 18, 1922); Betty Eaton, quoted in *The Real Julia: The Muriel Gardiner Story*.
20. Wellesley College Alumnae Association, "The Class of 1922"; *Wellesley Alumnae Quarterly Alumnae Notes*, January 1, 1922, 224, Wellesley College Archives, Margaret Clapp Library, Wellesley College, Wellesley, MA.
21. "Radio Messages Give News of Interest to 1922—Prominent Members Describe Futures at Class Supper," Wellesley College Archives.
22. Muriel Gardiner, quoted in *The Real Julia: The Muriel Gardiner Story*.

CHAPTER 5   SCHOLARS AND LOVERS

1. Muriel Gardiner, interview by Lucille Ritvo; Muriel Gardiner, interview by Brenda Webster, December 1975.
2. Muriel Gardiner, interview by Lucille Ritvo; REMINISCENCES, 111.
3. David Clay Large, *Between Two Fires: Europe's Path in the 1930s* (New York: Norton, 1990), 13; *1914–1918: The Great War*, http://www.pbs.org/greatwar/resources/casdeath_pop.html.
4. Connie Harvey, interview by author, November 7, 2008.
5. *The Real Julia: The Muriel Gardiner Story*; "October 24–30, 1922: Mussolini, Fascists March on Rome," http://www1.yadvashem.org/about_HOLocaust/chronology/before_1933/chronology_before_1933_9.html.
6. Marjorie Reeves, *St. Anne's College, Oxford, An Informal History* (Oxford: The College, 1979), 1–2; David Smith, archivist, St. Anne's Society Library, Oxford, interview by author, March 23, 2009. For more on women at Oxford, see Jane Howarth, "Women," in *The History of the University of Oxford*, vol. 8, *The Twentieth Century*, ed. Brian Harrison (Oxford: Clarendon Press, 1994). For more on the Society of Oxford Home-Students, see Ruth F. Butler, *A History of Saint Anne's Society*, vol. 2, *1921–1946*, printed for private circulation (Oxford: University Press, 1949).
7. Reeves, *St. Anne's College, Oxford*, 18; Howarth, "Women," 355.
8. MGN.
9. Ibid.
10. Reeves, *St. Anne's College, Oxford*, 25; Peter Riviere, ed., *A History of Oxford Anthropology* (New York and Oxford: Berghahn Books, 2007), 52.
11. Connie Harvey, telephone interview by author, May 8, 2009. Harvey said that Muriel likely used Wellesley to facilitate her anonymous gifts to her friends since the college had seemed agreeable to hiding her identity as a benefactor. She said that even when Muriel's friends knew she was underwriting their travels, they shared an unspoken arrangement that no one would mention it; Gardiner, *Code Name "Mary,"* 29; Muriel Gardiner, letter to granddaughter Ann Harvey, July 2, 1978.
12. "Dr. Ruth Bakwin Dies; Professor of Pediatrics," *New York Times*, August 2, 1985; E. M. "Pete" Bakwin, telephone interview by author, December 11, 2008.
13. Elisabeth Young-Bruehl, *Anna Freud: A Biography* (New York: Summit, 1988), 53; Peter Gay, *Freud: A Life for Our Time* (New York: Norton, 1998), 3–4; Freud, quoted in Gay, 207.
14. Gardiner, *Code Name "Mary,"* 29; MGN; REMINISCENCES, 12.
15. Notations on Muriel Morris's Oxford record in small letters and very faint pencil indicate that she was "removed" and had "failed." Society of Oxford Home Students, Register III, original handwritten register, Library, St. Anne's College, March 2009.
16. Muriel Gardiner, interview by Brenda Webster, December 1975; Henry P. Albarelli, phone and email interviews by author, November 13 and 14, 2009.
17. Muriel Gardiner, interview by Brenda Webster, December 1975; marriage license: Helen Muriel Morris and Harold A. Abramson.
18. Muriel Gardiner, interview by Lucille Ritvo; REMINISCENCES, 21.

19. Muriel Gardiner, interview by Brenda Webster, December 1975; Gardiner, *Code Name "Mary,"* 31.

CHAPTER 6   VIENNA: ON THE OEDIPAL BED

1. Gardiner, *Code Name "Mary,"* 31; Muriel Gardiner, interview by Lucille Ritvo, December 1968: "We both went to Vienna."
2. E. J. Hobshawm, Introduction, in Ilona Duczynska, *Workers in Arms: The Austrian Schutzbund and the Civil War of 1934* (New York: Monthly Review Press, 1978), 22.
3. MGN; REMINISCENCES, 12; Gardiner, *Code Name "Mary,"* 31.
4. Muriel Gardiner, interview by Brenda Webster, December 1975.
5. Muriel Gardiner, interview by Lucille Ritvo, December 1968.
6. Muriel Gardiner, "Mary Shelley and John Howard Payne," *London Mercury* 22, no. 131 (September 1930): 450.
7. "Ruth Mack Brunswick, 1897–1946," *Jewish Women: A Comprehensive Historical Encyclopedia*, http://jwa.org/encyclopedia/article/brunswick-ruth-mack; "Silver Ring with Blue Glass Intaglio," Freud Museum Collection, http://www.freud.org.uk/about/collections/detail/10158/.
8. REMINISCENCES, 15; Muriel Gardiner, interview by Brenda Webster, December 1975.
9. REMINISCENCES, 24, 25.
10. Muriel Gardiner, "My Friendship with Konenkov, 1926–1945," in *The Uncommon Vision of Sergei Konenkov, 1874–1971: A Russian Sculptor and His Times*, ed. Marie Turbow Lampard, John E. Bowlt, and Wendy R. Salmond (a co-publication of Rutgers University Press, New Brunswick, NJ, and London, and The Jane Voorhees Zimmerli Art Museum, Rutgers, The State University of New Jersey, 2001), 2.
11. Peter Loewenberg, telephone interview by author, June 2, 2009; REMINISCENCES, 18–20, 261–262.
12. REMINISCENCES, 241.
13. "287,000 Receive U.S. Tax Refunds of $174,120,177," *Chicago Daily Trib*une, December 29, 1926; "103,858,687 in Taxes Handed Back by U.S; Many Chicagoans on Mellon's List," *Chicago Daily Tribune*, December 29, 1927.
14. Muriel Gardiner, interview by Lucille Ritvo, December 1968.
15. "The Press: Reunion in Vienna," *TIME* Magazine, http://www.time.com/time/magazine/article/0,9171,776091,00.html#ixzz0oh4GoUMs; "The Foundation of the First Republic," Library of Congress Country Studies: Austria, http:countrystudies.us/austria/34.htm.
16. Henry Leichter, *Childhood Memories*, 8, privately printed, in private family collection; G. E. R. Gedye, *Betrayal in Central Europe: Austria and Czechoslovakia, The Fallen Bastions* (New York and London: Harper and Brothers, 1939), 29, 30–31; Hobshawm, Introduction, in Duczynska, *Workers in Arms*, 21.
17. Large, *Between Two Fires*, 62.
18. Loewenberg, *Decoding the Past*, 21; H. Leichter, *Childhood Memories*, 8; Gedye, *Betrayal in Central Europe*, 29, 53, 98.
19. Otto Alfred Snyder, "Reflections: The Background and Experiences of Two Immigrants, A Partial History of Our Family," Memoir Collection, Leo Baeck Institute, Center for Jewish History, 1986; H. Leichter, *Childhood Memories*, 10.
20. Loewenberg, *Decoding the Past*, 162; Brenda Webster, phone interview by author, January 17, 2009; E. J. Hobshawm, Introduction, in Duczynska, *Workers in Arms*, 22; "Dora—A Botched Case: Ida Bauer (1882–1945)." The patient Freud wrote about as 'Dora,' was sent to him in 1900 suffering from so-called 'hysterical' symptoms: a nervous cough, depression, and unsociability. The teenager had been resisting the advances of a family friend—the husband of a woman with whom Dora's father was having an affair. Rather than interpreting what these hysterical symptoms meant to Dora, Freud insisted that they must have the significance that his theory of the sexual roots of hysteria required. Dora rejected Freud and his ideas and left the treatment." http://www.loc.gov/exhibits/freud/freud02.html.
21. Muriel Gardiner, interview by Lucille Ritvo.
22. Bruce Watson, "Sacco and Vanzetti: 80 Years After Their Execution, A Look At The Men, the Murders, and the Judgment of Mankind," Democracy Now! August 27, 2007, www.democracynow.org/2007/8/22/sacco_and_vanzetti_80_years_after+august+1923+sacco&cd=4&hl=en&

ct=clnk&gl=us. "Around the world, there were protests, there were riots. The people threw—uprooted lampposts in Paris, threw them through plate-glass windows. They attacked embassies. The Moulin Rouge was damaged. In Geneva, people took it out on American targets. They targeted stores selling Lucky Strike cigarettes and theaters showing Douglas Fairbanks films. There were strikes all over South America, shut down transportation. The American flag was burned on the steps of the American embassy in Johannesburg. The riots went on. Three people were killed in riots in Germany. The riots went on for a few days, and then finally they stopped."

23. Loewenberg, *Decoding the Past,* 128–129.
24. Phil Rosner, interview by author, April 6, 2009.
25. Gedye, *Betrayal in Central Europe,* 19, 34; Loewenberg, *Decoding the Past,* 174; Rosner, interview by author, April 6, 2009; Duczynska, *Workers in Arms,* 144.
26. Muriel Gardiner, interview by Brenda Webster, December 1975.
27. Connie Harvey, telephone interview by author, May 20, 2009.
28. REMINISCENCES, 270–277.
29. Ibid.
30. MGN.
31. Muriel Gardiner, interview by Brenda Webster, December 1975; REMINISCENCES, 22.
32. Muriel Gardiner, interview by Lucille Ritvo, Oral History Workshop no. 4, American Psychoanalytic Association, "Americans Trained Abroad," December 13, 1975, APA Archives; Muriel Gardiner, interview by Lucille Ritvo, December 1968.
33. REMINISCENCES, 23; Gardiner, *Code Name "Mary,"* 41; Muriel Gardiner, interview by Lucille Ritvo, December 13, 1975.

CHAPTER 7   REDS VS. BLACKS

1. Gay, *Freud,* 292; Muriel Gardiner, "Meetings with the Wolf-Man (1938–1949) in "The Wolf-Man in Later Life," *The Wolf-Man by the Wolf-Man: The Double Story of Freud's Most Famous Case.* edited, with notes, introduction, and chapters by Muriel Gardiner (New York: Basic Books, 1971), 311.
2. Iris Meder, email to author, September 14, 2009.
3. Spender, *World within World,* 214.
4. C. H. Feinstein, Peter Temin, and Gianni Toniolo, *The World Economy between the World Wars* (New York: Oxford University Press, 2008), 98.
5. George Czuzka, unpublished novella, in private collection; Gedye, *Betrayal in Central Europe,* 63.
6. Connie Harvey, telephone interview by author, May 20, 2008; Muriel Gardiner, interview by Brenda Webster, December 1975; MGN.
7. Connie Harvey, telephone interview by author, May 20, 2008. Personal Recollections of Anna Freud, Box 3, Muriel Gardiner Papers, Sigmund Freud Collection, Manuscript Division, Library of Congress, Washington, D.C. "In Vienna, where I lived from autumn 1926 until late June 1938, I did not know Anna Freud well, seeing her only a few times for consultation, and, the last several years, at the famous Wednesday evening meetings. I knew fairly well some of the young kindergarten teachers whom Anna Freud had taught or influenced. Several of them served as governess to the children of analysts, and I was lucky enough to have Fini Wodak (later Hyndman) with me to help with my daughter Connie."
8. Muriel Morris—Julian Gardiner marriage license, in private collection.
9. Trudy Jeremias, interview by author, December 16, 2008; Connie Harvey, interview by author, November 6, 2008; Muriel Gardiner, interview by Brenda Webster, December 1975.
10. MGN.
11. Feinstein, Temin, and Toniolo, *The World Economy between the World Wars,* 98; "International: Gold Over Europe," *Time,* November 2, 1931; Connie Harvey, telephone interview by author, May 20, 2008.
12. Muriel Gardiner, interview by Lucille Ritvo, December 1968. After the *Anschluss,* Dr. Robert Waelder lived in Philadelphia where Muriel reconnected with him.
13. Connie Harvey, interview by author, November 4, 2008; Muriel Gardiner Papers, Box 3, Personal Recollections of Anna Freud, Sigmund Freud Collection, Manuscript Division, Library of Congress, Washington, D.C.

14. Guttman, "In Memoriam," 1–7.
15. REMINISCENCES, p 330; Shiela Grant Duff, *The Parting of Ways: A Personal Account of the Thirties* (London: Owen, 1932), 43–45.
16. Guttman, "In Memoriam," 1–7; Muriel Gardiner, "The Seven Years of Dearth" in *The Bulletin of The Philadelphia Association for Psychoanalysis* 12, no. 4 (December 1962).
17. Gedye, *Betrayal in Central Europe*, 61; Duczynska, *Workers in Arms*, 140; Loewenberg, *Decoding the Past*, 161.
18. When Alexander Rogowski made it to the United States after years spent in other European countries, he lived in a small apartment in New York City where he studied for his medical boards. It was a tiny place, with the window below street level. One day, as he sat at his table studying, he looked out the window and saw a pair of legs go by, walking a dog. He could only see the legs but, although Muriel had always worn pants to classes, he recognized those legs. He ran outside and the two reunited. He told her about his studies, about his apartment, and she said, "This is perfect. You must take my apartment, because I'm going on vacation. You will have much more room to spread out." So the young man moved into Muriel's large apartment for a period of time. His wife later asked him how he recognized her legs. He said, "She was wearing slippers." Not a very satisfying answer, but that's what Rogowski said. Elise Rogowski, interview by author, August 25, 2009.
19. Muriel Gardiner, curriculum vitae, in private collection; Muriel Gardiner, "The Seven Years of Dearth."
20. Muriel Gardiner, interview by Lucille Ritvo, December 13, 1975; Dr. Herbert Posch, interview by author, March 22, 2009.
21. Stephen Spender, Preface, in Muriel Gardiner, *The Deadly Innocents: Portraits of Children Who Kill* (New York: Basic Books, 1976), ix.

CHAPTER 8   BLOOD IN THE STREETS

1. Gedye, *Betrayal in Central Europe*, 68.
2. H. Leichter, *Childhood Memories*, 111.
3. Loewenberg, *Decoding the Past*, 185.
4. Connie Harvey, interview by author, November 6, 2008; Muriel Gardiner, interview by Brenda Webster, December 1975.
5. Muriel Gardiner, interview by Brenda Webster, December 1975.
6. H. Leichter, *Childhood Memories*, 82.
7. United States Holocaust Memorial Museum: Holocaust Encyclopedia, http://www.ushmm.org/wlc/en/article.php?ModuleId=10007499; Christopher Andrew, *Defend the Realm: The Authorized History of MI5* (New York: Alfred A. Knopf, 2009), 189.
8. Gedye, *Betrayal in Central Europe*, 64, 69.
9. Cable to FF, March 28, 1933, Box 1, Ruth Mack Brunswick Papers, Sigmund Freud Collection, Manuscript Division, Library of Congress, Washington, D.C.
10. Paul Roazen, *The Historiography of Psychoanalysis* (New Brunswick, NJ: Transaction Publishers, 2001), 74; Gedye, *Betrayal in Central Europe*, 68; MGN.
11. Muriel Gardiner, "My Friendship with Konenkov, 1926–1945," 186.
12. Gedye, *Betrayal in Central Europe*, 71–72; MGN; The "Horst-Wessel-Lied," or song, composed in 1929 by an SA commander, was the anthem of the Nazi Party. In 1933, it became a second national anthem for Germany:
    > The flag high! Ranks closed tight! / The stormtroopers march with bold, firm step.
    > Comrades shot by Reds and Reactionaries / March in spirit within our ranks.
    > Clear the streets for the brown battalions. / Clear the streets for the stormtroop men!
    > Millions already look hopefully up to the swastika. / The day is breaking for freedom and bread!
    > For the last time now the call is sounded! / Already we stand all ready to fight!
    > Soon the Hitler banners will flutter over the barricades. / Our bondage won't last much longer!
    > Flag high! Ranks closed tight! / The stormtroopers march with calm, firm step.
    > Comrades shot by Reds and Reactionaries / March in spirit within our ranks.

13. Gedye, *Betrayal in Central Europe,* 93; Frank Knox, publisher of the *Chicago Daily News,* quoted in Large, *Between Two Fires,* 90-91.
14. Gedye, *Betrayal in Central Europe,* 34; Guttman, "In Memoriam"; Karl Seitz, quoted in Gedye, *Betrayal in Central Europe,* 96.
15. REMINISCENCES, 55.
16. *The Real Julia: The Muriel Gardiner Story.*
17. Snyder, "Reflections," 55; Loewenberg, *Decoding the Past,* 187; Gedye, *Betrayal in Central Europe,* 43, 102; Large, *Between Two Fires,* 90; Phil Rosner, interview by author, April 6, 2009; Kurt Sonnenfeld, email to author, July 9, 2010. Vienna's sewers were immortalized in Graham Greene's *The Third Man.*
18. Naomi Mitchison, *Naomi Mitchison's Vienna Diary* (London: Gollancz, 1934), 56, 65; Gus Papanek, interview by author, February 2009. Otto Alfred Snyder's memory: "In a couple of days it was all over except for a central fire station in the 21st District, where a group of firemen, supported by a small contingent of the Schutzbund still held out. The men…had to capitulate after holding off the military for 4 days, vainly waiting for outside help. [Their leader]…was taken into custody, put before a military tribunal and convicted of treason and rebellion. Sentenced to be hanged, he was executed the following day. His request for death by firing squad rather than by hanging was denied. Today he is considered a hero, a street in Vienna carries his name and a monument stands in the 21st District." From "Reflections."
19. *The Real Julia: The Muriel Gardiner Story.*
20. REMINISCENCES, 56, 57.
21. Muriel Gardiner, interview by Brenda Webster, December 1975.
22. REMINISCENCES, 58; Mark Anderson, ed., *Hitler's Exiles: Personal Stories of the Flight from Nazi Germany to America* (New York: New Press, 1998), 8; Mitchison, *Naomi Mitchison's Vienna Diary,* 146–147; Large, *Between Two Fires,* 195. About the American Jewish Joint Distribution Committee (JDC), or The Joint, as it was called: "Hitler's rise to power in 1933 and the passage of the economically restrictive Nuremberg Laws pauperized the Jewish community in Germany, and JDC's support became critical. Emigration aid soon became the priority, as JDC focused on helping Jews fleeing from Nazi Germany, Austria, and Czechoslovakia. JDC provided food, shelter, and medical care for stranded refugees; it helped cover travel expenses and landing fees; and it secured travel accommodations and all-important visas for countries of refuge. By the end of 1939, JDC-supported organizations had helped some 110,000 Jews emigrate from Germany—30,000 in 1939 alone. In 1940, JDC was helping refugees in transit in more than 40 countries. From the outbreak of World War II through 1944, JDC enabled over 81,000 Jews to emigrate.

    "From its wartime headquarters in Lisbon, JDC chartered ships and continued to help thousands of refugees escape from Europe through various routes. In France, JDC financed legal and illegal organizations. It funneled in funds to support some 7,000 Jewish children in hiding and to smuggle over 1,000 more to Switzerland and Spain, and it smuggled aid to Jewish prisoners in labor camps." http://www.jdc.org/jdc-history/years/1930.aspx.
23. Mitchison, *Naomi Mitchison's Vienna Diary,* 35; Snyder, "Reflections."
24. Jeremias, interview by author, December 16, 2008; REMINISCENCES 57.

CHAPTERS 9   LOVE IN TIME OF WAR

1. Stephen Spender, quoted in John Sutherland, *Stephen Spender: The Authorized Biography* (London: Viking Penguin, 2005), 528.
2. Gardiner, *Code Name "Mary,"* 47; Stephen Spender, *World within World,* 212–213.
3. Spender, *World within World,* 213.
4. MGN; Gardiner, *Code Name "Mary,"* 47-48, 54.
5. Duczynska, *Workers in Arms,* 243.
6. Sutherland, *Stephen Spender,* 165.
7. "Austria to Crush Nazis' Terrorism: Leaders Will Be Returned to Concentration Camp if Their Violence Continues. Heavy Penalties Ordered. Two Women Are Hurt by Bombs in Cars in the Centre of Vienna—Five Hitlerites Arrested," May 13, 1934, *New York Times;* Anderson, ed., *Hitler's Exiles,* 8; Mitchison, *Naomi Mitchison's Vienna Diary,* 146–147.

8. Spender, unpublished journal material, from entry August 2–3, 1980, 336–7, in private collection, reprinted by kind permission of the Estate of Stephen Spender.

9. Spender quoted in Sutherland, *Stephen Spender,* 169.

10. Stephen Spender, "Experience," *Ruins and Visions: Poems 1934–1942* (New York: Random House, 1942), 16. Reprinted by kind permission of the Estate of Stephen Spender.

11. Spender, *World within World,* 210.

12. Ibid.

13. Ibid., 216, 215.

14. Joseph Buttinger and Muriel Gardiner, *Damit Wir Nicht Vergessen: Unsere Jahre 1934–1947 in Wein, Paris und New York* (Vienna: Verlag der Wiener Volksbuchhandlung, 1978), 175.

15. Spender, *World within World,* 218.

16. Stephen Spender, "Ice," in *Stephen Spender: Collected Poems 1928–1985* (Oxford University Press, 1987), 179. Reprinted by kind permission of the Estate of Stephen Spender.

17. Gardiner, *Code Name "Mary,"* 50; Ernst Glaser, "The Time of Illegality, Muriel Gardiner (1901–1985) and Ilse Kulczar (1902–1976)," in Doris Ingrisch, Ilse Erika Korotin and Charlotte Zwiauer, *Die Revolutionierung des Alltags: zur intellektuellen Kultur von Frauen im Wien der Zwischenkriegszeit* (Frankfurt am Main: P. Lang, 2004), 57–73. According to David Clay Large, when Philby visited Muriel in Vienna, "he was already working for Moscow," helping to set up a courier service between the underground communists in Austria and exiled communists in Prague and the Soviet Union. Large, *Between Two Fires,* 95.

18. Ron Rosenbaum, "Kim Philby and the Age of Paranoia," *New York Times Magazine,* July 10, 1994; Andrew, *Defend the Realm,* 169.

19. Sutherland, *Stephen Spender,* 167.

20. William Shirer, *The Rise and Fall of the Third Reich: A History of Nazi Germany* (New York: Simon and Schuster, 1960), 386; Walter B. Maass, *The Years of Darkness: The Austrian Resistance Movement 1938–1945* (Vienna: Federal Press Service, 1975), 6–7.

21. G. E. R. Gedye, "Two Rebels Hanged after Swift Trial," wireless to the *New York Times,* July 31, 1934.

22. Gardiner, *Code Name "Mary,"* 55–56.

23. Ibid., 49.

24. Trudy Jeremias, interview by author, December 16, 2008; REMINISCENCES, 60.

25. Spender, *World within World,* 217.

26. Ibid.

27. REMINISCENCES, 330–331; Christian Reder, "Twilight of Socialism: Drei Biografien Österreichs Zeitgeschichte," *Falter* 20 (1983): 11.

28. Spender, quoted in Sutherland, *Stephen Spender,* 168–169.

29. Sutherland, *Stephen Spender,* 174; Gardiner, quoted in Sutherland, *Stephen Spender,* 174.

30. Spender, quoted in Sutherland, *Stephen Spender,* 174; Gardiner, *Code Name "Mary,"* 55; REMINISCENCES.

31. Muriel Gardiner, interview by Brenda Webster, December 1975.

32. Sutherland, *Stephen Spender,* 175; Spender, *World within World,* 216. During Tony Hyndman's later career as a stage manager, his lover was Michael Redgrave, the father of Vanessa Redgrave, who would play the title role in the 1977 film *"Julia,"* from Lillian Hellman's fictionalized story based in part on Muriel Gardiner's life.

CHAPTER 10   CLEAR AND DECIDED

1. Hugh David, *Stephen Spender: A Portrait with Background* (Portsmouth, NH: Heinemann, 1992), 177; Joseph Buttinger, "Mary," *The Bulletin of the Philadelphia Association of Psychoanalysis* 22, no. 2 (June 1972): 105–109; Christian Reder, "Twilight of Socialism."

2. Stephen Spender, *World within World,* 220. An opposite point of view about Joe's openness was expressed by a fellow Austrian, Kurt Sonnenfeld: "Joe never saw anyone else's point of view." Kurt Sonnenfeld, e-mail to author, February 15, 2009.

3. Gedye, *Betrayal in Central Europe,* 112; Duczynska, *Workers in Arms,* 208.

4. Buttinger, *In the Twilight of Socialism,* 229.

5. Gardiner, *Code Name "Mary,"* 67; Spender, *World Within World,* 220.
6. REMINISCENCES, 345; Christian Reder, "Twilight of Socialism."
7. REMINISCENCES 345.
8. Ibid., 346.
9. Herbert Steiner, "The Role of the Resistance in Austria, with Special References to the Labor Movement," *The Journal of Modern History* vol. 64, Supplement: *Resistance against the Third Reich* (December 1992): S132.
10. Gedye, *Betrayal in Central Europe,* 114–115.
11. Ernst Glaser, "The Time of Illegality," 3, 59; Buttinger, *In the Twilight of Socialism,* 229.
12. Buttinger, *In the Twilight of Socialism,* 229.
13. REMINISCENCES, 349; Spender, *World within World,* 219.
14. Spender, *World within World,* 219.
15. Stephen Spender, "If It Were Not Too Late!" *Collected Poems, 1928–1953* (London, Faber, 1955). Reprinted by kind permission of the Estate of Stephen Spender.
16. Spender, *World within World,* 220.
17. Buttinger and Gardiner, *Damit Wir Nicht Vergessen,* 186.
18. Ibid.
19. Peter Unterweger, interview by author, March 19, 2008.
20. Spender, *World within World,* 219.
21. Christian Reder, "Twilight of Socialism"; "Americans Trained Abroad," Oral History Workshop no. 4, American Psychoanalytic Association, December 13, 1975.
22. Buttinger, "Mary."
23. Spender, *World within World,* 214.
24. Brenda Webster, interview by Jack Foley, 2000, on *Cover to Cover,* KPFA. Also, "The Perfect Freudian Child: An Interview with Brenda Webster." *Women's Studies* 32, issue 5 (July 2003).
25. Ibid.
26. Glaser, "The Time of Illegality," 62; Bruno Kreiskly, quoted in Glaser, 63.
27. Ibid., 64.
28. Sutherland, *Stephen Spender,* 177.
29. Gedye, *Betrayal in Central Europe,* 122.
30. Stephen Spender, quoted in *Letters to Christopher: Stephen Spender's Letters to Christopher Isherwood 1929–1939, with "The Line of the Branch"—Two Thirties Journals,* ed. Lee Bartlett (Santa Barbara, CA: Black Sparrow Press, 1980), 79; Buttinger, *In the Twilight of Socialism,* 258.
31. Buttinger and Gardiner, *Damit Wir Nicht Vergessen,* 188.
32. Paul Streeten, "Aerial Roots, An Autobiographical Sketch," *Banca Nazionale del Lavoro Quarterly Review* no. 157 (1986): 135-159, Austrian Heritage Collection, Leo Baeck Institute; H. Leichter, *Childhood Memories,* 11.
33. Spender, *World Within World,* 378. On the feud between Joe and Otto Leichter, Leichter wrote: "In [Joe's] manuscript, his lies turned a heroic and enlightened epoch of social democratic fulfillment of duty and loyalty into a time of ugly group and power struggles." He also wrote about Joe's early release from prison in 1934: "The serious nervous breakdown he suffered after a few weeks of arrest in 1934, and the declaration of loyalty he signed in order to be released early from arrest." From the estate of Otto Leichter, letter from Otto Leichter to several unidentified recipients, comments regarding Buttinger's manuscript of *The Example of Austria,* New York, October 4, 1951, in Dokumentationsarchiv des österreichischen Widerstandes (DöW), Archives of the Resistance (DOEW), Vienna.
    How Joe got his passport: "A Socialist from a German-Bohemian town called Landskron, Dr. Ernst Janisch, who was about my age and who looked somewhat similar, gave up his passport for me. A talented document forger changed the photograph and added a seal.... This passport helped me on numerous travels back and forth from then on until November of 1939 when I came to the United States as Muriel's husband." Buttinger and Gardiner, *Damit Wir Nicht Vergessen,*173.

CHAPTER 11   IN HIDING, IN LOVE

1. Franz Leichter, interview by author, April 16, 2009; H. Leichter, *Childhood Memories,* 94.
2. REMINISCENCES, 257.

3.   Stephen Spender, *Letters to Christopher*, 9.

4.   H. Leichter, *Childhood Memories*, 119.

5.   Buttinger and Gardiner, *Damit Wir Nicht Vergessen*, 262.

6.   Phil Rosner, interview by author, April 6, 2009.

7.   Ibid.

8.   Kurt Sonnenfeld, email to author, February 28, 2010; Radomir V. Luža, *The Resistance in Austria: 1938–1945* (Minneapolis: University of Minnesota Press, 1984), 84.

9.   Buttinger and Gardiner, *Damit Wir Nicht Vergessen*, 184.

10. Gustav Papanek, telephone interview by author, March 1, 2009; Stephen Spender, *Vienna* (New York: Random House, 1934). Reprinted by kind permission of the Estate of Stephen Spender.

> From VIENNA (1934)
> To Muriel
>
> …
>
> Lucky: those who were shot dead:-
> Outright not being and not being those
> Thrown down cellar and trampled with nailed boots;
> Made to swallow the badge with three arrows
> That excellently deflect harmless into
> A ground pegged out for making decent houses;
> Beaten to death; left frozen
> In the so gentle snow breeding all iron
> Solid with their clenched rifles; or hanged
> By an ignoring justice, fit only for colonies,
> Our fatal unconfidence attempted a bridge
> Between revolution and the already providing
> World.
>
> …
>
> I think often of a woman
> With dark eyes neglected, a demanding turn of the head
> And hair of black silky beasts.
> How admirable it is
> They offer a surface bright as fruit in rain
> That feeds on kissing. Loving is their conqueror
> That turns all sunshine, fructifying lemons.
> Our sexes are the valid flowers
> Sprinkled across the total world and wet
> With night…

11. Shirer, *The Rise and Fall of the Third Reich*, 405.

12. Gardiner, *Code Name "Mary,"* 79.

13. Muriel Gardiner, interview by Brenda Webster, December 1975.

14. Gardiner, *Code Name "Mary,"* 79-80; Ira Nelson Morris, *Heritage from My Father: An Autobiography*, 251–256. In late April 1937, Nelson met his friend Burtis Dolan in Paris and suggested they travel home together on the *Hindenberg*. After Dolan died in the crash, Nelson established a trust fund for his family. Facesofthehindenberg.blogspot.com2009/…/nelson-morris.html. For more information on the Nazi-sponsored Hindenberg, see http://www.airships.net/hindenburg.

15. E. M. "Pete" Bakwin, interview by author, December 11, 2008. Shortly after their marriage, Ruth and Harry Bakwin began purchasing many famous paintings. Included in the Bakwin Collection was Van Gogh's painting, *Madame Ginoux*, which was held in the collection until it was sold by Christie's for more than $40 million. http://www.christies.com/Lotfinder/lot_details.aspx?intObjectID=4701806

16. H. Leichter, *Childhood Memories*, 116.

17. Shirer, *The Rise and Fall of the Third Reich*, 414.

18. Buttinger and Gardiner, *Damit Wir Nicht Vergessen*, 178.

19. Shirer, *The Rise and Fall of the Third Reich*, 422.

20. Buttinger and Gardiner, *Damit Wir Nicht Vergessen*, 179. Robert Danneberg would die in 1942: "Robert Danneberg was born in Wien in 1885. During the war he was in Wien, Austria. Deported

with transport to Dachau on 02/04/1938. Robert perished in 1942 in Auschwitz Camp. This information is based on a List of victims from Austria found in the Namentliche Erfassung der oesterreichischen Holocaustopfer, Dokumentationsarchiv des oesterreichischen Widerstandes (Documentation Centre for Austrian Resistance), Wien." From http://www.yadvashem.org/wps/portal/IY_HON_Welcome.

21. Buttinger and Gardiner, *Damit Wir Nicht Vergessen*, 181; Buttinger, *In the Twilight of Socialism*, 421; MGN.
22. Buttinger and Gardiner, *Damit Wir Nicht Vergessen*, 179–181.
23. REMINISCENCES, 73–74; Gardiner, *Code Name "Mary,"* 83.
24. REMINISCENCES, 75; Shirer, *The Rise and Fall of the Third Reich*, 450. For details of Berchtesgaden meeting, see Shirer, 444–451.
25. Buttinger, "Mary," 105–109.

CHAPTER 12   INVASION

1. Donald G. Daviau, ed., *Austrian Writers and the Anschluss: Understanding the Past—Overcoming the Past* (Riverside, CA: Ariadne Press, 1991), xv, viii.
2. Connie Harvey, REMINISCENCES, interview by Dr. Bluma Swerdloff.
3. Ibid.
4. Ibid.
5. William Shirer, *The Rise and Fall of the Third Reich*, 451.
6. Ibid., 454
7. Luža, *The Resistance in Austria*, 20.
8. Large, *Between Two Fires*, 91.
9. Shirer, *The Rise and Fall of the Third Reich*, 457.
10. Buttinger, *In the Twilight of Socialism,* 470–471.
11. Ibid, 471. Joe's resolution: "Resolution of a special illegal party conference of the Revolutionary Socialists of Austria:
    Workers! Comrades!
       The form of plebiscite Schuschnigg dictates places you before the vote to either vote "yes" or to help Hitler Fascism to power. A victory for Hitler is not only bloody suppression and limitless exploitation of the Austrian workers, but also means a defeat of the workers in the whole world and a strengthening of the inhuman dictatorship, that national fascism has established over the German worker class.
       The Austrian working class may therefore not vote with "no" on Sunday, because they thereby aid Hitler fascism. It cannot on this day get even with the authoritarian regime for what it perpetrated in February, 1934 and thereafter, and would thereby bring itself to greater ruin.
       The 13th of March is not the day of reckoning of the workers with the Austrofascists—
       The 13th of March is for them only a day of demonstrating their fanatical enmity against Hitler fascism.
       Therefore, the working class must vote with "yes" on Sunday, March 13.
       The yes vote of the Austrian workers, who have no other choice, is no vote for the authoritarian regime and Schuschnigg, but is rather a vote against Hitler and the unification. The February battle and the sacrifice rich struggle in the four years of the illegality have shown the world where the working class stands in relation to this regime. The vote on Sunday will not change this, nor the few concessions that the regime has to make the workers in its current plight.
       The vote will not decide Austria's fate. Schuschnigg can win it with the help of the workers, but Austria is still lost if the working class does not continue its fight with strengthened force for full political and unionist freedom. Not a sham vote, not a ballot cast on Sunday, but only a radical, liberal battle of destruction against national fascism can save Austria's independence.
       Therefore an end to authoritarian catastrophic politics!
       Down with Hitler fascism!
       Freedom!"

12. Shirer, *The Rise and Fall of the Third Reich,* 462.
13. Ibid., 465.
14. Otto Bauer, quoted in Buttinger and Gardiner, *Damit Wir Nicht Vergessen,* 193.
15. Gardiner, *Code Name "Mary,"* 91.
16. MGN.
17. Sutherland, *Stephen Spender: The Authorized Biography,* 180.
18. Buttinger, "Mary"; REMINISCENCES, 137–138.
19. MGN.
20. REMINISCENCES, 82.
21. MGN.
22. Gardiner, *Code Name "Mary,"* 93; REMINISCENCES, 84.
23. Buttinger and Gardiner, *Damit Wir Nicht Vergessen,* 195.
24. Muriel Gardiner to Anna Freud, October 2, 1979, Anna Freud Papers, Box 34, Folder 10, Sigmund Freud Collection, Library of Congress, Washington D. C.
25. Shirer, *The Rise and Fall of the Third Reich,* 441, 471–472.
26. REMINISCENCES, 358–359.
27. Gardiner, *Code Name "Mary,"* 94.
28. MGN.
29. Lizzy Rapp-Bauer, "Lest We Forget—The Nazi Era," memoir, January 25, 1991, Austrian Heritage Collection, Leo Baeck Institute, New York.
30. Brenda Webster, *Paradise Farm* (Albany: State University of New York Press, 1999), 154; H. Leichter, *Childhood Memories,* 125.
31. Gedye, *Fallen Bastions,* 9.
32. Ann Kathrin Hamber, interviewed by Martin Horvath, October 10, 1996, Austrian Heritage Collection Interview, Leo Baeck Institute.
33. H. Leichter, *Childhood Memories,* 124-5.
34. George Czuczka, interview by author, April 29, 2009.
35. Jennifer E. Michaels, "The *Anschluss* Remembered: Experiences of the *Anschluss* in the Autobiographies of Elisabeth Castonier, Gina Kaus, Alma Mahler-Werfel, and Hertha Pauli," in *Austrian Writers and the Anschluss: Understanding the Past—Overcoming the Past,* ed. Donald G. Daviau (Riverside CA: Ariadne Press, 1991), 258.
36. Luža, *The Resistance in Austria,* 13; *Inside: The Vienna Jewry, Austrian Information,* New York vol. 36, no. 7/8 (1983); Gertrude Schneider, *Exile and Destruction: The Fate of Austrian Jews 1938–1945* (Westport, CT: Praeger, 1995), 10; Walter B. Maass, *The Years of Darkness: The Austrian Resistance Movement 1938–1945* (Vienna, unknown binding, 1979), 9.
37. Shirer, *The Rise and Fall of the Third Reich,* 473.
38. Luža, *The Resistance in Austria,* 84.
39. Buttinger, *In the Twilight of Socialism,* 482. As a result of the expulsion of the Jews from Austria, entire scientific schools and cultural movements came to an end:
    Neopositivists: Rudolf Carnap; Kurt Godel; Otto Neurath; Edgar Zilsel
    Psychology/Psychoanalysis: Paul Federn; Karl and Charlotte Buhler
    Theoretical Physics: Erwin Schrödinger; Wolfgang Pauli; Lise Meiner
    Social Sciences: Marie Jahoda; Paul Lazarsfeld
    Art History: Ernst Gombrich; Hild Zaloscer
    Theater: Max Reinhardt; Otto Tausig
    Film: Leon Askin; Billy Wilder
    Cabaret: Karl Farkas
    Music: Arnold Schönberg; Ernst Krenek; Robert Stolz; Bruno Walter; Herbert Zipper
    Dance: Otto Werberg
    Painting: Oskar Kokoschka; Josef Floch
    Sculpture: Fritz Wotruba; Anna Schindler
    Architecture: Herbert Eichholzer; Margarete Schütte-Lihotzky; Josef Frank; Oskar Wlach
    Photography: Trude Fleishmann
    Well-Known Authors: Hermann Broch; Elias Canetti; Ödön von Horvath; Robert Musil; Robert Neumann; Josef Roth; Manes Sperber; Hilde Spiel; Friedrich Troberg; Franz Werfel; Stefan Zweig

CHAPTER 13   THE THIRD WOMAN

1. Spender, *World within World*, 377–378.
2. *The Real Julia: The Muriel Gardiner Story*; Wagner and Tomkowitz, *Anschluss*, 209; Luža, *The Resistance in Austria*, 8.
3. Buttinger, *Twilight of Socialism*, 481; Wagner and Tomkowitz, *Anschluss*, 16; http://www.yad-vashem.org/wps/portal/IY_HON_Welcome.
4. Wagner and Tomkowitz, *Anschluss*, 8.
5. Paul Streeten, An Autobiographical Sketch, "Aerial Roots," 1917–1986, in *Banca Nazionale del Lavoro Quarterly Review* no. 157 (1986): 135–159, Austrian Heritage Collection, Leo Baeck Institute, New York.
6. Wagner and Tomkowitz, *Anschluss*, 13.
7. REMINISCENCES, 96.
8. Ibid., 97.
9. Ibid., 98.
10. Ibid.
11. Ann Kathrin Hamber, interviewed by Martin Horvath, October 10, 1996, Austrian Heritage Collection Interview, Leo Baeck Institute; Saul Friedländer, *Nazi Germany and the Jews,* vol. 2, *The Years of Extermination, 1939–1945* (New York: HarperCollins, 2007), 91.
12. Connie Harvey, interview by author, November 4, 2008.
13. *The Real Julia: The Muriel Gardiner Story.*
14. "Germany: Rothschild Ransomed," *Time*, May 22, 1939.
15. Franz Leichter, interview by author, April 16, 2009; H. Leichter, *Childhood Memories*, 122.
16. REMINISCENCES, 105–106.
17. Ibid., 106.
18. Steiner, "The Role of the Resistance in Austria, S129; H. Leichter, *Childhood Memories*, 123; Friedländer, *Nazi Germany and the Jews*, vol. 1, *The Years of Persecution*, 239.
19. Grant McConnell, letter to Ann Harvey, August 6, 1983, in private collection.
20. REMINISCENCES, 108.
21. Ibid., 109.
22. Ibid., 110–111.
23. Senator Müller, quoted in REMINISCENCES, 114.
24. Kurt Sonnenfeld, email to author, March 6, 2010; Otto Franz Bauer (son of Little Otto Bauer), interview by author, December 19, 2008.
25. REMINISCENCES, 116–117.
26. Shirer, *The Rise and Fall of the Third Reich*, 477; http://www.country-data.com/frd/cs/attoc.html.
27. Shirer, *The Rise and Fall of the Third Reich*, 476; Luža, *The Resistance in Austria*, 8.
28. H. Leichter, *Childhood Memories*,125.
29. REMINISCENCES, 89.
30. *Encyclopaedia Britannica Online*, "League of Nations Passport," http://search.eb.com.online.library.marist.edu/eb/article-9063038, accessed March 12, 2010.
31. Gardiner, "The Wolf-Man in Later Life," in *The Wolf-Man by the Wolf-Man*, 311–315.
32. REMINISCENCES, 118.
33. Ibid., 122–123.
34. Ibid., 124.
35. Ibid., 125.
36. Otto Franz Bauer, interview by author, December 10, 2008.
37. *The Real Julia: The Muriel Gardiner Story.*
38. Gardiner, *Code Name "Mary,"* 123–126.
39. Ibid., 127.
40. Buttinger, *In the Twilight of Socialism*, 483.
41. Joseph Buttinger, letter to Friedrich Adler, April 13, 1938, DöW; David Gil, interview by Christian Lerch, February 28, 2005, Austrian Heritage Collection, Leo Baeck Institute; Herbert Steiner, "The Role of the Resistance in Austria," S129. David Gil's story: "The problem was that most people didn't have any place to go. [When my father was arrested] then my mother took over the running of affairs. And she registered my brother and me for Youth-Aliyah. Now I was too young

for going to Palestine. My brother was going to Palestine straight, he was older. And I was sent to Sweden. I was there for a year and then in March 1940 I was able to go to Palestine. This was just a few weeks before Holland and Belgium and France were occupied. We flew from Sweden to Holland, Amsterdam, and from there by train to Marseilles. From there we sailed by boat to Palestine. My mother said she would need to get my father out. Then she was able to get transit on an illegal transport to Palestine. That was in 1941. They were caught by the British in the Mediterranean. They were to be deported to a British colony in Africa. They were put on a boat, the Patria, which the Jewish underground blew up. I guess 200 people died in that event, they were 2000 people on that boat to be deported.

[Question] The Jewish underground blew up a boat with Jewish people on it?

Yes. In order to prevent the deportation. Their calculus was: we will save some, some will die. My parents swam to shore, were arrested and were put into a British internment camp in Atlit. My mother died in that camp shortly after they arrived. She had typhus."

42. Joseph Buttinger, letter to Friedrich Adler, envelope 7632, letter no. 2, Buttinger papers, DöW; MGN.
43. REMINISCENCES, 130–131.
44. Ibid., 129–130.
45. H. Leichter, *Childhood Memories*, 123.
46. Franz Leichter, interview by author, April 16, 2009; Luža, *The Resistance in Austria*, 85.
47. H. Leichter, *Childhood Memories*, 128–129.
48. http://www.yadvashem.org/wps/portal/IY_HON_Welcome.
49. Otto Alfred Snyder, "Reflections: The Background and Experiences of Two Immigrants. A Partial History of Our Family," Memoir Collection, Leo Baeck Institute, 1986. From "Jews in Vienna," in *Inside: The Vienna Jewry, Austrian Information, New York* vol. 36, no. 7/8: "The history of the Vienna Jewry can be traced back to the time of the Romans…Jews lived in Vienna at the beginning of the 10th century, with a ghetto instituted in the 13th century, situated around the square called 'Judenplatz' today. At the close of the 13th and during the 14th century, the community of Vienna was recognized as the leading community of German Jewry…There were cruel persecutions in 1421 in the course of which many Jews died as martyrs and some were expelled…Only a small number of Jews lived in Vienna in the 15th and 16th centuries. Jewish community life was revived at the beginning of the 17th century…The Jews returned slowly under special license after 1675…It was Maria Theresa's son, Emperor Joseph II, who by issuing his 'Toleranzpatent' in 1781 paved the way in many respects for 19th century emancipation…Jews participated in the revolution of 1848 and were granted equal rights in 1849 and finally in 1867.

"After centuries of oppression, after the revolution of the year 1848, the Jews of Vienna enjoyed a golden age, once they had been granted their freedom, which was of extraordinary cultural importance and which enriched not only the Jews, but Vienna and Austria too. At the end of the 19th and first quarter of the 20th century, Vienna was a center of Zionism…Jews were among the founders of the first political parties in the monarchy, and occupied leading positions in both the liberal and the social democratic parties…The federal constitution of the Republic of Austria, established in 1918 after the collapse of the empire, was drawn up by the Jewish constitutional lawyer Hans Kelson, and the exemplary social achievement of the First Republic would have been inconceivable without…men like Victor Adler, Otto Bauer, Hugo Breitner, Robert Danneberg, Julius Deutsch [and others].

"…The share of the Jewish citizens of Vienna in the technical and industrial development of the country was outstanding…they helped to make Vienna one of the most beautiful and modern cities in Europe. [Some names:] Astronomy—Samuel Oppenheim; biochemistry—Max F. Perutz (Nobel Prize 1962), Ernst Pribam; biology—Hans Pribam; botany—Julius von Wiesner; chemistry—Fritz Feigl, Otto von Fürth, Leo Grünhut, Reginald O. Herzog, Edmund von Lippmann (founder of the German sugar industry, Eduard Lippmann; physics—Martin Deutsch, Felix Ehrenhaft, Otto R. Frisch, Sulamit Goldhaver, Lise Meitner, Wolfgang Pauli (Nobel Prize 1945), Victor F. Weiskopf; zoology—Berthold Hatschek. As well as Lise Meitner, Isidor Isaac Rabi…awarded the Nobel prize for physics in 1944. Other Jewish Nobel prizewinners of Austrian origin include: Alfred Hermann Fried, Nobel prize for peace 1911; Karl Landsteiner (1930) and Otto Loewi (1936), Nobel Prize for medicine; Robert Bárány, Nobel prize for physiology in 1941; Elias Canetti, Nobel prize for literature 1981…

"The Jews of Vienna in the arts, literature and journalism…were active in the theatre as dramatists, actors and producers [including] Max Reinhardt, Berthold Viertel, Billy Wilder "and others. In music, above all Gustav Mahler, and then Arnold Schönberg, as initiator and creator of the Vienna School [and] Johann Strauss senior, who was half-Jewish…the blossoming of Austrian culture, reaching from the middle of the last century until the annexation of Austria in 1938, was for the most part determined by artists and scholars of Jewish origin.

"…In the year 1938 there were 180,000 Jews in Vienna. This figure sank due to persecution, expulsion and extermination to the present 8,000–10,000."

50.   David Cohen, *The Escape of Sigmund Freud* (London: JR Books Ltd, 2009), 159.
51.   Muriel Gardiner to Anna Freud, October 2, 1979, Anna Freud Papers, Sigmund Freud Collection, Library of Congress.
52.   REMINISCENCES, 132, 134.
53.   Ibid., 135.
      DEFINITION OF A JEW: The Reich Citizenship Law: First Regulation (November 14, 1935): Article 5
      1. A Jew is anyone who is descended from at least three grandparents who are racially full Jews. Article 2, para. 2, second sentence will apply.
      2. A Jew is also one who is descended from two full Jewish parents, if (a) he belonged to the Jewish religious community at the time this law was issued, or joined the community later, (b) he was married to a Jewish person, at the time the law was issued, or married one subsequently, (c) he is the offspring of a marriage with a Jew, in the sense of Section I, which was contracted after the Law for the Protection of German Blood and German Honor became effective, (d) he is the offspring of an extramarital relationship with a Jew, according to Section I, and will be born out of wedlock after July 31, 1936.
      http://www.jewishvirtuallibrary.org/jsource/Holocaust/nurmlaw4.html.
54.   REMINISCENCES, 353–354.
55.   Gardiner, *Code Name "Mary,"* 130-131.
56.   Friedländer, *Nazi Germany and the Jews,* vol. 1, *The Years of Persecution, 1933–1939,* 247; H. Leichter, *Childhood Memories,* 123.

CHAPTER 14   AMERICA: HOME FROM THE WARS

1.   MGN.
2.   REMINISCENCES, 160; MGN.
3.   Connie Harvey, interview by author, November 6, 2008.
4.   Franz Goldner, *Austrian Emigration, 1938–1945* (New York: F. Ungar, 1979), 8–9.
5.   MGN.
6.   Joseph Buttinger, letter to Friedrich Adler, letter no. 2, pages 4–6, Envelope 7632, Buttinger material, DöW; Sigline Bolbecher and Konstantin Kaiser, eds. *Lexikon der österreichischen Exilliteratur* (Vienna: Deuticke, 2000), 21–22.
7.   REMINISCENCES, 141.
8.   Buttinger, "Mary."
9.   Franz Leichter, email to author, July 10, 2010; H. Leichter, *Childhood Memories,* 135–136.
10. Luža, *The Resistance in Austria,* 84–85.
11. Gardiner, *Code Name "Mary,"* 136.
12. Ibid.
13. Friedländer, *Nazi Germany and the Jews,* vol. 1, *The Years of Persecution, 1933–1939,* 267.
14. MGN: Joseph Buttinger and Hans Pav communicated by letter in February and April 1939 with no hint that Joe knew that Pav was a spy. This is somewhat confusing since Pav's name was given to Henry Leichter by his mother, Käthe, when he visited her just before his escape to Paris in August 1938. But in the correspondence between Joe and Pav, dated February 9, 1939, and April 3, 1939, warm greetings are exchanged, and Pav sends regards to Muriel. From Joseph Buttinger, letter to Hans Pav, September 2, 1939, and October 2, 1939, Joseph Buttinger correspondence, envelope # 16145/40, DöW. The envelope is labeled: "Correspondence between Buttinger (Paris) and Hans Pav (Arosa/Switzerland) regarding questions concerning Austria; it is well known that Pav worked for the Gestapo. The correspondence took place between February 9 and April 3,

1939." Hans Pav was later tried and convicted of war crimes. Kurt Sonnenfeld, email to author, March 19, 2010.

15. Gardiner, *Code Name "Mary,"* 137.

16. "Kristallnacht: The November 1938 Pogroms," United States Holocaust Memorial Museum, http://www.ushmm.org/museum/exhibit/focus/kristallnacht/; "Kristallnacht: A Nationwide Pogrom, November 9-10, 1938," United States Holocaust Memorial Museum, http://www.ushmm.org/wlc/en/article.php?ModuleId=10005201.

17. William French, "Code Name Mary," *The Globe and Mail* (Canada), May 26, 1983.

18. MGN.

19. It is understandable that Muriel would be nervous in the vicinity of the notorious Mauthausen camp. "On August 8, 1938, just a few [months] after the Nazi occupation of Austria, prisoners from the Dachau concentration camp near Munich, were transferred to the Austrian town of Mauthausen, near Linz. They were brought to the rock quarry there, known as the 'Wiener Graben,' where they began to build the granite fortress-prison of the main camp, mostly with their blood, bodies, bare hands and backs. It was known as the 'mother camp' for all of Austria, comprising some 49 sub-camps. Between Aug. 8, 1938 and May 5, 1945, about 195,000 persons, men and women, were forced into these camps. Most of the people were imprisoned under the Nazi 'protective custody' laws, that is, they were considered dangerous to the Third Reich of Germany and Austria, and therefore, these two nations, now joined, had to be 'protected' from these people because of their racial origin, nationality, political affiliation or religious belief. It should be noted that Austria contributed more volunteers for the SS, per capita, than did Germany.

The Mauthausen camp was one of the most infamous in the entire Nazi alternate universe of human destruction. Many people, most of whom were innocent of any crimes, were tortured to death in its rock quarry, and in the tunnels of Mauthausen-Gusen, the most infamous of the sub-camps. The policy of death through work was instituted by Chief of SS Reichsfuhrer Heinrich Himmler. Prisoners were to be given only the most primitive tools, and also, whenever possible, they were to work with their bare hands. This policy was known as 'Primitivbauweise.' In Mauthausen it resulted in a harsh, stone world, deprived of any human kindness and compassion. It is there today still...sitting on a small mountain-top in the astonishingly beautiful and bucolic Austrian countryside, maintained by the Austrian government." From http://remember.org/camps/mauthausen/mau-introduction.html.

20. REMINISCENCES, 151–152.

21. REMINISCENCES, 152; Gardiner, *Code Name "Mary,"* 144.

22. Gardiner, *Code Name "Mary,"* 145–146.

23. Ibid.,146.

24. Gardiner, *Code Name "Mary,"* 147; Anderson, *Hitler's Exiles*, 12; Hitler's speech to the Reichstag on January 30, 1939, http://www.holocaust-history.org/der-ewige-jude/hitler-19390130.shtml.

25. "Munich Agreement," *Encyclopedia Britannica* (online), http://www.britannica.com/EBchecked/topic/397522/Munich-agreement.

26. Joseph Buttinger, letter to Friedrich Adler, March 8, 1939, Envelope 7632, Buttinger papers, DöW.

27. MGN.

28. Ibid.

29. Connie Harvey, interview by author, November 5, 2008; Buttinger, *In the Twilight of Socialism*, 541.

30. Sutherland, *Stephen Spender*, 238, 244.

31. REMINISCENCES,160; MGN.

32. REMINISCENCES, 162.

33. Gardiner, *Code Name "Mary,"* 151.

34. Connie Harvey, interview by author, November 7, 2008.

35. REMINISCENCES, 162.

36. Ibid., 163.

37. Gardiner, *Code Name "Mary,"* 153; REMINISCENCES, 170.

38. Connie Harvey, interview by author, November 7, 2008.

39. REMINISCENCES, 170.

40. Kurt Sonnenfeld, email to author, March 23, 2010.
41. Buttinger, *In the Twilight of Socialism*, 514.
42. Kurt Sonnenfeld, email to author, May 1, 2010; Goldner, *Austrian Emigration*, 24.
43. Goldner, *Austrian Emigration*, 25–26.
44. Ernst Glaser, "The Time of Illegality," 66.
45. REMINISCENCES, 171–174.
46. MGN.
47. REMINISCENCES, 173.

CHAPTER 15   A HEALING TIME

1. MGN. Goldner writes in *Austrian Immigration, 1938-1945*, that at this point not many under Nazi control would find a way out, although Sweden continued to be a safe haven. Switzerland apparently changed its earlier attitude and took in many people fleeing France after 1942. Other countries that took people in, often in tightly controlled numbers, included Canada, Australia, the Union of South Africa, Kenya, British dominions such as India, some South American, Central American, and Caribbean countries, especially the Dominican Republic, Palestine, and even Shanghai.
2. MGN.
3. E. M. "Pete" Bakwin, interview by author, December 11, 2008.
4. MGN.
5. Ibid.
6. Buttinger and Gardiner, *Damit Wir Nicht Vergessen*, 151–158.
7. REMINISCENCES, 185–186.
8. Ibid., 187–188.
9. Anderson, *Hitler's Exiles*, 1; Sheila Isenberg, *A Hero of Our Own: The Story of Varian Fry* (New York: Random House, 2001), 9.
10. Goldner, *Austrian Immigration*, 4; "Immigration Policies," Jewish Virtual Library, http://www.jewishvirtuallibrary.org/jsource/Holocaust/grobim.html.
11. This was a practice Muriel continued all her life, even providing a loan to Nobel Prize-winning writer Czesław Miłosz after he emigrated to the United States. (Connie Harvey, interview by author, November 5, 2008).
12. Buttinger and Gardiner, *Damit Wir Nicht Vergesssen*,158; Heiden, quoted in *Damit Wir Nicht Vergessen*, 156.
13. MGN.
14. Joseph Buttinger, letter to Oskar Pollak, January 19, 1940, Envelope 7824, Buttinger papers, Dokumentationsarchiv des österrichischen Widerstandes (Documentary Archives of the Austrian Resistance (DöW).
15. Gertrude Danneberg to Muriel Gardiner, July 16, 1940, Buttinger papers, DöW.
16. Connie Harvey, telephone interview by author, January 19, 2002.
17. Aaron Levenstein, *Escape to Freedom: The Story of the International Rescue Committee* (Westport, CT: Greenwood Press, 1983), 9.
18. Siglinde Bolbecher and Konstantin Kaiser, eds. *Lexikon der österreichischen Exilliteratur* (Vienna: Deuticke, 2000), 21–22; Isenberg, *A Hero of Our Own*, 17.
19. H. Leichter, *Childhood Memories*, 172-3.
20. Buttinger and Gardiner, *Damit Wir Nicht Vergessen*, 153–154; Joseph Lash, quoted in Levenstein, *Escape to Freedom*, 21; Eleanor Roosevelt, quoted in Levenstein, *Escape to Freedom*, 22.
21. Joseph Buttinger, Report, "Attempts to Organize Assistance for Political Refugees in France and England," June 26–27, 1940, Buttinger papers, DöW; Isenberg, *A Hero of Our Own*, 8.
22. Kurt Sonnenfeld, interview by author, February 15, 2009.
23. Ibid.
24. Franz Leichter, interview by author, April 16, 2009; Buttinger and Gardiner, *Damit Wir Nicht Vergessen*, 151–158; Joseph Buttinger, letters to Loisl Buttinger, August 23, 1940, and September 11, 1940, Buttinger papers, DöW.
25. Joseph Buttinger, letter to Harry Kriszhabers, December 6, 1940, Buttinger papers, DöW.

26. "Seven Ways to Compute the Relative Value of a U.S. Dollar Amount, 1774 to Present," Measuring Worth website, http://www.measuringworth.com/uscompare/.

27. Connie Harvey, interview by author, November 4, 2008.

28. Gardiner, *Code Name "Mary,"* 173.

29. Brenda Webster, telephone interview by author, July 1, 2009; "Seven Ways to Compute the Relative Value of a U.S. Dollar Amount, 1774 to Present," Measuring Worth website, http://www.measuringworth.com/uscompare/; Connie Harvey, interview by author, November 5, 2008.

30. Dennis Buttinger, telephone interview by author, August 26, 2009.

31. "Classification System in Nazi Concentration Camps," United States Holocaust Memorial Museum, *Holocaust Encyclopedia*, http://www.ushmm.org/wlc/en/article.php?ModuleId=10005378; Anderson, *Hitler's Exiles*, 14.

32. REMINISCENCES, 43–44.

33. Muriel Gardiner, essays about New Jersey State Hospital at Trenton: "Accident Ward," "Ambulance Call," "Awful Light for a Nigger," "Blackout," "DOA," "Hospital Bed," "The Newborn," "No Harm Has Been Done," "What Does It Matter?" unpublished, in private collection.

34. Muriel Gardiner, "I Didn't Ask to Have It," unpublished, in private collection.

35. Goldner, *Austrian Emigration*, 55–56; J. Buttinger and Gardiner, *Damit Wir Nicht Vergessen*, 157.

36. Spender, *World within World*, 330–331.

37. "http://www.ushmm.org/wlc/en/article.php?ModuleId=10005477.

38. Allgemeine correspondence to General Jewish Council, New York City, October 6, 1942, Envelope 18890/3, Buttinger papers, DöW.

39. Letter to Joseph Buttinger from Gurs, March 14, 1941, envelope 18882/24, Buttinger papers, DöW; "Wannsee Conference and the 'Final Solution,'" United States Holocaust Memorial Museum, *Holocaust Encyclopedia*, http://www.ushmm.org/wlc/article.php?lang=en&ModuleId=10005298; http://www.yadvashem.org/wps/portal/IY_Hon_Welcome.

40. Anderson, *Hitler's Exiles*, 14; H. Leichter, *Childhood Memories*, 189, 213.

41. REMINISCENCES, 229.

42. REMINISCENCES, 229. The New-Land Foundation identifies its five grant-making program areas as: Civil Rights/Justice, Population Control, Peace/Arms Control, Leadership Development, and Environment. The foundation today supports the anti-capitalist agendas of radical environmentalism. In recent years, the leading recipients of New-Land environmental grants have been: the Environmental Working Group; the Tides Foundation and Tides Center; Environmental Defense; the Union of Concerned Scientists; the Rainforest Alliance; Earthjustice; the Northern Plains Resource Council; Earth Island Institute; the Natural Resources Defense Council; Green Corps; the League of Conservation Voters; Conservation International; and Earth Day Network. Another priority is the foundation's effort to shrink, and to alter the nature of, the American military and to that end, it is a member organization of the Peace and Security Funders Group. Muriel's grandson, Hal Harvey, is the president of New-Land's Board of Directors. http://www.discoverthenetworks.org/funderprofile.asp?fndid=5370&category=79.

43. Connie Harvey, interview by author, November 6, 2008.

44. Ernst Langendorf (who would become the director of Radio Free Europe), May 5, 1945.

45. Muriel Gardiner, letter to Connie Harvey, May 13, 1945, in private collection.

46. Muriel Gardiner, letter to Joseph Buttinger from Paris, undated, in private collection.

47. Muriel Gardiner, letter to Sheba Strunsky, May 13, 1945; Muriel Gardiner, letters to Joseph Buttinger, May 12 and 13, 1945, in private collection.

48. Muriel Gardiner, letter to Joseph Buttinger, undated, in private collection.

49. Muriel Gardiner, letters to Joseph Buttinger, June 27, July 8, July 18, and July 23, 1945, in private collection.

50. Muriel Gardiner, letter to Joseph Buttinger, June 2, 1945, in private collection.

51. Muriel's mother, Helen Swift Morris Neilson, was a patron of the arts. During her lifetime, along with her second husband, Francis Neilson, she endowed charities and made contributions to many institutions, including the University of Chicago. At her death, she bequeathed much of her vast art collection, including works by Rembrandt and John Singer Sargent, to museums, including the Metropolitan Museum of Art in New York City and the Boston Museum of Fine

Art. Helen also left an estate of $2 million, worth more than $22 million in today's money. http://www.measuring worth.com/calculators/uscompare/index.phpl.

52. Muriel Gardiner, letter to Joseph Buttinger, July 4, 1945, in private collection.
53. Ibid., July 5, 1945.
54. Ibid., July 9, 1945.
55. Ibid., July 16, 1945.
56. Ibid., July 23, 1945.
57. Ibid., July 28, 1945.
58. Ibid., August 15, 1945.
59. Ibid., August 26, 1945.
60. Ibid., September 1, 1945.

CHAPTER 16   A FULLNESS OF LIVING

1. Partial summary kept by Joseph Buttinger of thank-you letters and requests sent to Muriel and Joe from European refugees after the war. All information from Buttinger Material, Dokumentationsarchiv des österreichischen Widerstandes (DöW) or Documentation Center of the Austrian Resistance (DOEW) in Vienna:
   1946: 14 thank-you letters for care packages
   1946–48: 25 thank-you letters for care packages
   1946–49: 40 thank-you letters for care packages
   1947: 85 thank-you letters for care packages; 54 thank-you letters
   1947–49: 420 thank-you letters for care packages
   1947–48: 151 thank-you letters for care packages
   Requests for care packages: 16
   * request help to stay in Switzerland
   * request for balls & trainer for sports club
   1948: 66 thank-you letters; 44 thank-you letters for care packages
   Requests for care packages: 14
   1948–49: 85 thank-you letters for care packages
   * 2 requests for help for apartment exchange
   * 2 letters from Anna Schon-Kuffner- requesting medicine.
   * request suit for wedding
   * request to help get choir singing music
   * request medicine
   * request for stockings
   * thanks for gift to sports club
   1949: 20 thank-you letters
   List of recipients of care packages: Austria, Germany, France, England
   Oct. 1950: 10 packages to Germany; 12 packages to Austria; 1 package to France
   Christmas 1950: 9 packages to Germany; 18 packages to Austria; 3 packages to France; 1 package to England
   Dec. 1953: 13 packages to Austria; 3 packages to Germany; 4 packages to France
   Undisclosed date: 21 packages to Austria; 9 Packages to Germany; 3 packages to England; 3 packages to France
   List of more than 50 additional packages (no date or country listed—only addresses).
2. Buttinger and Gardiner, *Damit Wir Nicht Vergessen*, 163–164.
3. Ibid., 161.
4. CARE was begun in 1945. CARE packages were paid for by donations from individuals, like Muriel, and from American companies. The first packages included one pound of beef in broth; one pound of steak and kidneys; eight ounces each of liver loaf, corned beef and bacon; twelve ounces of luncheon loaf (like Spam); two pounds each of coffee, whole milk powder, margarine, and sugar; one pound each of lard, fruit preserves, honey, raisins, and chocolate; eight ounces of egg powder. Later CARE packages included food for different cultural diets and non-food items such as carpentry tools, blankets, school supplies and medicine. www.care.org/index.asp

5. Buttinger and Gardiner, *Damit Wir Nicht Vergessen*, 162, 165; Peter Unterweger, interview by author, March 19, 2009.

6. Eric Thomas Chester, *Covert Network: Progressives, the International Rescue Committee, and the CIA* (Armonk, NY: M. E. Sharpe, 1995), 1–4.

7. There are conflicting reports on the causes of Ruth Mack Brunswick's death. The first is that it had to do with her drug addition: "The worst of Ruth's drug addiction occurred in America…Ruth's death in 1946 was the end-result of a pattern of self-destructive behavior. She had been drinking paregoric the way an alcoholic consumes whiskey. Her health was undermined, and the federal authorities had taken note of her drug-taking. She caught pneumonia, recovered, and then died from the combination of too many opiates and a fall in the bathroom; she had hit her head and fractured her skull. The full tragedy was for many years not publicly known. The cloudy circumstances associated with Ruth's medical troubles, and the misfortune of her early death, have obscured both her scientific contributions and her immense personal standing with Freud." From Paul Roazen, "Brunswick, Ruth Mack [1897–1946]," in *International Dictionary of Psychoanalysis*, 2005, http://www.encyclopedia.com.

    But her obituary in the *New York Times* stated that she died of a heart attack brought on by pneumonia. "Ruth Brunswick, Freud Associate," *New York Times*, January 26, 1946.

8. Connie Harvey, interview by author, November 6, 2008.

9. Ibid.

10. Ibid.

11. Larkin Warren, telephone interview by author, April 14, 2009.

12. Muriel Gardiner, letter to Margarita Konenkov, December 12, 1947, in private collection.

13. Muriel Storfer, telephone interview by author, January 27, 2009; Gerda Gray, telephone interview by author, April 5, 2010; Lady Natasha Spender, interview by author, March 24, 2009.

14. Larkin Warren, telephone interview by author, April 14, 2009.

15. Charles Silberstein, telephone interview by author, November 29, 2008.

16. Muriel Gardiner, last will and testament, January 21, 1985.

17. Brenda Webster, telephone interview by author, July 1, 2009; Connie Harvey, interview by author, November 6, 2008.

18. Joseph Buttinger, letter to Muriel Gardiner, January 29, 1947, quoted in Buttinger and Gardiner, *Damit Wir Nicht Vergessen*, 165.

19. Robin Pogrebin, "Love Letters by Einstein at Auction," *New York Times*, June 1, 1998; Martin Kettle, "Letters reveal scientist's compromising passion: Einstein's affair with a spy from Moscow; Evidence found in Russia shows that the father of modern physics had a long relationship with a Soviet agent who was trying to extract nuclear secrets while the US was developing the atom bomb," *The Guardian* (London), June 2, 1998, 3; Muriel Gardiner, quoted in introduction to *The Uncommon Vision of Sergei Konenkov, 1874–1971*, 50.

20. Was Margarita Konenkov a Soviet spy? Opinions vary. First, Einstein met Margarita and Sergei Konenkov through his wife, Margot, who was also a sculptor. Einstein became romantically involved with Margarita after his wife died, creating more complications than he could have at that time foreseen. Einstein biographer Walter Isaacson wrote, "Margarita, unbeknown to Einstein, was a soviet spy." From Walter Isaacson, *Einstein: His Life and Universe* (New York: Simon & Schuster, 2007), 436–437.

    But another Einstein biographer, Thomas Levenson, was not so certain: "The lover in question, a Russian émigré named Margarita Konenkova, was listed by a Russian intelligence officer as one of his agents. The full list included a wide range of alleged spies, even Niels Bohr, which has led to the suspicion that the entire file was fake, a real-life version of Graham Greene's *Our Man in Havana*. From Thomas Levenson, *Einstein in Berlin* (New York: Bantam Books, 2003), 437.

    The Russians said Muriel's friend Margarita was indeed a Soviet spy: "…our veteran agent Margaret Konenkova (code name "Lukas"), the wife of the famous Russian sculptor Sergei Konenkov, who was working in Princeton on a bust of Einstein, to influence Oppenheimer and other prominent American scientists whom she met frequently in Princeton from 1943 to 1945." From Pavel Sudoplatov and Anatoli Sudoplatov, with Jerrold L. and Leona P. Schecter, *Special Tasks: The Memoirs of an Unwanted Witness, a Soviet Spymaster*, updated ed. (Boston: Little, Brown, 1995), 493.

21. Brenda Webster, telephone interview by author, July 1, 2009.
22. Mitchell Cohen, "Decades of Dissent," *Dissent* (Winter 2004).
23. "Son Asked Study of Einstein Brain, Scientist's Will Includes No Specific Bequest of Body—Neighbors Mourn," *New York Times,* April 20, 1955.
24. Connie Harvey, interview by author, November 5, 2008.
25. Ibid.
26. Ibid.
27. Connie Harvey, email to author, April 7, 2010.
28. Quoted in Levenstein, *Escape to Freedom,* 56.
29. MGN.
30. Otto Franz Bauer, interview by author, December 10, 2008.
31. Chester, *Covert Network,* 160.
32. Ibid., 162.
33. Ibid., 169–173.
34. Larkin Warren, telephone interview by author, April 14, 2009; Chester, *Covert Network,* 175.
35. Todd Gitlin, *The Sixties: Years of Hope, Days of Rage* (New York: Bantam, 1993), 171, 173.
36. Muriel Gardiner, letters to Berta Bornstein, Muriel Gardiner Papers, the Sigmund Freud Collection, Library of Congress.
37. MGN.
38. Dr. Daniel Jacobs, telephone interview by author, February 6, 2009.
39. Ibid.
40. Muriel Storfer, telephone interview by author, January 27, 2009.
41. Muriel Gardiner, letter to Fred Stackpole, August 30, 1962, in private collection; Muriel Gardiner, quoted in Johnson, "Obituary of Dr. Muriel Gardiner," Princeton, New Jersey, Town Topics, February 13, 1985.
42. Dr. Daniel Jacobs, telephone interview by author, February 6, 2009.
43. Muriel Gardiner, letter to Clara and Pavel Thalmann, December 3, 1962, in private collection; Guntram Weissenberger, telephone interview with author, December 10, 2008; Peter Unterweger, interview with author, March 20, 2009; Jessica Lohnes, interview with author, July 7, 2009; Anne Nowak, telephone interview with author, September 10, 2009.
44. Information about Muriel's travels from her letters to Anna Freud, Box 34, Anna Freud Papers, Sigmund Freud Collection, Library of Congress; Stephen Spender, unpublished journal material, January 1, 1994, reprinted by kind permission of the Estate of Stephen Spender; Muriel Gardiner, letter to Clara Thalmann, May 27, 1969, in private collection.
45. *Wellspring,* The Quarterly Newsletter of the Stony Brook-Millstone Watershed Association 46, no. 3 (Fall 1999).
46. Muriel Gardiner, "To C," unpublished, in private collection.
47. Connie Harvey, REMINISCENCES, interview by Dr. Bluma Swerdloff.
48. Muriel Gardiner, note to Joseph Buttinger, October 1959, in private collection.

CHAPTER 17 "ARE YOU JULIA?"

1. Muriel Gardiner, *curriculum vitae,* in private family collection.
2. Muriel Gardiner, letter to Anna Freud, October 19, 1979, Anna Freud Papers, Sigmund Freud Collection, Library of Congress.
3. Gerda Gray, telephone interview by author, April 5, 2010.
4. Gardiner, Introduction, *The Wolf-Man by the Wolf-Man,* v; Anna Freud, Foreword, *The Wolf-Man by the Wolf-Man,* xi.
5. Larkin Warren, interview by author, April 14, 2009.
6. Ibid.
7. Mark Harvey, interview by author, November 5, 2008; Hal Harvey, phone interview by author, April 20, 2009.
8. Mark Harvey, interview by author, November 5, 2008.
9. Marc Wortman, "The Muses On the Couch," *Yale Alumni Magazine, LII, no. 2,* (November 1988): 27–31.

10. Brenda Webster, telephone interview by author, October 22, 2008; *The Real Julia: The Muriel Gardiner Story*; Gardiner, *Code Name "Mary,"* 178.
11. Gardiner, *Code Name "Mary,"* 178.
12. Nancy Olson, interview by author, August 26, 2009; Dennis Buttinger, letter to Muriel Gardiner, July 6, 1978; Jessica Lohnes, interview by author, May 11, 2009.
13. Stephen Spender, unpublished journal material, August 2–3, 1980, 335, reprinted by kind permission of the Estate of Stephen Spender,
14. Ibid.
15. David Garrard Lowe, "'Julia' and Muriel Gardiner," *Dissent* 33 (Summer 1986): 367, http://www.dissentmagazine.org/article/?article=3455.
16. *The Real Julia: The Muriel Gardiner Story*; Lillian Hellman, "Julia," in *Pentimento* (Boston: Little, Brown, 1973), 107, 114, 118, 138–9.
17. Timothy Dow Adams, "Lillian Hellman: 'Are You Now or Have You Ever Been?'" *Telling Lies in Modern American Autobiography* (Chapel Hill: University of North Carolina Press, 1990), 139–153.
18. Lillian Hellman, *An Unfinished Woman: A Memoir* (Boston: Little, Brown, 1969), 44.
19. *The Real Julia: The Muriel Gardiner Story.*
20. William Wright, *Lillian Hellman: The Image, the Woman* (New York: Simon & Schuster, 1986), 407.
21. Marcia Burick, "Moment of Friendship," *Wellesley Magazine* (Spring 1985).
22. Muriel Gardiner, letter to Anna Freud, March 10, 1977, Anna Freud Papers.
23. Gardiner, introduction to *Code Name "Mary,"* xvi.
24. Muriel Gardiner, letter to Lillian Hellman, October 26, 1976, in private collection.
25. John Simon, "Pentimental Journey," *The Hudson Review* 26, no. 4 (Winter 1973–1974): 743–752.
26. Katie Roiphe, "Imagining Enemies: Nora Ephron's Theory of Mary McCarthy vs. Lillian Hellman," *Slate* Magazine (online), Tuesday, December 10, 2002, http://www.slate.com/id/2075251/.
27. Stephen Spender, unpublished journal material, September 2, 1980–January 21, 1981, November 6–18, 1981, 135, reprinted by kind permission of the Estate of Stephen Spender; Connie Harvey, interview by author, November 6, 2008.
28. Muriel Gardiner, letter to Anna Freud, April 10, 1980, Anna Freud Papers.
29. Burt A. Folkart, "Dr. Muriel Gardiner Dies; Helped Anti-Fascists Flee Austria," *Los Angeles Times*, February 8, 1985, http://articles.latimes.com/1985-02-08/news/mn-4906_1_muriel-gardiner.
30. Muriel Gardiner, letter to Anna Freud, March 7, 1981, Anna Freud Papers; Muriel Gardiner, letter to Martha (no last name given), September 10,1983, in private collection; Muriel Gardiner, letter to Anna Freud, March 7, 1981, Anna Freud Papers.
31. Quoted in "Old Mortality" by Sir Walter Scott, 375, as Anonymous, but actually from "The Call" by Thomas Osbert Mordaunt (1730–1809); Dr. Herbert Steiner, quoted in Edwin McDowell, "Publishing: New Memoir Stirs 'Julia' Controversy," *New York Times*, April 29, 1983.
32. Gladys Topkis, letter to Muriel Gardiner, May 25, 1982, in private collection.
33. Victoria Lubin, "Muriel Gardiner and Anna Loeb on the Resistance," *Valley News*, September 3, 1983, 15; Hal Harvey, phone interview by author, April 20, 2009.
34. Gladys Topkis, interview by author, December 17, 2008.
35. McDowell, "Publishing: New Memoir Stirs 'Julia' Controversy."
36. *Vogue* (Fall 1983); Gladys Topkis, interview by author, December 17, 2008.
37. Stephen Spender, quoted in Sutherland, *Stephen Spender,* 528; Arthur Zitrin, interview by author, May 7, 2009.
38. Wright, *Lillian Hellman,* 408–409. The last word, or almost, about Muriel Gardiner and Lillian Hellman: The "Julia" controversy outlived both women. Much of Hellman's obituary would be devoted to rehashing her lawsuit against McCarthy, and the charges that Julia was based on Muriel. Hellman got the last word in her obituary, however, which quoted the line about Muriel's not being the model for Hellman's Julia. But over the decades since her death, the Muriel/Julia discussion would be revisited, with filmmakers, cultural critics, journalists, essayists, playwrights, and others weighing in on the question. Most came in on the side of truth: "Hellman had falsely made herself the heroine of somebody else's story," wrote Richard Bernstein, in the "Critic's Notebook," *New York Times,* November 12, 1998.

Sixty years after *Watch on the Rhine*, another play, *Imaginary Friends: A Play with Music* by Nora Ephron, imagined a relationship of sorts between adversaries Hellman and McCarthy, along with a third character, Muriel Gardiner, about whom Mary McCarthy's character says: "This person is the gun over the mantel." The gun would go off, shooting holes in Hellman's story.

Ephron wrote: "It was quite a while before I began to suspect that the fabulous stories [Hellman] entertained her friends with were, to be polite about it, stories....the story of Julia...was certainly a total invention." Introduction, *Imaginary Friends*, xiii, xiv.

Most recently, Muriel had the final say: "Whether Hellman's 'Julia' existed or not, there was an American heiress who bravely resisted the Nazis in Austria. She managed to escape. Her name was Muriel Gardiner. She never met Lillian Hellman." Jim Dwyer, "Tales of Love and Terror, with Very Few Facts," *New York Times*, September 29, 2007.

CHAPTER 18   THE CHOICE

1. Hal Harvey, phone interview by author, August 14, 2009.
2. Gladys Topkis, letter to Marcia Burick, April 3, 1984, in private collection.
3. Jeffrey Masson, quoted in Janet Malcolm, *In the Freud Archives* (New York: Vintage, 1985), 36; New York: *The New York Review of Books*, 1983; quoted in Elisabeth Young-Bruehl, *Anna Freud: A Biography* (New York: Summit Books, 1988), 437.
4. Young-Bruehl, *Anna Freud*, 437.
5. Muriel Gardiner, quoted in Malcolm, *In the Freud Archives*, 136–137; Ralph Blumenthal, "Freud Archives Research Chief Removed in Dispute over Yale Talk," *New York Times*, November 9, 1981.
6. Malcolm, *In the Freud Archives*, 137.
7. Hal Harvey, phone interview by author, August 14, 2009.
8. Malcolm, *In the Freud Archives*, 135, 154,162.
9. Hal Harvey, telephone interview by author, April 20, 2009.
10. Michael Molnar, email to author, April 1, 2009.
11. Muriel Gardiner, letter to Ann Harvey, January 20, 1984, in private collection.
12. Sari Staver, "MD Reflects on Years in Anti-Nazi Underground," *American Medical News*, March 23–30, 1984.
13. Marcia Burick, phone interview by author, August 6, 2009.
14. Gerda Gray, phone interview by author, April 5, 2010.
15. *The Courage to Care: Rescuers of Jews During the Holocaust*, 1986. This video originated from the conference "Faith in Humankind: Rescuers of Jews During the Holocaust," sponsored by the United States Holocaust Memorial Council, September 1984. The documentary, nominated for an Academy Award in 1986, included a commentary by Elie Wiesel.
16. Connie Harvey, letter about memorial service for her mother, in private collection; Connie Harvey, interview by author, November 6, 2008; Charles Silberstein, phone interview by author, December 11, 2008.
17. Connie Harvey, interview by author, November 6, 2008; Dennis Buttinger, phone interview by author, August 29, 2009.
18. Jessica Lohnes, interview by author, May 11, 2009.
19. Connie Harvey, interview by author, November 6, 2008.
20. Mark Harvey, interview by author, November 4, 2008.
21. Muriel Gardiner, letter to Martha (no last name given), September 10, 1983, in private collection.
22. Anna Freud, letter to Muriel Gardiner, September 15, 1979, Anna Freud Papers, Sigmund Freud Collection, Library of Congress.
23. Stephen Spender, unpublished journal material, August 8, 1980, 338, reprinted by kind permission of the Estate of Stephen Spender.
24. Ibid., 126.
25. Lady Natasha Spender, interview with author, March 24, 2009. Muriel's influence on those who knew and loved her was varied and deep. Stephen Spender, who outlasted her by a decade, dedicated his *Journals 1939–1983* to her after she died. From Sutherland, *Stephen Spender*, 530.

Muriel's lifelong generosity to friends and acquaintances and students needing funds for their education, extended far and wide. Even the famous knew her kindness: She once provided a loan to Nobel prize—winning Polish poet and novelist, Czesław Miłosz, a friend of Stephen Spender's, for a home mortgage.

At her death, the bulk of Muriel's estate went to her daughter, Connie Harvey, to Connie's six children, to the New-Land Foundation, and to the Maki Foundation, an environmental organization founded by Connie. Muriel also left bequests to countless friends and relatives and others for schooling. In addition, she left a small legacy to a former lover of Joe's, Jeanette Roderick.

Muriel's New-Land Foundation showed fair market value assets in 2007 of $38,167,249 based on tax returns (publicly available information). The tax returns also indicate that the foundation granted awards totaling between $1.69 million and $1.93 million each year, between 2001 and 2007.

Muriel died three weeks before she could receive the Wellesley Alumnae Achievement Award. On February 21, 1985, Connie attended the ceremony at Wellesley, along with her daughter Muriel; the two women accepted the gold oak leaf pin in Muriel Gardiner's name.

Muriel, as she had wished, had no funeral or burial service but Connie organized a memorial ceremony for her mother at the Westbury Hotel in New York City at 2 P.M. on March 9, 1985.

Guests were invited to come and tell how they knew Muriel, and talk of their memories of her. Many did.

BIBLIOGRAPHY

Muriel Gardiner was a private woman who left behind few records of her inner thoughts and feelings, with two notable exceptions: one is a collection of outlines, notes, and sketches in preparation for a memoir. However, the 1983 memoir *Code Name "Mary"* left out most of Gardiner's intimate reflections as expressed in these early, unpublished writings. They are here referred to as Muriel Gardiner Notes (MGN).

The other is a lengthy interview of Gardiner conducted by Dr. Bluma Swerdloff for the Psychoanalytic Movement Oral History Project, "The Reminiscences of Muriel Gardiner," referred to in the notes as REMINISCENCES. Significant interviews of Gardiner were also done by Lucille Ritvo and Brenda Webster.

Other major primary sources include the archives at Wellesley College; Vienna's Dokumentationsarchiv des österreichischen Widerstandes (DöW) or Documentation Center of the Austrian Resistance (DOEW); the Joseph Buttinger papers at the Harvard-Yenching Library; the Austrian Heritage Collection at the Leo Baeck Institute; the library at St. Anne's College, Oxford; and the Sigmund Freud Collection in the Library of Congress. Within the Freud Collection are papers of eminent psychoanalysts, including Anna Freud and Muriel Gardiner.

I was fortunate to be able to conduct interviews with many people who knew Gardiner during her lifetime, including her years in Austria, and including those who lived through the *Anschluss*. I offer here as much documentation as possible for each statement that I make about Gardiner's life. If there are absences in documentation, or errors in facts, the fault is, of course, my own.

BOOKS

Albarelli, Henry. *A Terrible Mistake: The Murder of Frank Olson.* Walterville, OR: Trine Day, 2009.

Anderson, Mark M., ed. *Hitler's Exiles: Personal Stories of the Flight from Nazi Germany to America.* New York: New Press, 1998.

Andrew, Christopher. *Defend the Realm: The Authorized History of MI5.* New York: Alfred A. Knopf, 2009.

Bolbecher, Siglinde, and Konstantin Kaiser, eds. *Lexikon der österreichischen Exilliteratur.* Vienna: Deuticke, 2000.

Brailsford, H. N. *Shelley, Godwin and Their Circle.* London: Oxford University Press, 1951.

Bukey, Evan Burr. *Hitler's Austria: Popular Sentiment in the Nazi Era, 1938-1945.* Chapel Hill: University of North Carolina Press, 2000.

Burlingham, Michael John. *The Last Tiffany: A Biography of Dorothy Tiffany Burlingham.* New York: Atheneum, 1989.

Butler, Ruth. *A History of Saint Anne's Society, formerly The Society of Oxford Home-Students.* Vol. 2, *1921-1946.* Printed for private circulation. Oxford: University Press, 1949.

Buttinger, Joseph. *In the Twilight of Socialism: A History of the Revolutionary Socialists of Austria.* Translated by E. B. Ashton. New York: F. A. Praeger, 1953.

—— and Muriel Gardiner. *Damit Wir Nicht Vergessen: Unsere Jahre 1934-1947 in Wein, Paris und New York.* Vienna: Verlag der Wiener Volksbuchhandlung, 1978.

Buttinger, Louis. *An Updated Letter for My Grandchildren: Autobiographical Notes and Commentary.* Self-published and privately printed.

Cabot, Ella Lyman. *Everyday Ethics.* New York: Henry Holt & Co, 1906.

Chester, Eric Thomas. *Covert Network: Progressives, the International Rescue Committee, and the CIA.* Armonk, NY, and London: M.E. Sharpe, 1995.

Churchill, Winston. *The Second World War: The Gathering Storm*. Cambridge, MA: Riverside Press, 1948.

Cohen, Bernard, and Luc Rosenzweig. *Waldheim*. Translated by Josephine Bacon. New York: Adama Books, 1987.

Cohen, David. *The Escape of Sigmund Freud*. London: JR Books Ltd, 2009.

Cohen, Stanley. *States of Denial: Knowing about Atrocities and Suffering*. Cambridge, UK: Polity, 2001.

Cutler, Irving. *The Jews of Chicago: From Shtetl to Suburb*. Urbana: University of Illinois Press, 1996.

Czuzka, George. Unpublished novella.

Dainty, Ralph B. *Darling-Delaware Centenary: 1882-1982*. Chicago: Darling-Delaware Company, 1981.

Danto, Elizabeth Ann. *Freud's Free Clinics: Psychoanalysis and Social Justice 1918-1938*. New York: Columbia University Press, 2005.

David, Hugh. *Stephen Spender: A Portrait with Background*. Portsmouth, NH: Heinemann, 1992.

Decker, Hannah S. *Freud, Dora, and Vienna 1900*. New York: Free Press, 1991.

Dorman, Joseph. *Arguing the World: The New York Intellectuals in Their Own Words*. Chicago: University of Chicago Press, 2000.

Duczynska, Ilona. *Workers in Arms: The Austrian Schutzbund and the Civil War of 1934*. New York and London: Monthly Review Press, 1978.

Duff, Shiela Grant. *The Parting of Ways: A Personal Account of the Thirties*. London: Peter Owen, 1982.

Ephron, Nora. *Imaginary Friends, A Play with Music*. New York: Vintage, 2002.

Fedder, Ruth, and Muriel Gardiner. *The Troubled Child Can Learn: Psychological Insight for Teachers*. Flagstaff, AZ: Sir Speedy Printing Center, 1979.

Feibleman, Peter. *Lilly: Reminiscences of Lillian Hellman*. New York: William Morrow, 1988.

Feichtlbauer, Hubert. *The Austrian Dilemma: An Inquiry into National Socialism and Racism in Austria*. Vienna: Holzhausen, 2001.

Feinstein C. H., Peter Temin, and Gianni Toniolo. *The European Economy between the Wars*. New York: Oxford University Press, 1997.

Fleck, Christian, and Heinrich Berger. *Gefesselt vom Sozialismus: Der Austromarxist Otto Leichter (1897-1973)*. Frankfurt and New York: Campus, 2000.

Freeman, Lucy, and Marvin Small. *The Story of Psychoanalysis*. New York: Pocket Books, 1960.

Freud, Sigmund. *A General Introduction to Psychoanalysis*. Translated by Joan Riviere. Garden City, NY: Garden City Publishing Company, 1943.

Friedländer, Saul. *Nazi Germany and the Jews*. Vol. 1, *The Years of Persecution, 1933-1939*. Vol. 2, *The Years of Extermination, 1939-1945*. New York: HarperCollins, 1997–2007.

Frischauer, Willi. *Twilight in Vienna: The Capital without a Country*. Boston: Houghton Mifflin, 1938.

Fuchs, Martin, and Charles Hope Lumley. *Showdown in Vienna: The Death of Austria*. New York: G. P. Putnam's Sons, 1939.

Gardiner, Muriel. *Code Name "Mary": Memoirs of an American Woman in the Austrian Underground*. Introduction by Anna Freud. New Haven: Yale University Press, 1983.

——. *The Deadly Innocents: Portraits of Children Who Kill*. Preface by Stephen Spender. New York: Basic Books, 1976.

——, ed., *The Wolf-Man by the Wolf-Man: The Double Story of Freud's Most Famous Case*, with *The Case of the Wolf-Man* by Sigmund Freud. Supplement by Ruth Mack Brunswick. Edited, with notes, an introduction, and chapters by Muriel Gardiner. Foreword by Anna Freud. New York: Basic Books, 1971.

Gay, Peter. *Freud: A Life for Our Time*. New York: W. W. Norton, 1988.

Gedye, G. E. R. *Betrayal in Central Europe: Austria and Czechoslovakia: The Fallen Bastions*. New York and London: Harper & Brothers, 1939.

Geisst, Charles R. *Wheels of Fortune: The History of Speculation from Scandal to Respectability*. New York: J. Wiley, 2002.

Gitlin, Todd. *The Sixties: Years of Hope, Days of Rage*. New York: Bantam, 1993.

Goldner, Franz. *Austrian Emigration 1938-1945*. New York: F. Ungar,1979.

Grosskurth, Phyllis. *The Secret Ring: Freud's Inner Circle and the Politics of Psychoanalysis*. New York: Addison-Wesley, 1991.

Gunther, John. *The Lost City*. New York: Harper & Row, 1964.

Hellman, Lillian. *Pentimento: A Book of Portraits*. New York: New American Library, 1973.

——. *An Unfinished Woman: A Memoir*. Boston: Little Brown, 1969.

——. *Watch on the Rhine*. In *Six Plays by Lillian Hellman*. New York: Vintage, 1979. First produced in New York City by Herbert Shumlin, 1941.

Herzstein, Robert Edwin. *Waldheim: The Missing Years*. New York: Arbor House, 1988.

Horn, Gerd-Rainer. *European Socialists Respond to Fascism: Ideology, Activism, and Contingency in the 1930s*. New York: Oxford University Press, 1996

——, ed. *Letters from Barcelona: An American Woman in Revolution and Civil War; Lois Orr*. New York: Palgrave Macmillan, 2009

Horowitz, Helen Lefkowitz. *Culture and the City: Cultural Philanthropy in Chicago from the 1880s to 1917*. Chicago: University of Chicago Press, 989.

Isaacson Walter, *Einstein: His Life and Universe*. New York: Simon & Schuster 2007.

Isenberg, Sheila. *A Hero of Our Own: The Story of Varian Fry*. New York: Random House, 2001.

Jaher, Frederic Cople. *The Urban Establishment: Upper Strata in Boston, New York, Charleston, Chicago, and Los Angeles*. Urbana: University of Illinois Press, 1982.

Josephson, Matthew. *The Robber Barons:* The Great American Capitalists, 1861-1901. New York: Mariner Books, 1962.

Kershaw, Ian. *Hitler: 1936-45; Nemesis*. New York and London: Allen Lane, 2000.

Kramer, Edith. *Art As Therapy with Children*. Introduction by Muriel Gardiner. New York: Schocken, 1971.

Kreisky, Bruno. *The Struggle for a Democratic Austria*. New York: Berghahn, 2000.

Large, David Clay. *Between Two Fires: Europe's Path in the 1930s*. New York: W. W. Norton, 1990.

Leeming, David. *Stephen Spender: A Life in Modernism*. New York: Henry Holt, 1999.

Leichter Henry, *Childhood Memories*, privately printed.

Leichter, Otto. *Glanz und Ende der Ersten Republik*. Vienna: Europa-Verlag Wien. 1964.

Legenda of Wellesley College. Poole's Index. 1922. http://www.archive.org/stream/wellesleylegenda 1922bost#page/n5/mode/2up

Levenson, Thomas. *Einstein in Berlin*. New York: Bantam, 2003.

Levenstein, Aaron. *Escape to Freedom: The Story of the International Rescue Committee*. Westport, CT: Greenwood Press, 1983.

Lieberman, J. Nina. *The Salzburg Connection: An Adolescence Remembered*. New York: Vantage Press, 2004.

Loewenberg Peter. *Decoding the Past: The Psychohistorical Approach*. Piscataway, NJ: Transaction Publishers, 1996.

Low, Alfred. *The Anschluss Movement, 1931-1938, and the Great Powers*. Boulder, CO: East European Monographs, 1985.

Luža, Radomir V. *The Resistance in Austria: 1938-1945*. Minneapolis: University of Minnesota Press, 1984.

Marshall, Bruce. *Vespers in Vienna*. Boston, Houghton Mifflin, 1947.

Maass, Walter B. *The Years of Darkness: The Austrian Resistance Movement 1938-1945*. Vienna, unknown binding, 1979.

Malcolm, Janet. *In the Freud Archives*. New York: New York Review of Books, 1983, 1997.

McCarthy, Kathleen D. *Noblesse Oblige: Charity and Cultural Philanthropy in Chicago, 1849-1929*. Chicago: University of Chicago Press, 1982.

Mellen, Joan. *Hellman and Hammett: The Legendary Passion of Lillian Hellman and Dashiell Hammett*. New York: HarperCollins, 1996.

Mitchison, Naomi. *Naomi Mitchison's Vienna Diary*. New York: H. Smith and R. Haas, 1934.

Molden, Fritz. *Exploding Star: A Young Austrian Against Hitler*. New York: William Morrow, 1979.

Morris, Ira Nelson. *Heritage from My Father: An Autobiography*. Privately published by Constance Lily (Rothschild) Morris, 1947.

Neilson, Francis. *The Makers of War*. New Orleans: Flanders Hall Publishers, 1950.

——. *My Life in Two Worlds*. Appleton, WI: C. C. Nelson, 1952.

Neiman, Robert. "The Anschluss: A Study of the Methodology of the Third Reich's Policy toward Austria." Ph.D. diss., New York University, 1958.

Palmieri, Patricia Ann. *In Adamless Eden: The Community of Women Faculty at Wellesley*. New Haven and London: Yale University Press, 1995.

Papanek, Ernst with Edward Linn. *Out of the Fire*. New York: William Morrow, 1975.

Pauley, Bruce F. *From Prejudice to Persecution: A History of Austrian Anti-Semitism*. Chapel Hill: University of North Carolina Press, 1992.

———. *Hitler and the Forgotten Nazis: A History of National Socialism*. Chapel Hill: University of North Carolina Press, 1981.

Pelinka, Anton. *Austria: Out of the Shadow of the Past*. Boulder, CO: Westview Press, 1998.

Perkins, Agnes Frances. *Vocations for the Trained Woman: Opportunities Other Than Teaching*. University of Michigan Library, January 1, 1910.

Persico, Joseph E. *Piercing the Reich: The Penetration of Nazi Germany by American Secret Agents during World War II*. New York: Viking, 1979.

Reeves, Marjorie. *St Anne's College Oxford: An Informal History: 1879-1979*. Oxford: The College, 1979.

Riviere, Peter, ed. *A History of Oxford Anthropology*. New York and Oxford: Berghahn Books, 2007,

Roazen, Paul. *The Historiography of Psychoanalysis*. New Brunswick, NJ: Transaction Publishers, 2001.

Roth, Joseph. *The Wandering Jews*. Translated by Michael Hofmann. New York: W. W. Norton, 2001.

Sargent, Porter E. *A Handbook of American Private Schools: An Annual Survey* (The Sargent Handbooks, 9th edition: 1924–1925). Unknown Binding.

Schmidt, Elfriede. *1938…And The Consequences: Questions And Responses: Interviews*. Translated by Peter J. Lyth. Riverside, CA: Ariadne Press, 1922.

Schneider, Gertrude. *Exile and Destruction: The Fate of Austrian Jews 1938-1945*. Westport, CT: Praeger, 1995.

Schuschnigg, Kurt von. *Austrian Requiem*. Translated by Franz von Hildebrand. New York: G. P. Putnam's Sons, 1946.

———. *The Brutal Takeover: The Austrian ex-Chancellor's Account of the Anschluss by Hitler*. Translated by Richard Perry. London: Weidenfeld and Nicolson, 1971.

Shirer, William L. *The Rise and Fall of the Third Reich*. New York: Simon & Schuster, 1960.

———. *Twentieth Century Journal: A Memoir of a Life and the Times.*,Vol. 2, *The Nightmare Years, 1930-1940*. Boston and Toronto: Little Brown, 1984.

Shugaar, Antony. *I Lie for a Living: Greatest Spies of All Times*. Washington, DC: National Geographic, 2006.

Sinclair, Upton. *The Jungle: The Uncensored Original Edition*. Introduction by Kathleen De Grave. Tucson, AZ: See Sharp Press, 2003.

Sorin, Gerald. *Irving Howe: A Life of Passionate Dissent*. New York and London: New York University Press, 2002.

Spender, Stephen. *Collected Poems 1928-1985*. Oxford University Press, 1987.

———. *Journals 1939-1983*. Edited by John Goldsmith. London: Faber & Faber, 1985.

———. *Letters to Christopher: Stephen Spender's Letters to Christopher Isherwood 1929-1939, with "The Line of the Branch"—Two Thirties Journals*. Edited by Lee Bartlett. Santa Barbara: Black Sparrow Press, 1980.

———. *New Collected Poems of Stephen Spender*. Edited by Michael Brett. London: Faber and Faber, 2004. Reprinted by kind permission of the Estate of Stephen Spender.

———. *Ruins and Visions: Poems 1934-1942*, New York: Random House, 1942.

———. *Vienna*. New York: Random House, 1935.

———. *World within World: The Autobiography of Stephen Spender*. Introduction by John Bayley. New York: Modern Library edition, 2001.

———. Unpublished journal material. Reprinted by kind permission of the Estate of Stephen Spender.

Spiel, Hilde. *Vienna's Golden Autumn: 1866-1938*. New York: Weidenfeld and Nicolson, 1987.

Sutherland, John. *Stephen Spender: The Authorized Biography*. New York: Oxford University Press, 2005.

Swift, Helen. *My Father and My Mother*. Chicago: Privately Printed, 1937.

——. *Where Green Lanes End: A Collection of Nature Studies, Essays, and Fictional Character Sketches, Emotional Experiences with Nature, Impressions of Seasons & Wonders of Outdoor World.* New York: B. W. Huebsch, 1924.

Swift, Louis F. *The Yankee of the Yards: The Biography of Gustavus Franklin Swift.* Chicago: A.W. Shaw, 1927.

Wade, Louise C. *Chicago's Pride: The Stockyards, Packingtown and Environs in the Nineteenth Century.* Urbana: University of Illinois Press, 1987.

Wagner, Dieter, and Gerhard Tomkowitz. *Anschluss: The Week Hitler Seized Austria.* Translated by Geoffrey Strachan. New York: St. Martin's Press, 1971.

Webster, Brenda. *The Last Good Freudian.* New York: Holmes & Meier, 2000.

——. *Paradise Farm.* Albany: State University of New York Press, 1999.

Weissenberger, Guntram. *My Town: A Builder's Life.* Pine Plains, N. Y.: Swan Books, 2006.

Wimmer, Adi, ed. *Strangers at Home and Abroad: Recollections of Austrian Jews Who Escaped Hitler.* Jefferson, NC: McFarland, 2000.

Wright, William. *Lillian Hellman: The Image, the Woman.* New York: Simon and Schuster, 1986.

Young-Bruehl, Elisabeth. *Anna Freud: A Biography.* New York: Summit Books, 1988.

ARTICLES

"287,000 Receive U.S. Tax Refunds of $174,120,177." *Chicago Daily Tribune*, December 29, 1926.

"103,858,687 in Taxes Handed Back by U.S; Many Chicagoans on Mellon's List." *Chicago Daily Tribune*, December 29, 1927.

Adams, Timothy Dow. "Lillian Hellman: 'Are You Now or Have You Ever Been?'" In his *Telling Lies in Modern American Autobiography.* Chapel Hill: University of North Carolina Press, 1990.

"Americans Trained Abroad," Oral History Workshop #4, American Psychoanalytic Association, December 13, 1975, Boston Psychoanalytic Society and Institute Archives and Oral History Transcripts. The Archives of the Boston Psychoanalytic Society and Institute (BPSI). Hans Sachs Library. Boston Psychoanalytic Society and Institute, Boston, MA

"Austria to Crush Nazis' Terrorism; Leaders Will Be Returned to Concentration Camp if Their Violence Continues. Heavy Penalties Ordered. Two Women Are Hurt by Bombs in Care in the Centre of Vienna—Five Hitlerites Arrested." *New York Times*, May 12, 1934.

Backman, Marjorie. "A Nation's Lost Holocaust History, Now on Display." *New York Times*, June 2, 2007, section B, p. 7.

Bernstein, Richard. "Critic's Notebook," *New York Times*, November 12, 1998.

Blumenthal, Ralph. "Freud Archives Research Chief Removed in Dispute over Yale Talk." *New York Times*, November 9, 1981.

Burick, Marcia. "Moment of Friendship: A Visit with Muriel Morris Gardiner, '22, M. D.," *Wellesley Magazine*, Spring 1985.

Buttinger, Joseph. "Mary." *The Bulletin of the Philadelphia Association of Psychoanalysis* 22, no.2, (June 1972).

Cain, Louis P. "Innovation, Invention, and Chicago Business." http://www.encyclopedia.chicagohistory.org/pages/643.html

"Charity Bazaar a Winner When these Girls Run Booths." Photo caption. *Chicago Daily Tribune*, November 10, 1912.

"Chicago to Honor Dead Fire Chief." *New York Times*, December 24, 1910.

"Clothing Wet, Ardor Undampened, 5,000 Women March." *Chicago Tribune*, June 8, 1916.

Cockburn, Alexander. "Who Was Julia?" *The Nation*, February 23, 1985.

Cohen, David. "The Escape of Sigmund Freud." *The Evening Citizen* [Ottawa, Ontario], July 9, 1938.

Cohen, Mitchell. "Decades of Dissent." *Dissent*, Winter 2004.

"College Commemorates Armistice Day." *Wellesley College News* 30, no. 8 (November 17, 1921).

"College Votes to Discard Honor System as Impractical." *Wellesley College News* 30, no.28 (May 18, 1922).

"Death Comes to Nelson Morris." *Chicago Tribune*, August 28, 1907.

"Dr. Ruth Bakwin Dies; Professor of Pediatrics." *New York Times*, August 2,1985.

Dwyer, Jim. "Tales of Love and Terror, With Very Few Facts," *New York Times*, September 29, 2007.

"Ed. Morris Dead: Left $40,000,000." *New York Times,* November 4, 1913.

"Edward Morris, Packer, is Dead; End Comes as Surprise to Friends, Though He Had Been Ill Long Time; Estate of $40,000,000." *Chicago Tribune,* November 4, 1913.

Exenberger, Herbert. "Dr. Käthe Leichter." In *The World on Fire: An Anthology of Murdered Socialist Writers,* edited by Herbert Exenberger. Vienna: Mandelbaum, 2000.

French, William. "Code Name Mary." Review. *The Globe and Mail* [Canada], May 26, 1983.

Gardiner, Beth. "Einstein's Letters Indicate Affair with Suspected Spy. Newly Discovered Writings Reveal Strong Feelings for Margarita Konenkova." *Philadelphia Inquirer,* June 2, 1998.

Gardiner, Muriel, and James Jan-Tausch. "Homicidal Acts of School Age Children and Their Implication for Education." Trenton, NJ: State of New Jersey Department of Education, 1971.

——. "Mary Shelley and John Howard Payne." *The London Mercury* 22, no. 131 (September 1930): 450. [as Muriel Morris]

——. "Memoirs of the Wolf-Man, 1938, Introduction and Postscript," *The Bulletin of the Philadelphia Association for Psychoanalysis* 20, no. 2 (June 1970).

——. "My Friendship with Konenkov, 1926-1945." In *The Uncommon Vision of Sergei Konenkov, 1874-1971: A Russian Sculptor and His Times,* edited by Marie Turbow Lampard, John E. Bowlt, and Wendy R. Salmond. A co-publication of Rutgers University Press, New Brunswick, NJ, and London, and The Jane Voorhees Zimmerli Art Museum, Rutgers, The State University of New Jersey, 2001.

——. "A Note on Accreditation." *Bulletin of the Philadelphia Association for Psychoanalysis* 10, no. 2 (June 1960).

——. "The Seven Years of Dearth." *The Bulletin of The Philadelphia Association for Psychoanalysis* 12, no. 4 (December 1962).

——. "To C," unpublished poem. In private collection.

Glaser, Ernst. "The Time of Illegality: Muriel Gardiner (1901-1985) and Ilse Kulczar (1902-1976)." *Die Revolutionierung des Alltags: zur intellektuellen Kultur von Frauen im Wien der Zwischenkriegszeit* by Doris Ingrisch, Ilse Erika Korotin and Charlotte Zwiauer. Frankfurt am Main: P. Lang, 2004.

Greeley, Horace. "Editorial." *New York Tribune, July 13, 1865.*

"Gustavus F. Swift Dead, Well Known Chicago Packer Expires Suddenly." *Chicago Daily Tribune,* March 30, 1903.

Gutman, Israel. "Anschluss." *Encyclopedia of the Holocaust,* New York: MacMillan, 1990.

Guttman, Samuel A. "In Memoriam: Muriel M. Gardiner, M.D. (1901-85)." *The Psychoanalytic Study of the Child* 40 (1985): 1–7.

"Hats Off to the Weather Man." *Chicago Tribune,* November 23, 1916.

Holden, Stephen. "12 Witnesses to History at Its Most Frightening." *New York Times,* October 8, 1996.

Howarth, Janet. "Women." In *The History of the University of Oxford.* Vol. 8, *The Twentieth Century,* edited by Brian Harrison. Oxford: Clarendon Press, 1994.

Kettle, Martin. "Letters reveal scientist's compromising passion: Einstein's affair with a spy from Moscow; Evidence found in Russia shows that the father of modern physics had a long relationship with a Soviet agent who was trying to extract nuclear secrets while the US was developing the atom bomb." *The Guardian* [London]. June 2, 1998.

Lissner, Will. "Memories of Nock and Neilson." *Fragments,* April-June 1982, www.cooperative individualism.org.

Loewenberg, Peter. "Karl Renner and the Politics of Accommodation: Moderation versus Revenge." *Austrian History Yearbook* 22 (1991): 35–56. Originally given as the Kann Memorial Lecture at the University of Minnesota, 1985.

Lowe, David. " 'Julia' and Muriel Gardiner," *Dissent,* vol. 33, Summer 1986.

Lubin, Victoria. "Muriel Gardiner and Anna Loeb on the Resistance." *Valley News,* September 3, 1983, p. 13.

Lumsden, Linda J. "The Life and Times of Inez Milholland." *Inez Milholland: A Thanatography of the Suffrage Martyr,"* Professor Barbara Babcock's Women's Legal History Project, April 3, 2000.

McDowell, Edwin. "Publishing: New Memoir Stirs 'Julia' Controversy." *New York Times,* April 29, 1983.

Michaels, Jennifer E. "The Anschluss Remembered: Experiences of the Anschluss in the Autobiographies of Elisabeth Castonier, Gina Kaus, Alma Mahler-Werfel, and Hertha Pauli." In *Austrian Writers and the Anschluss: Understanding the Past—Overcoming the Past*, edited by Donald G. Daviau. Riverside CA: Ariadne Press, 1991.

"Morris Millions in Trust, Packer's Widow Controls—Will Be One of World's Wealthiest Women." *New York Times*, November 12, 1913.

"Morris-Swift Nuptials." *Chicago Tribune*, October 2, 1890.

"Mrs. Edw. Morris Marries Briton; Surprises Son. Widow of Packer Bride of Francis Neilson, Statesman." *Chicago Daily Tribune*, September 5, 1916.

Nava, Mica. "The Unconscious and Others: Rescue, Inclusivity and the Eroticization of Difference in 1930s Vienna." In *Culture and the Unconscious*, edited by C. Bainbridge, S. Radstone, M. Rustin, and C. Yates. London: Palgrave, 2006, 41–57.

"Nelson Morris Dead: Financier and Meat Packer Dead at His Home in Chicago." *New York Times*, August 28, 1907.

"Obituary of Dr. Muriel Gardiner," *Princeton, New Jersey, Town Topics*, February 13, 1985.

Pogrebin, Robin. "Love Letters by Einstein at Auction." *New York Times*, June 1, 1998.

Rapp-Bauer, Lizzy. "Lest We Forget—The Nazi Era," January 25, 1991. Austrian Heritage Collection, Leo Baeck Institute, New York.

Reder, Christian. "Twilight of Socialism: Drei Biografien Österreichs Zeitgeschichte (Three Biographies of Austria's Contemporary History)." *Falter*, Wien, no. 20, 1983.

Roiphe, Katie. "Imagining Enemies: Nora Ephron's Theory of Mary McCarthy vs. Lillian Hellman." Posted Tuesday, December 10, 2002, on slate.com.

Rosenbaum, Ron. "Kim Philby and the Age of Paranoia." *New York Times Magazine,* July 10, 1994.

Rosenkranz, Herbert. "Austria." *Encyclopedia of the Holocaust*, 126–132. New York: MacMillan, 1990.

Roth, Walter. "Judge Julian W. Mack: The Court and the Community." *Chicago Jewish Historical Society Newsletter* 31, no. 3 (Summer 2007).

——. "Nelson Morris and 'The Yards,'" *Chicago Jewish Historical Society* 32, no. 2 (Spring 2008).

Russell, Paul L. Review of *The Wolf-Man. Psychosomatic Medicine* 35, no. 3 (May-June 1973).

Simon, John. "Pentimental Journey." Review of *Pentimento*, by Lillian Hellman. *The Hudson Review* 26, no. 4 (Winter 1973–1974).

Snyder, Otto Alfred: "Reflections: The Background and Experiences of Two Immigrants. A Partial History of Our Family." Memoir Collection, Leo Baeck Institute, New York.

"Son Asked Study of Einstein Brain." *New York Times*, April 20, 1955..

Staver, Sari. "MD Reflects on Years in Anti-Nazi Underground," *American Medical News*, March 23/30, 1984.

Steinacher, Gerald. "The Special Operations Executive (SOE) in Austria, 1940-1945." *International Journal of Intelligence and Counterintelligence* 15, no. 2 (Summer 2002): 211–221.

Steiner, Herbert. "The Role of the Resistance in Austria, with Special Reference to the Labor Movement." *The Journal of Modern History*. Supplement: *Resistance against the Third Reich* 64 (December 1992).

Streeten, Paul. An Autobiographical sketch, "Aerial roots," 1917-1986. in *Banca Nazionale del Lavoro Quarterly Review* no. 157, (1986), 135–159. Austrian Heritage Collection. Leo Baeck Institute, New York.

Ty, Eleanor. "Mary Wollstonecraft Shelley." In *Dictionary of Literary Biography 116: British Romantic Novelists, 1789-1832*, edited by Bradford K. Mudge. Detroit: Gale Research, 1992.

"U.S. Lists Stock Embargo; Show to Boom Today—Government Authorities Find Plague to be Stomatitis." *Chicago Tribune*, December 2, 1916.

"Vassar Girl, Aid in Strike, in Cell." *Chicago Tribune*, January 18, 1910.

Webster, Brenda. Interview by Jack Foley on *Cover to Cover*, KPFA, 2000. Also, "The Perfect Freudian Child: An Interview with Brenda Webster." *Women's Studies* 32, issue 5 (July 2003).

"Weeds Too Thick for Pack to Follow the Hunt." Photo. *Chicago Tribune*, September 21, 1913.

Wellspring Online, The Quarterly Newsletter of the Stony Brook-Millstone Watershed Association 46, no. 3 (Fall 1999).

"Will Is Broken by Morris Heirs; Agreement Made Out of Court to Divide $30,000,000 among Widow and Four Children." *Chicago Daily Tribune*, October 15, 1907.

"Women Students To Confer; Nineteen Colleges to Join in Armament Discussion at Vassar." *New York Times*, Oct. 15, 1921.

"Working Girl; Sister of Packing Company Head Hold Clerical Position in General Offices of Firm in Stockyards." *Chicago Tribune*, August 30, 1919.

Wortman, Marc. "The Muses on the Couch: Sigmund Freud's Theories Have Provided Common Ground for Scholars of the Mind and the Humanities." *Yale*, November 1988.

ARCHIVAL COLLECTIONS

Anna Freud Papers. The Sigmund Freud Collection, Manuscript Division, the Library of Congress, Washington D.C.

Archives & Special Collections. A C. Long Health Sciences Library. Columbia University Medical Center, New York.

Austrian Heritage Collection. Leo Baeck Institute. Center for Jewish History, New York.

Boston Psychoanalytic Society and Institute Archives and Oral History Transcripts. The Archives of the Boston Psychoanalytic Society and Institute (BPSI). Hans Sachs Library. Boston Psychoanalytic Society and Institute, Boston, MA.

Civilian Agency Records, State Department and Foreign Affairs Records, "Records of the Foreign Service Posts of the Department of State" RG 84, Austria. National Archives. Washington, DC.

Dokumentationsarchiv des österreichischen Widerstandes (DöW), Archives of the Resistance (DOEW), Vienna.

Gardiner, Muriel. Outlines, notes and drafts for memoirs, unpaginated and undated, typed and hand-written (MGN). In private collection.

Gardiner, Muriel. "Reminiscences." Interview by Dr. Bluma Swerdloff. Psychoanalytic Movement Oral History Project. Oral History Research Office. Butler Library, Columbia University, 1981.

Gardiner, Muriel. Interview by Lucille Ritvo, December 1968. Mp3, in the Oral History Interview Records. The Boston Psychoanalytic Society and Institute, Boston MA.

Gardiner, Muriel. Interview by Lucille Ritvo, Oral History Workshop no. 4, American Psychoanalytic Association, "Americans Trained Abroad," December 13, 1975, APA Archives.

Gardiner, Muriel. Interview by Brenda Webster, APA Workshop, December 1975. Digital only, in the Oral History Interview Records, The Boston Psychoanalytic Society and Institute, Boston MA.

Harvey, Connie. "Reminiscences." Interview by Dr. Bluma Swerdloff. Psychoanalytic Movement Oral History Project. Oral History Research Office. Butler Library, Columbia University, 1981.

"Hitler Arrives in Vienna." CBS. March 14, 1938. Museum of Broadcast Communications. http://archives.museum.tv/archives. CBS broadcast its "News Roundup" via shortwave radio from five European capitals, anchored by Bob Trout in New York and Edward R. Murrow in London. Hitler's takeover of Austria in March 1938 was recorded live for these broadcasts.

Muriel Gardiner Papers. The Sigmund Freud Collection, Manuscript Division, Library of Congress, Washington, D.C.

DOCUMENTARIES, FILMS

Chicago: City of the Century. American Experience. WGBH-Boston. January 2003.

Julia. Directed by Fred Zinnemann. 1977.

The Real Julia: The Muriel Gardiner Story. Produced by Dan Klugherz. Distributed by Altana Films. 1987.

INDEX